The Pastor as Friend?

The Pastor as Friend?

Understanding Dynamics of Friendship and Friendliness Within a Pastoral Ministry

Dan Holder

Foreword by John Swinton

◆PICKWICK *Publications* • Eugene, Oregon

THE PASTOR AS FRIEND?
Understanding Dynamics of Friendship and Friendliness Within a Pastoral Ministry

Copyright © 2025 Dan Holder. All rights reserved. Except for brief quotations in critical publications or reviews, no part of this book may be reproduced in any manner without prior written permission from the publisher. Write: Permissions, Wipf and Stock Publishers, 199 W. 8th Ave., Suite 3, Eugene, OR 97401.

Pickwick Publications
An Imprint of Wipf and Stock Publishers
199 W. 8th Ave., Suite 3
Eugene, OR 97401

www.wipfandstock.com

PAPERBACK ISBN: 979-8-3852-1387-0
HARDCOVER ISBN: 979-8-3852-1388-7
EBOOK ISBN: 979-8-3852-1389-4

Cataloguing-in-Publication data:

Names: Holder, Daniel F., author. | Swinton, John, 1957–, foreword.
Title: The pastor as friend? : understanding dynamics of friendship and friendliness within a pastoral ministry / Dan Holder ; foreword by John Swinton.
Description: Eugene, OR : Pickwick Publications, 2025 | Includes bibliographical references.
Identifiers: ISBN 979-8-3852-1387-0 (paperback) | ISBN 979-8-3852-1388-7 (hardcover) | ISBN 979-8-3852-1389-4 (ebook)
Subjects: LCSH: Pastoral theology. | Clergy—Office. | Friendship—Religious aspects—Christianity. | Theology, Practical.
Classification: BV4011.3 .H65 2025 (paperback) | BV4011.3 .H65 (ebook)

VERSION NUMBER 01/22/25

For my parents Len and Phyl Holder

It was you who first taught me that the "chief end of man" is to "glorify God and enjoy him forever." I am constantly learning more of what this means in my life—and what it has to do with friendship.

For me, friendship is not merely an "experience." Rather friendship is at the heart of my understanding of the moral life.

—Stanley Hauerwas

Friendship is a negotiated space between two parties who care for one another. It does not require that we collapse ourselves into the other in a way that smothers the self or forces it to take on unnatural shapes and forms. It also does not mean that the other always takes priority over the needs of the self.

—John Swinton

Contents

Foreword by John Swinton | ix

Acknowledgments | xi

1. Approaching the Topic of Friendship in a Pastoral Setting | 1
2. Inquiring into Lived Experiences of Friendship Amongst Ordained Pastors | 26
3. Theological Reflection Around Friendship in Scripture and the Elements of Friendliness as Found Within the Experience of the Interviewed Pastors | 85
4. Theological Reflection on the Essential Elements of Friendship and Their Interwovenness Within the Experience of the Interviewed Pastors | 127
5. Envisioning Revised Forms of Practice in Pastoral Friendship Within a Local Congregation | 195
6. Summary and Closing Thoughts | 223

Bibliography | 231

Foreword

HAVE YOU EVER WONDERED what it means for pastors to be friends with people in their churches? This is the fascinating question that Dan Holder dives into in this thought-provoking book. As a pastor himself in the Swiss Reformed Church, Dan brings a wealth of personal experience and insight to the table. He gets up close and personal with this topic, using in-depth interviews to unpack the real-life joys and struggles of pastoral friendships.

One of the great strengths of this book is the way in which Dan boils down the essence of these unique relationships into four key elements: mutuality, affection, freedom, and openness. This allows us to understand the nature of friendship and to explore not only the friendships that are laid out in the book, but also our own network of friendship. Readers will be surprised at what they discover. The book shows how these qualities are all woven together in the rich tapestry of pastoral life in ways that bring out both sadness and joy. In highlighting the everyday traits of friendliness that help these deeper relationships to take root and flourish Dan helps us to see what it looks like to live as relational creatures made in the image of a relational God. The book is a reminder that the big, life-changing moments of friendship are often built on a foundation of small, consistent acts of kindness and care.

This isn't just a book of anecdotes and observations. Dan digs deep into the theological foundations of friendship, wrestling with big ideas from important theologians such as Dietrich Bonhoeffer and Jürgen Moltmann. He explores paradoxes like the tension between closeness and professional distance, the interplay of different kinds of love, and the risks and rewards of vulnerability. In the process, Dan unearths some beautiful gems of wisdom for pastors seeking to cultivate authentic, life-giving relationships in their ministries. Another strength of this book is the way it grapples with the complexities and grey areas of pastoral friendships. Dan doesn't shy away from the tough questions or try to offer easy answers. Instead, he invites readers into a nuanced, thoughtful exploration of the topic, one that acknowledges both the potential pitfalls and the profound opportunities of these relationships. Through vivid stories and examples, the book illustrates how friendships can enrich and deepen a pastor's ministry, providing a source of support, encouragement, and mutual growth. At the same time, it is honest about the challenges and risks involved, from the temptation to favoritism to the danger of blurred boundaries. Dan's insights offer a roadmap for navigating these tricky waters with wisdom, discernment, and grace.

At its heart, this book is an invitation to reflect on the power of friendship in the context of pastoral care. Dan argues convincingly that pastors who can navigate the complexities of these relationships with grace, humility and dependence on God's leading can discover a whole new depth of meaning and joy in their ministries. His insights have the potential to breathe fresh life into the relational heart of the church. Whether you're a pastor, a church leader, or just someone who cares about the health and vitality of the Christian community, this book is well worth your time. Dan's warm, down-to-earth writing style makes even the weightiest topics engaging and accessible. And his knack for storytelling brings the challenges and delights of pastoral friendship to vivid life. As you read, you may find yourself nodding in recognition, chuckling at a relatable anecdote, or pausing to ponder a particularly insightful observation. You may even find yourself challenged to rethink some of your assumptions about what it means to be a friend and a pastor. But one thing is certain: you'll come away with a deeper, richer understanding of the joys and complexities of pastoral friendships—and a renewed appreciation for the power of these relationships to shape lives and communities for the better.

So prepare to be inspired, challenged, and encouraged. Who knows? You may just discover a new vision for the role of friendship in your own life and ministry. And in the process, you might just find yourself becoming a better friend—and a better pastor—along the way.

John Swinton
University of Aberdeen
May 2024

Acknowledgments

THIS BOOK IS THE fruit of my doctoral thesis in practical theology. My thanks go to my supervisors John Swinton and Leon van Ommen at the University of Aberdeen for their encouragement, their humour, and their skill in guiding me through my dissertation. They helped me to develop both my understanding of the field as well as my theological acumen, and they kept me on track when I was tempted to wander.

Thanks go also to other staff members at the theological faculty in Aberdeen, whose interest in my work and kindness in encouraging me I have appreciated greatly over these past few years.

I am grateful to any number of colleagues in Church ministry and some in theological faculties, to theology students as well as members of Church congregations I have met who have been interested in my work and have been happy to ponder and discuss with me their thoughts on friendship in the pastoral setting.

I am indebted to those research participants who shared with me their personal experiences, feelings, and thoughts around friendship in their professional environments.

I thank my family members, my children Sophia and her husband Tim, along with David, Benedict, and John, and friends who have supported me over the last years and whose love and prayerful support have been a source of strength and motivation for me.

Finally, my profound thanks go especially to my wife Martina, also an ordained pastor in the Swiss Reformed Church, who I regard as my best friend and with whom it is both an honour and joy to work, laugh, live, and be.

1

Approaching the Topic of Friendship in a Pastoral Setting

BACKGROUND—WHERE I COME FROM

FRIENDSHIP SEEMS TO BE a word which many people think they intuitively understand and also something many would regard as a phenomenon they have experienced and enjoyed. If asked what is most important in their lives, many people will invariably talk about their friends, along with their family and their health. Friendship may also be a word which readily comes to mind when Christians think about some of the relationships they have with others in their local church. According to some sociologists, there seem to be three significant factors which make the formation of a friendship possible: *proximity*—nearness or having a place or places to interact; *repeated, unplanned interactions*; and a *setting* that encourages people to let down their guard and confide in each other. Similarly there is a tendency to come to like a person simply as a result of having regular personal contact with them. With this in mind, weekly Sunday services at a local church with coffee afterwards would seem to be an excellent place in which to make and develop friendships.

Such was the case for me as I was growing up. I had two sets of people I would call friends: Church friends and school friends—school being the other close-by place in my life where repeated, unplanned interactions and regular personal contact occurred, and where every now and then there was the possibility of confiding in someone, to a degree. For me, these two sets of friends did not really converge, as none of my school friends went to the Church of which my family and I were members, and none of my Church friends were in the same year at school. I cannot remember this bothering me much at the time. My Church friends were, in general, those I valued more highly as we shared more of who we and our families were together.

Growing up in a small, nonconformist, evangelical Church in the 1970s in England meant being aware from an early age that serious Christians, those who really wanted to follow Jesus, were probably few and far between. Neither my parents nor the Church was sectarian in the sense that we knew that our form of Christian worship and living was not the only way to do it. But my identity growing up was of belonging to a community which was different from the mainstream, living in the world and for the world but not of the world. This meant for me, in my formative years, that any friendships I would classify as more than merely superficial would have to be with people who at the least understood and in the best case shared this. My father was a lay pastor and preacher who, having been raised as member of a strict Baptist chapel, had joined the young people's group at a local Brethren Church and had met my mother there and married her. Both my parents came from a background where there was not necessarily a formal, paid pastor at church, the worship services and Bible studies being led either by the elders or by itinerant preachers from the region. The role of pastoring was either taken on by the elders or delegated to those in the congregation regarded as trustworthy and suitable for the task.

My parents often, as I recall, took on a pastoral role in our Church communities, my father more as the Bible teacher and evangelist and my mother as the empathetic listener and counsellor. My mother especially had a gift for befriending people who did not seem to fit in.[1] The people involved, as far as I was aware, regarded themselves as friends of my mother, and my mother, in mentioning them, talked of them as friends. In retrospect, perhaps the fact that my parents took on a pastoral role in their Church communities and were acknowledged in this role, but

---

1. I use the word "befriend" consciously in the context of this study but aware of the complexities surrounding it. Making friendship the "goal" of a relationship is, by some definitions of friendship, a contradiction in terms. See for instance, Lewis, *The Four Loves*, 103: "I have no duty to be anyone's friend, and no man in the world has a duty to be mine. No claims, no shadow of necessity."

were neither employed to do it, nor formally given a mandate, made it easier for them to form relationships which could be regarded as friendships from both sides. As John Tiemstra, a Christian professor emeritus of economics and business at Calvin College, puts it in a short article he wrote dealing with professionality and friendship, "the difference between professional help and help from friends is in part the difference between paying for help and getting it free."[2] This brings up a number of interesting questions regarding the nature of freedom within relationships, something I shall discuss in more detail in the fourth chapter while reflecting theologically on the findings of my research.

My own studies and my calling, as I have understood it, to serve in the kingdom of God have led me to be an ordained pastor, together with my wife who is also an ordained pastor, in the Swiss Reformed Church, where I have served and worked for over twenty-five years, first of all in a semi-rural setting and then in a suburban area very close to the city of Basel. My wife and I presently work in a parish with some 1,800 nominal members who pay church taxes, of whom around 130 come to worship each Sunday. Pastoral work in this setting means relatively close involvement with those members of the congregation whom we meet and worship with weekly, as with the team involved in keeping the church community "running." It involves counselling with members of the congregation as well as with others who wish to meet with us for a "talk," whether nominal members of the church or not. Further, such pastoral work involves occasional involvement with whole families and others in the taking of funerals and weddings, and all that is involved in those occasions. There are weekly confirmation classes for young people, prayer meetings, Bible groups and other duties, as well as various meetings to initiate and organize events.[3]

MOTIVATION—THE QUESTION OF THE PASTOR AS FRIEND AND AN INITIAL LOOK AT ITS RELEVANCE

For those of us, such as myself and my wife, who are in formal, paid, pastoring positions in parochial churches, friendship has not necessarily been a word which immediately springs to mind when reflecting on

---

2. Tiemstra, "Professional Friends," 11.

3. In chapter 2 I give more detail about the setting of the Swiss Reformed Church and my own social location within it.

relations with those with whom we associate. In our training and in further education courses over the years, we have reflected extensively on how to conduct ourselves professionally as pastors and counsellors. And yet I cannot remember one instance in which the concept of friendship as a form of relationship was talked about or discussed in such a course in anything but a passing manner. Friendships were private relationships you either had or did not have outside of your profession and calling as a pastor. In conversation with colleagues, if the topic of friendship arose, it was recognized to be a limited, difficult term in the pastoral context. This was taken for granted, and we did not find it in any way surprising. The claim to friendship with the pastor in established churches, in our experience often seemed to be bound up with issues of power and influence, exclusivity and the need for people to feel somehow superior to others. And thus, for the pastors themselves the use of the word friendship had connotations which sounded threatening or tricky and often had the character of an imposition.

The position in which I found myself for many years regarding friendship as a pastor is well summed up by M. Craig Barnes, the former president of Princeton Theological Seminary. He writes that in his view pastors are not, and indeed cannot be, a friend to members of their congregations, no matter the extent to which members of the congregation might themselves regard their relationship with the pastor as such and wish it were so.[4] In describing his experience of the relationship with a specific elder in his own congregation while he was a Presbyterian pastor, he remarks that it "sounds like friendship. But it can't be." The reason he gives for this is that it is necessary to maintain a distinction between relationships of free mutuality and those of service as a pastor. Ordination to being a pastor, he writes, must necessarily create a holy distance which is grounded in a love which is strong and high enough to no longer to expect the mutuality of a special relationship to a particular person. On the one hand, this seems to echo the high calling of love to which Jesus calls his disciples when he commands them to love not just those who love them but everyone, even their enemies.[5] Yet on the other hand, it is

---

4. Barnes, "Pastor, not Friend."

5. "You have heard that it was said, 'Love your neighbour and hate your enemy.' But I tell you, love your enemies and pray for those who persecute you, that you may be children of your Father in heaven. He causes his sun to rise on the evil and the good and sends rain on the righteous and the unrighteous. If you love those who love you, what reward will you get? Are not even the tax collectors doing that? And if you greet only your own people, what are you doing more than others? Do not even pagans do that? Be

hard to see how such an idea of "holy distance" love fits with the biblical account of Jesus stating that there is no greater love than that of one who gives his life for his friends.[6]

Friendship, understood as a freely chosen and mutual relationship, would seem to contradict the general benevolence of love which expects nothing in return, the relationship to which Jesus calls his followers in Matthew's Gospel. And yet Jesus himself talks in a positive and particular manner about his friends in John's Gospel. This tension has tended to be discussed in theological literature with reference to different Greek terms for forms of love, in this context those of *agape* love and of *philia* love, and in that literature *agape* has generally been preferred.[7] As the American feminist Christian theologian Sallie McFague writes regarding the way in which the term *philia* (which is most often translated as friendship love) has been treated within Christian literature:

> (friendship) has had a bad press in Christian circles. *Philia* is often compared unfavourably with *agape*: the former is preferential and exclusive, the latter is nonselective and inclusive. One should not, the argument goes, think of God's love as *philia*, for God has no favourites, chooses no friends.[8]

As an example of this way of thinking, here McFague refers to the ethicist Joseph Fletcher, who contrasts the use of *philia* love in John's Gospel with what he sees as the better form of love as *agape* in the synoptics and in Paul's epistles, and who finds friendship love to be in direct contrast with justice.[9] This is the type of thought which we find echoed in M. Craig Barnes' essay, which leads him to conclude that the love required as a pastor is the love of service to others, equally and justly, and not the love required in the mutuality of a particular friendship relationship.

In the last few years, however, through contact with the work of John Swinton and Hans Reinders,[10] and specifically through their emphasis

---

perfect, therefore, as your heavenly Father is perfect." Matt 5: 43–48 NIV.

6. "Greater love has no-one than this: to lay down one's life for one's friends. You are my friends if you do what I command." John 15:13–14 NIV.

7. I take up the terms *philia* and *agape* in more detail in chapter 4.

8. McFague, *Models of God*, 160.

9. Fletcher, *Moral Responsibility*, 53.

10. My wife's first profession was as an educator with people with physical and mental disabilities. After her ordination as a pastor, she became involved with the European Society for the Study of Theology and Disability and attended a number of ESSTD conferences, where she met John Swinton and Hans Reinders.

on the need for relationships of friendship within the Church, especially for the most vulnerable,[11] I began to question the absence of a concept of friendship for ordained pastors within a congregation. It seemed to me that the constant drive for professionalization within the pastoral ministry had led to a downgrading of those attributes of interpersonal relationships most often equated with friendship—such as affection, trustful and honest speech, and indeed mutuality.[12] The "higher way" of a love to all, a love committed to justice, which overcame the need for mutuality, sounded good and right. But in practice, rather than enhancing pastoral relationships, it seemed to involve reducing one's personal involvement with people and encouraging an approach of professional distance—the type of hierarchy involved in the counsellor–client setting thus becoming the norm for a pastoral way of relating to others. This was mirrored, for instance, in the way my wife and I, as young theologians on our way to becoming pastors, were encouraged to take courses in Clinical Pastoral Education (CPE)[13] to enhance our general pastoral skills, in which we as pastors would be called counsellors and the person to whom we were talking would be called the client. I remember at the time of my first encounter with CPE in the late 1980s how fascinated I was by the carefulness and exactness of the method, and yet also how strange and incongruent it felt to refer to the other person in the encounter as a client.

11. See for instance: Swinton, *From Bedlam to Shalom*; Swinton, *Raging with Compassion*; Swinton, *Resurrecting the Person*; Reinders, *Receiving the Gift of Friendship*.

12. The Oxford English Dictionary, for instance, presently defines a friendship as a relationship between friends, and a friend as, "A person with whom one has developed a close and informal relationship of mutual trust and intimacy." www.oed.com. And the German Duden, which is regarded as the definitive dictionary of the German language, defines friendship, *Freundschaft*, as a relationship between people grounded on mutual affection ("auf gegenseitiger Zuneigung beruhendes Verhältnis von Menschen zueinander"). www.duden.de. For a short contemporary summary of what has been understood by friendship in the Euro-Western world, see Ellithorpe, *Towards Friendship-Shaped Communities*, 26–27.

13. In Switzerland and Germany known as KSA—*Klinische Seelsorge-Ausbildung*, but sometimes also referred to using the English abbreviation CPT, Clinical Pastoral Training. CPE, developed in a hospital setting among chaplains in the United States and associated with the names of Richard Cabot and Anton Boisen, is widely regarded as a general method for developing personal and professional growth in ministry. It usually involves supervision and involvement in an intervisionary group, as well as the communal discussion of verbatim accounts of pastoral encounters. In the German and Swiss setting, people such as the practical theologian Hans Christoph Piper were instrumental in establishing CPE as a recognized form of pastoral education. See Piper, *Klinische Seelsorge-Ausbildung*; Piper, *Gesprächsanalysen*. Compare also Campbell, *Dictionary of Pastoral Care*, 36–37.

Janet Ruffing, Professor for Spirituality at Fordham University, New York, refers to something similar in her particular field of pastoral work, that of spiritual direction, when she writes:

> it appears that the prevailing operative model of the spiritual direction relationship increasingly resembles a clinical model of therapy with many of the conventions and contracts which govern this relationship—fifty-minute hours, restriction of the relationship to the clinical setting, including time, place, and frequency of meetings, one-sided self-disclosure by the directee of intimate details of his or her life to a director who maintains clinical distance, . . . Despite the growth in skill current directors may experience from this professionalization of spiritual direction, we might well raise the question [of] whether or not other features of this complex relationship are being compromised or neglected by this growing dominance of the therapeutic relationship as the model for all relationships in our culture![14]

As she rightly points out, those involved in such a focus towards a therapeutic model of understanding one's work and ministry, may well experience a growth in skill. Yet this move towards expertise, although beneficial in terms of developing counselling skills tends to leave other areas of a relationship underdeveloped, albeit perhaps inadvertently.[15] In many cases in everyday life there is no problem with this, as the type of relationship needed and thus the expectations involved are clearly defined. I do not expect my physiotherapist, for instance, necessarily to be anything else to me than a skilful physiotherapist. But what about the pastoral relationship within a community which understands itself as the body of Christ? What type of relationship with each other does communal discipleship of Jesus require of those ordained to a pastoral ministry within a congregation? How, indeed, did Jesus himself describe his relationship to his disciples? What did it have to do with forms of friendship? And what, if anything, does that have to do with relations pastors have in the contemporary setting of their ministry in a local congregation?

14. Ruffing, "Spiritual Direction," 65.

15. This is ably noted by the Anglican theologian Vanessa Herrick, to whom I refer in more detail in chapter 5, when she writes similarly to Ruffing: "Professionalism in pastoral ministry—particularly over the last twenty years—has tended to promote detachment, problem-centredness, dependency and individualism, whereas true pastoral care is "involved," growth-centred, mutually upbuilding and rooted in the community of faith. It is nevertheless true that "professionalism" in Christian pastoral ministry has been beneficial in terms of developing counselling skills and a deeper understanding of the psychological dimensions of caring." Herrick, *Limits of Vulnerability*, 18.

The Bible text most often referred to in theological literature on friendship is in the fifteenth chapter of the Gospel of John. Here Jesus, according to John, uses the term friends (philon) to describe the way he relates to the disciples, who are following him:

> Greater love has no one than this: to lay down one's life for one's friends. You are my friends if you do what I command. I no longer call you servants, because a servant does not know his master's business. Instead, I have called you friends, for everything that I learned from my Father I have made known to you. (John 15;13–15, NIV).

Friendship here is not portrayed as an early stage of spiritual relations with Jesus, one which will gradually be superseded by a higher form of love as his disciples grow and mature in their faith. Indeed, it is servanthood which is overcome as Jesus practices a kind of love, shown for instance in the way he is affected by the presence of his friends such as Lazarus or Peter, which exhibits the characteristic of openness and frankness of speech associated with the equality, mutuality, and vulnerability of the way in which friends relate to each other. Brian Edgar, professor for theological studies at Asbury Seminary, notes in *God is Friendship* that in much Christian teaching and praxis Jesus' call to servanthood, as in Mark 10:42–44,[16] is interpreted as a step up from a lower or more childish form of friendship with Jesus.

> Mature faith, it seems, must leave behind the childish approach. It is just as though Jesus had called the disciples to a new level of relationship by saying, "I no longer call you friends, but servants." However, to think in this way is to reverse the actual trend of Jesus' thought and to guarantee the development of a works-related and duty-orientated view of discipleship, rather than one permeated by the grace and love of friendship.[17]

Further, he notes the contemporary significance of a model of friendship within the Church, contending that:

> Friendship is an inclusive relationship that can be adult in form, reflecting a partnership rather than childish reliance. It is

---

16. "Jesus called them together and said, 'You know that those who are regarded as rulers of the Gentiles lord it over them, and their high officials exercise authority over them. Not so with you. Instead, whoever wants to become great among you must be your servant, and whoever wants to be first must be slave of all'" (NIV).

17. Edgar, *God Is Friendship*, loc. 248.

gender-neutral and completely unrelated to any office or position. It is an expression of faithfulness and even of the kind of sacrifice where the greatest love is to die for one's friends. In addition to all this, friendship can provide a theoretical and practical foundation for ecclesiology and mission; it is relevant to the life of the Church in wider society, and it can become a vision of God's future for the world.[18]

There is a tension here. On the one hand, the limits of working with or even encouraging the term friendship in the practical work and relations of people in formal and professional forms of Christian pastoring is an experiential reality. Furthermore, there is a widely held Christian position, echoed for instance by M. Craig Barnes, grounded in Jesus' command to love impartially, even one's enemies, which shuns the particularity and open mutuality of a friendship relationship and seeks a professional distance in pastoral work. Friendships, which are understood by their very nature as having to do with partiality (so goes the argument), will compromise a pastor's ministry, and only through keeping professional distance will the universal love and justice to which pastors are called be able to be lived out. On the other hand, Jesus' openness in revealing "everything that I learned from my Father" with a particular group of people, his disciples, and calling them friends and no longer servants if they love as he has commanded them to do, points to a dynamic in the love required in discipleship, which cannot be contained in the confines of a relationship of professional distance, and which will necessarily have repercussions in the way Christians relate to each other and to the world.

The context in John 15 is not one which refers to the calling to pastoral ministry or indeed ordination. And making too straightforward an analogy between Jesus and his disciples and the practice of ordained ministry in the particular context of this study within the Swiss Reformed Church[19] may be misleading. And yet there are uncomfortable questions here in regard to how pastors should relate to members of their congregations and those in their parishes, especially for those who favour a counsellor-client relationship for pastoral ministry or a calling to maintaining professional distance, which sees little room for friendship within that ministry.

18. Edgar, *God Is Friendship*, loc 327.

19. In chapter 5 I look at the specific context of the Swiss Reformed Church in terms of pastoral education, direction, and expectation.

- If the Church can be understood as a gathering place of Jesus' disciples, those he has chosen to call friends, would it not be strange if that did not also have meaning for the way in which we think about and practice Christian pastoring?

- If part of the vocation of pastors is to encourage and enable others within the body of Christ to live lives which reflect Jesus' call to discipleship, and thus lives open to friendliness and friendship with each other, what might this entail in their own relationships with those in their congregations?

- Could there be types of friendliness and friendship which can and should be actively sought and deepened in the ministry that ordained pastors have within their congregations? And if so, what might the dynamics of such friendliness and those of such friendships look like?

- If pastors have such friends, how do they experience having a friend or friends within their congregations, and what do these friendships mean to them?

The aim of this study is to search for understanding around the questions outlined above within the context of pastoral ministry by ordained pastors within their congregations within the specific framework of the Swiss Reformed Church, with which I am familiar and in which I myself work. Using the research findings, I then reflect theologically upon the understanding of friendliness and friendship which has emerged, and consider what potential it may have in being helpful for those in pastoral positions and their relationships within their congregations.

INITIAL THOUGHTS AROUND METHOD— PRACTICAL THEOLOGY

This is a study in practical theology. The task of the practical theologian is complex. Pete Ward, Professor of Practical Theology at Durham University, defines it extremely broadly but helpfully as "study, that takes both practice and theology seriously."[20] In wishing to take both practice and theology seriously I have chosen to use an approach to practical theology suggested by John Swinton as an orientation point. He describes the task of practical theology as

20. Ward, *Introducing Practical Theology*, 5.

to excavate the hidden layers of meaning that indwell the praxis of Christian communities and to test the authenticity of the praxis of the Church against the vision of the coming kingdom.[21]

Although in the academic setting practical theology has been understood largely as a prescriptive discipline since the reformed German theologian Friedrich Schleiermacher defined it as such, a discipline that seeks to apply theology to the specific needs of the governance and leadership of the Church,[22] the last sixty years since the 1950s and 1960s have seen a major shift away from the restriction of practical theology to the application of doctrine to pastoral situations.[23] This shift has moved toward understandings that focus on the description of and theological reflection around not only the actions of the Church in the world but also around that of actions in society in general.[24] With this in mind, for a study such as this one to gain understanding around pastors' experience and thought regarding friendship in their congregations, such a descriptive approach to research in practical theology is useful. The shift towards a focus on description has meant that the actual lived experience of a person, whom the theologian Anton Boisen called the "living human document,"[25] has been given more weight and authority in academic thought and discussion within theology over the last fifty years than it had traditionally, and is now closely studied and regarded by many as a "valid text" for theological study, comparable to traditional texts of Scripture and doctrine.[26] Critically, however, this "living human document" is not an island, but always part of a community. Thus, more recent literature emphasizes what Bonnie Miller-McLemore calls the "living human web" of life,[27] which the individual "living human document" is moulded by but also moulds itself.

21. Swinton, *Resurrecting the Person*, 12.

22. Compare, for instance, Woodward and Pattison, *Blackwell Reader in Pastoral and Practical Theology*, 24.

23. For an excellent summary of this shift from a personal viewpoint of experience in the British context, see Oliver, "Speaking Christian," 454–66.

24. Compare, for instance, Miller-McLemore, *Wiley Blackwell Companion to Practical Theology*, 1–4; Woodward and Pattison, *Blackwell Reader in Pastoral and Practical Theology*, 1–19; Osmer, *Practical Theology*, viii–x; Ward, *Introducing Practical Theology*, 2–7; Bennett et al., *Invitation to Research in Practical Theology*, 1–11.

25. Compare Gerkin, *Living Human Document*. Gerkin uses the phrase from Anton Boisen.

26. Compare Miller-McLemore, *Wiley Blackwell Companion to Practical Theology*, 1.

27. See Miller-McLemore, "Living Human Web," 9–26; see also Osmer, *Practical Theology*, 16.

Harriet Mowat and John Swinton, in taking up an essay by Stanley Hauerwas, compare Christianity to the acting out of a drama, for instance Shakespeare's Lear. Lear must be performed for one to understand what it is—a drama. People often seek to make Christianity a text rather than a performance. Practical theology takes seriously the idea of performing the faith and seeks to explore the nature and in particular the faithfulness of that performance. There are many ways to interpret Lear, but there remains a fundamental plot, structure, storyline and outcome without which it would be unrecognizable.[28] Discovering what faithfulness to the "plot" of Christianity means is one of the main tasks of theology as a whole.

Swinton and Mowat write:

> the task of practical theology is to "remind" the Church of the subtle ways in which it differs from the world and to ensure that its practices remain faithful to the script of the gospel.[29]

For the work of a practical theologian, this means observation and study of the real lives and communal context of those endeavouring to perform the faith, intertwined with critical appraisal regarding the faithfulness of that praxis to the message and calling of Jesus Christ as witnessed to by the Scriptures.

Approaching this in the context of this study, I have chosen to use as a guideline the framework of the four stages of a research project in practical theology associated with the pastoral cycle. The pastoral cycle or spiral, often originally connected with forms of liberation theology and insights from the social sciences, is referred to, for instance, by the practical theologians Paul Ballard and John Pritchard in their book *Practical Theology in Action*. In looking at useful ways to approach research in practical theology, they use the terms experience, exploration, reflection, and action to describe the pastoral cycle.[30] Swinton and Mowat similarly suggest a four-stage model for research, one which begins with experience in a particular situation, moves to an exploration of the situation using qualitative research methods, then on to theological reflection and from there to suggestions of revised forms of practice.[31]

---

28. Swinton and Mowat, *Practical Theology and Qualitative Research*, 4.

29. Swinton and Mowat, *Practical Theology and Qualitative Research*, 9.

30. Ballard and Pritchard, *Practical Theology in Action*, 73–86. For a contemporary critique and discussion around the pastoral cycle, see Paterson, "Discipled by Praxis," 7–19.

31. Swinton and Mowat, *Practical Theology and Qualitative Research*, 94–97.

The first stage in the terms of the pastoral cycle is that of experiencing. This involves identifying a practice or situation in the experience of the researcher "in the more-or-less routine existence of a given context"[32] that requires reflection and critical challenge. This is an intuitive or what Swinton and Mowat call a pre-reflective phase in which the researcher attempts in exploring a situation to work out what they think may be the key issues involved. This may include an exploration of literature on the area and also an initial and provisional look at the historical and cultural background of the situation.[33] This first chapter in my study is concerned with this identifying of a practice in current praxis which I think, from my experience, requires reflection and critical challenge. And this chapter, dealing with the first stage of the pastoral cycle, after an initial description of the method I deem most suitable for my research, also includes a brief literature review around the theme of the pastor as friend.

The second stage in terms of the pastoral cycle is that of exploration. This involves the gathering of information with the goal of increasing understanding around the issue identified. Swinton and Mowat describe this stage in terms of the application of a qualitative research method involving engagement in "a disciplined investigation into the various dynamics (overt and covert) that underlie the forms of practice that are taking place within the situation."[34] Through such disciplined investigation, fresh insights surrounding the complexities of the hermeneutical dimensions of the situation emerge, some perhaps confirming our intuitive reflections, and others challenging and enhancing our understanding.

For the exploration in this study regarding the search for understanding around pastors' experience and thought regarding friendship in their congregations, I have chosen to carry out in-depth, semi-structured interviews in qualitative research amongst ordained pastors within the Swiss Reformed Church. Such interviews are a way of formally attending to a situation as they are investigative of the particular and the specific within that situation using empirical research. The method which I thought best as a disciplined way of attending to the particularity of the experience of pastors around their practice and understanding of friendship within their congregations is hermeneutic phenomenology, which I will describe below and then return to in chapter two.

---

32. Ballard and Pritchard, *Practical Theology in Action*, 77.
33. Swinton and Mowat, *Practical Theology and Qualitative Research*, 94.
34. Swinton and Mowat, *Practical Theology and Qualitative Research*, 96.

Amongst the various methods for research towards exploring and gaining understanding around an issue, a phenomenological approach lends itself well to such a complex, relational concept as friendship. Linda Finlay, an occupational therapist who has written widely on qualitative research within health care, describes succinctly in her book *Phenomenology for Therapists* the focus of a phenomenological research project:

> The phenomenological research project . . . aims to focus on the psychological reality of the lived experience (its givenness) rather than the "reality" (material or otherwise) itself.[35]

As each of the interviewees has talked to me, it is their reality and experience regarding the phenomenon of "friendship" within their congregations and work as pastors which is the focus of the research.[36]

Phenomenology is both a philosophical idea, originally associated with figures such as Edmund Husserl[37] and Martin Heidegger[38] working within a framework of German thought and language, and a family of qualitative research methodologies. The term *phenomenology* itself is used in regard to the study of phenomena, that which constitutes a phenomenon being "anything that appears to someone in their conscious experience."[39] Within such a study of the phenomenon, phenomenological philosophy challenges the treatment of subjectivity common to the natural sciences in that it rejects the Cartesian subject–object relationship, which carries such weight in the natural sciences. Dermot Moran, a professor of philosophy at Boston College and a specialist in phenomenology, usefully puts it as follows:

> the whole point of phenomenology is that we cannot split off the subjective domain from the domain of the natural world as scientific naturalism has done. Subjectivity must be understood as inextricably involved in the process of constituting objectivity.[40]

---

35. Finlay, *Phenomenology for Therapists*, 75.

36. As Mark Vernon writes, referring to Derrida's work on friendship: "one of the issues is that friendship presumes friendship to be friendship. Friendship is non-predicative, that is, it is not possible ahead of time to say conclusively to what group of people or things the predicate (in this case friendship) applies. Calling someone a friend makes them a friend." In Vernon, "Ambiguity of Friendship," 404.

37. See, for instance, Husserl, *Ideen zu einer reinen Phänomenologie und phänomenologischen Philosophie*.

38. See, for instance, Heidegger, *Sein und Zeit*.

39. Gill, "Phenomenology as Qualitative Methodology," 73.

40. Moran, *Introduction to Phenomenology*, 15.

The application out of this philosophy towards usable methods in qualitative research in other languages and settings is something to which generations of researchers after Husserl and Heidegger have been applying themselves, and which is connected to names such as Amedeo Giorgi,[41] Max Van Manen,[42] and others.[43] They have come up with differing approaches, and Michael Gill, a researcher at Oxford University, in his instructive essay "Phenomenology as qualitative methodology" lists a number of these, the main ones being descriptive phenomenological method as developed by Giorgi, hermeneutic phenomenology which he associates with van Manen, and interpretative phenomenological analysis (IPA) as developed by Smith.[44] Common to all of these approaches, says Gill, are

> a shared foundation of phenomenological philosophy; an explicit interest in the meaning of individuals' experiences; attempting to grasp the point of view of the "experiencer"; homogeneous sampling; and thematic analyses that necessitate creativity and imagination.[45]

In phenomenology in general the attempt is made to "bracket" the researcher's pre-assumptions, biases, and the like, allowing them to access the phenomenon being researched as purely as possible.[46] It is in this attempt that the main differences between the methods lie. Whereas those working with descriptive empirical phenomenology have reasonable confidence that they can access the essence of the phenomenon through pure description and "do not attempt to interpret meanings by

---

41. See, for instance, Giorgi, "Theory, Practice, and Evaluation," 235–60; Giorgi, *Descriptive Phenomenological Method in Psychology.*

42. See, for instance, Van Manen, *Researching Lived Experience*; Van Manen, *Phenomenology of Practice.*

43. For instance Sanders, Benner, and Smith: Sanders, "Phenomenology," 353–60; Benner, *Interpretive Phenomenology*; Smith, "Beyond the Divide between Cognition and Discourse," 261–71.

44. Gill, "Phenomenology as Qualitative Methodology," 77–84.

45. Gill, "Phenomenology as Qualitative Methodology," 86.

46. Van Manen, *Phenomenology of Practice*, 215: "The basic method is called the reduction. The reduction consists of two methodical opposing moves that complement each other. Negatively it suspends or removes what obstructs access to the phenomenon—this move is called the epoché or bracketing. And positively it returns, leads back to the mode of appearing of the phenomenon—this move is called the reduction."

bringing external theory to bear,"⁴⁷ those using hermeneutic phenomenology or IPA

> argue that as researchers we cannot help but bring ourselves into the research. All our understandings are inevitably based upon our situatedness (our unique personal history and circumstances) . . . While we should still attempt to disentangle our perceptions and understandings from the phenomenon being studied by adopting the phenomenological attitude, we have to recognize that interpretation cannot be exorcized from the ongoing revelation of the thing under scrutiny and should probably be acknowledged.⁴⁸

The phenomenological attitude is one which Max van Manen describes as "wonder at what gives itself and how something gives itself. It can only be pursued while surrendering to a state of wonder."⁴⁹ The aim of such a state of wonder, which has to do with curiosity, fascination, openness and a "disciplined naiveté," is to attempt to connect directly and immediately with the experienced world.⁵⁰ Within this state of wonder the researcher using hermeneutic phenomenology will constantly be aware of the need for reflexivity, which is "a difficult, continuous, iterative, layered and paradoxical" process which involves the need "to . . . reflect reflexively on meanings arising in our research and upon our role as (embodied) researchers in constituting those meanings."⁵¹ Such reflexivity is vital for the method of hermeneutic phenomenology, as it is perceived as inevitable that researchers cannot do otherwise than bring their own subjective selves into the research. Findings emerging from research mirror this and thus are understood as the result of a co-created relational process, in which both participant and researcher contribute.

What being reflexive means is portrayed usefully by, for instance, Bennett, Graham, Pattison, and Walton as "looking thoughtfully at one's own self, at what I am like, at how I see what is outside of myself, how I affect it, or how my seeing of it affects how I present it."⁵² They encourage

---

47. Finlay, *Phenomenology for Therapists*, 94. Here, she quotes extensively from the psychologists Amedeo Giorgi, mentioned above, and Frederick J. Wertz, both of whom she regards as leading figures in the area of descriptive empirical phenomenology.

48. Finlay, *Phenomenology for Therapists*, 113.

49. Van Manen, *Phenomenology of Practice*, 27.

50. Compare Finlay, *Phenomenology for Therapists*, 23.

51. Finlay, *Phenomenology for Therapists*, 79.

52. Bennett et al., *Invitation to Research in Practical*, 35.

researchers to ask a number of basic questions which open up the field to an understanding of what reflexivity involves. These include questions such as

- How does my personal history influence my approach to this topic?
- How does my social location (gender, class, ethnicity, sexual identity, religion, cultural location) affect my understanding?
- What is my own entanglement in what I am seeking to understand?
- Where do my allegiances lie, and how do my religious and moral values and political commitments guide my inquiry?
- What can my body and my emotional responses contribute to my attempts to understand this subject?[53]

Understanding something of our own impact as researchers on the research we are undertaking requires a reflexive self-awareness, which is both exciting and daunting in its complexity as it requires that researchers be reflexively aware of their use of the hermeneutic circle or spiral, "the process of coming to understand the being of something . . . through moving iteratively between the whole and parts and back again to the whole."[54] The method of hermeneutic phenomenology I contend is helpful towards the exploration needed in the second stage of the pastoral cycle, opening up a path to a gain in understanding around the friendships of the pastors interviewed. It allows for the discovery of elements and attributes of the experience of forms of friendship which are exhibited in the relational behavior described and reflected upon within the interviews.

In the present study, chapter two is concerned with this exploration. There I describe the design of the research and the way in which it was carried out, and I present my research findings, which involve a close, exploratory examination of the interviews, which were carried out using the hermeneutic phenomenological method. In keeping with the method, the resulting findings from the interviews emerge as a co-creation from the rich descriptions of experience around friendship by the interviewees and my own interpretation of those.

The third stage in terms of the pastoral cycle is that of reflecting theologically, which I will do in chapters three and four. This does not mean that theology was absent in stages one and two, but that a formal

---

53. Bennett et al., *Invitation to Research in Practical Theology*, 42.
54. Finlay, *Phenomenology for Therapists*, 115.

and intentional focus is given to theological reflection at this stage. I shall describe my approach to theological reflection at the beginning of chapter three and then reflect theologically first on the witness of Scripture around the terms and *topos* of friendship, and second, on those themes from the data analysis I identify as not essential attributes of friendship, but nonetheless as associated with friendliness. In chapter four, I then reflect theologically and comprehensively on the essential attributes of friendship and their interwovenness with each other as they have emerged from the research findings from the interviews.

In chapter five, I then formulate possible revised forms of practice which might be understood to emerge from the research and the theological reflection. This stage I refer to in the terms of the pastoral cycle as that of action or of responding. It involves drawing together the various other stages of the research to produce suggestions as to how a deepening of understanding regarding the dynamics involved in a situation may be helpful in transforming it in ways which are authentic and faithful to the gospel of Christ. Regarding this stage of formulating suggestions for revised forms of practice, I have found useful the different forms of pastoral leadership that Richard Osmer, practical theologian and professor of mission and evangelism at Princeton, himself an ordained pastor in the Reformed Presbyterian tradition in the United States, refers to in his *Practical Theology*, a book mainly aimed at leaders in congregations.[55] There he describes three forms of leadership within the Church which he considers useful in responding to the results emerging from practical theological research. These he calls task competence, transactional leadership, and transforming leadership. As the term suggests, task competence has to do with competent performance of the already defined tasks within a congregation, such as "teaching, preaching, running committees, leading worship and visiting the sick."[56] Doing such tasks competently and well is recognized as an important part of the leadership expected from an ordained pastor. Transactional leadership has to do with the ability to deal with others in the sense of mutual exchange or trade-offs. Thus, a good transactional leader might be a person who is capable of envisioning sensible compromises between parties with conflicting interests and then of striking the appropriate deals necessary for the continued running and indeed blossoming of the church. Transforming

---

55. Osmer, *Practical Theology*, x.
56. Osmer, *Practical Theology*, 176.

leadership involves "deep change,"[57] and is about the costly and risky work involved in modelling with integrity the sorts of change desired, even when these may involve something along the lines of a paradigm shift within a church or congregation. In my formulation of suggestions for revised practice, in responding to the research I shall consider whether the suggestions I make for envisioning forms of pastoral friendship have more to do with task competence, transactional leadership, or transformational leadership.

My hope in the fourth stage of responding to the research is that understanding around pastoral friendliness and friendship emerging from this thesis may be helpful in approaching anew some of the complexities and dynamics involved in friendship relationships within the pastoral setting. Such understanding may also be helpful in encouraging those in ordained pastoral ministry to consider nurturing forms of friendship as part of their own discipleship of Jesus within their congregations and may allow them to find ways of circumnavigating the traps of exclusivism, elitism, and jealousy, which so often have led pastors to avoid friendship altogether.

A BRIEF REVIEW OF THE LITERATURE

There has been discussion in recent years regarding the validity of a literature review within research that uses phenomenological methods, as the study of such literature may seem to assist in strengthening preconceived notions and detract from the desired phenomenological attitude which attempts for a while to bracket such notions.[58] Jane Fry, Janet Scammel, and Sue Barker, coming from phenomenological studies in the field of nursing and mental health, discuss the question helpfully in their article, "Drowning in Muddied Waters or Swimming Downstream?"[59] They conclude—and I follow them in this—that a preliminary discussion of the literature around a theme can indeed be helpful in undertaking a preparatory exploration of the dimensions of the phenomenon in order to delineate it, and indeed may be a necessary requirement to ensure

---

57. A phrase taken from the professor for organizational studies Robert E. Quinn. Quinn, *Deep Change*.

58. Compare, for instance, Cluett and Bluff, *Principles and Practice of Research in Midwifery*; Dunne, "Place of the Literature Review in Grounded Theory Research," 111–24.

59. Fry et al., "Drowning in Muddied Waters or Swimming Downstream?," 1–12.

methodological rigour in a research project. It is, however, necessary within a phenomenological study to enter consciously into a phenomenological attitude after one has studied the literature. As they point out, the "bracketing" involved in the phenomenological attitude does not entail the annihilation of knowledge but is about the conscious attempt to suspend or put out of play that knowledge for a period of time, before returning to it at a later point and deepening understanding through reflection within the hermeneutical cycle. The concern of researchers therefore should not so much be about consciously learning as little as possible about the field of research and the relevant literature before beginning the study, but more about consciously and reflexively giving themselves over to the state of wonder and of "disciplined naiveté" during the parts of their research where this is necessary to gain new understanding.

I turn thus to literature in practical theology specifically around the theme of pastoral friendship and how it is experienced within ordained, Christian, pastoral ministry within a church congregation. Such literature is surprisingly rare. This may well be due to the mostly nonverbalised consensus to which I referred in relating my own experience, a consensus that such friendships are not helpful in the calling of a pastor to a "higher love"[60] and are not healthy and appropriate for the standing of the pastor within a congregation.[61] It may also have to do with the notoriously difficult definition of what might be regarded as an expected form of friendliness and what might actually constitute a friendship.[62]

---

60. Compare, for instance, the story of "Snowy," who was needed as a vicar and not as a friend, in Carr, *Say One For Me*, 40; quoted in Bayes, "Making Friends," 23.

61. Compare Whipp, *SCM Studyguide Pastoral Theology*, 146; she refers to the "lure of the friendship model." I take this up further in chapter 5; compare also Bayes, "Making Friends," 16; he refers to Kenneth Childs, "In a sense, the more shy and retiring we are, the better. Nothing is more tiresome than the gregarious young priest who overwhelms his parishioners with 'friendship.'" Childs, *In his own Parish*, 15; compare also a number of verbalised discussions around the theme in blog posts such as https://reluctantxtian.com/2017/09/18/why-your-pastor-is-actually-not-your-friend/; or the commentaries on the aforementioned article by Craig Barnes, https://www.christiancentury.org/article/2012-12/pastor-not-friend.

62. The philosopher and theologian Mark Vernon, for instance, writes of the difficulty in defining friendship, and posits that even Aristotle, whose discussion of friendship has been pivotal in the history of western thought, probably knew "that ultimately a definitional approach to friendship has its limits." Vernon, *Philosophy of Friendship*, 4. And the social scientist and psychotherapist Lilian Rubin writes perceptively, "We have friends, and we have 'just' friends; we have good friends, and we have best friends. Yet such is the elusiveness of the idea of 'friend' that not even the people involved can always say which is which." Rubin, *Just Friends*, 7.

A literature search around the title of this study of the "pastor as friend" reveals only a few academic texts, none of which has the same focus as my research. Most recently, Joas Adiprasetya's article "Pastor as Friend: Reinterpreting Christian leadership"[63] takes up a critique of the current discussions of servant-leadership, or doularchy as he calls it,[64] and proposes a form of friendship-leadership, which he calls philiarchy, which should allow for less hierarchical authority and lead to a form of leadership of equal-standing amongst the followers of Jesus. His contention is that even when servant-leadership is authentically Christ centred and not just a somewhat camouflaged version of kyriarchy, or leadership by masters, it is a form of leadership which is oriented towards the cross. Philiarchy, however, is oriented towards the resurrection of Christ and towards the new creation in which Christ no longer calls his disciples servants but friends. It is oriented towards mutual *philia* love rather than *agape* love, and Adiprasetya shows this by discussing Jesus' encounter with Peter after the resurrection, where Jesus asks Peter three times if he loves him, the first two times using *agape* but the third time using *philia* to denote their friendship and a future of restored communion. Adiprasetya's positive use of *philia* as a fuller love than *agape*, in contrast to Anders Nygren's classic position, where *philia* is basically unimportant,[65] which encompasses both the cross and the resurrection of Christ is stimulating. Yet, what friendship in the pastoral setting actually means and entails Adiprasetya largely leaves undeveloped.

A further mention of the phrase "pastor as friend" is found in the *Baker's Dictionary of Practical Theology* of 1967, edited by Ralph Turnbull. Its pastoral section lists nine qualities associated with a pastoral calling. The last one mentioned is *The Pastor as Friend*, and the article by August W. Hintz, pastor of First Baptist Church in Seattle, begins in the fashion of classic applied theology with the words, "A minister of the gospel will be a friend to every man. He serves one who was a friend to all."[66] What is understood by the word "friend" is then described in terms of friendly pastoral behavior, such as visiting of those in need in the congregation, coming alongside of the disadvantaged, and the practice of loving and

---

63. Adiprasetya, "Pastor as Friend," 47–52.

64. A term borrowed from the Korean theologian Kim Yong Bock; Bock, "Minjung and Power," 628–30.

65. Nygren, *Agape and Eros*; for a discussion of this, see Holst, "Philia and Agape," 55–65.

66. Hintz, "Pastor as Friend," 326.

frank speech. Themes often associated with friendship, such as mutuality, vulnerability, and particular affection are not discussed, and thus the idea of friend is presented as a one-sided phenomenon on the part of the pastor who acts in a friendly way to others but does not appear to expect others to be actual friends.[67]

In terms of actual studies in qualitative research on how pastors experience friendship in their congregations, I have found only two that could be purported to come close to the question addressed in this dissertation. One is Deborah Fredericks' unpublished dissertation *The Leader's Experience of Relational Leadership: A hermeneutic phenomenological study of leadership as friendship*. Her research interests me in that it concluded that leaders can, and do, find ways to lead with friends, and in that she moreover demonstrates in the results of her research that leaders can have actual friendships (with each other and with what she calls their followers or subordinates), provided boundaries are maintained. Yet her work is not in practical theology, has a different focus not situated in the life of the Church, and is more concerned with leadership and women's studies.

The second is Stephen Murray Beaumont's *Pastor, Counsellor and Friend: exploring multiple role relationships in pastoral work*. Beaumont's context is Australian clergy, and his study is a descriptive one that uses both quantitative research and within qualitative research a grounded-theory analysis. Further, his focus is on how clergy juggle between their various roles, which they see as given, and not on how they experience and understand friendship within their role as pastor. Interesting, however, in the context of my study is one of his conclusions that some of the clergy who were involved in his study viewed friendship at times as both an image of pastoral relationships as well as a description of particular relationships, and that it was not always easy for them to differentiate between the two.

Regarding literature around friendship in pastoral theology, there are a number of texts which are helpful in the context of this study, but which also have a different focus. Concerning pastoral care, Alistair Campbell's *Paid to Care? The limits of professionalism in pastoral care* is instructive. Although he rarely uses the term "friendship," themes often associated with friendship, such as mutuality and openness are core to Campbell's thought and reflection around professionalism as well as his

---

67. In chapter 2 I explore further the qualities of friendliness as differentiated from the essential attributes of friendship.

criticism of it.[68] Samuel Southard's *Theology and Therapy: The wisdom of God in a context of friendship*[69] is concerned with discussing how the love of Christ can be lived within therapeutic pastoral relationships which are open to exhibiting some of the attributes of friendship as he understands it, such as particular affection, openness, and mutual freedom. Friendship, particularly in the context of those with mental or physical disabilities, is a recurring and essential theme in John Swinton's work, with his practical emphasis on the disciples of Christ learning to be capable of "being" rather than just "doing."[70] Gordon Lynch's *Pastoral Care and Counselling*, specifically chapters five "The boundaries of the pastoral relationship" and six "Friendship and the qualities of the pastoral relationship,"[71] is also useful in this regard for our context. Lynch points out the boundaries and limitations of an idea of friendship within the pastoral setting by describing a situation in which a person seeking pastoral care experienced such an encounter as exploitative and abusive. He suggests the conscious differentiation between therapeutic pastoral counselling, with clear boundaries and with a written code of ethics, and situations of pastoral care, where the response of the pastor may often need to be more flexible. Within this more flexible approach he sees the advantages and promise of a type of friendship, which, with reference to Alistair Campbell's phrase "moderated love" used in the context of professional medical care,[72] he calls "moderated friendship," a phrase at which I shall look more closely in chapter five.

In the field of leadership studies, two further works are of special interest in our context. Edward Zaragoza's *No Longer Servants, but Friends: A theology of ordained ministry*, a work from which Adiprasetya draws in his article, examines critically the servant-leadership movement, mostly associated with the work of Robert Greenleaf, and locates it as originating in the corporate context and, given its merely masked relinquishment of control and power, as only partially fit for the Church. Using trinitarian thought, he finds the egalitarian approach of friendship in leadership better for the Church, and encourages pastors to think

---

68. For a useful criticism of Campbell's criticism, see Lyall, *Counselling in the Pastoral and Spiritual Context*, 109–10.

69. In chapter 4 I look in detail at Southard's thought around pastoral freedom.

70. See for instance, Swinton, "Healing Presence"; Swinton, *From Bedlam to 'Shalom'*; Swinton, *Resurrecting the Person*; Swinton, *Raging with Compassion*.

71. Lynch, *Pastoral Care and Counselling*, 59–81.

72. Campbell, *Moderated Love*.

and relate more in embodied terms of who they are rather than just in terms of what they do,[73] and sees thus a shift in an understanding of what ordination should mean.

In Chloe Lynch's comprehensively researched dissertation, *Ecclesial Leadership as Friendship* she takes up the concept of friendship within Church leadership with the focus being once again a critique of the current forms of taught leadership within the Church. Building on the work of Ray S. Anderson, senior professor of theology and ministry at Fuller Theological Seminary, she envisions what she calls incarnational ecclesial leadership, where both incarnational ecclesiology and Christian friendship are understood and experienced as "deepening participation in the divine-human friendship," which is characterized by "all of us together loving and delighting in God and loving and delighting in one another in our mutual enjoyment of God."[74] This breaking into everyday life of an eschatological vision leads then to the idea that friendship-power becomes "power with" rather than "power over"; that is, it is understood as co-active rather than coercive. Although her work has a different focus from that of this study, the scope and energy of her discussion of friendship within the "tensive reality where the Church is both mystical reality and sociological institution"[75] is stimulating and helpful.

Regarding the wide discussion of friendship within theology in general, there is a number of authors whose works I have found particularly useful for my research. These are, in alphabetical order: the Anglican practical theologian Liz Carmichael;[76] the theologian and ordained minister in the Uniting Church in Australia, Brian Edgar;[77] the U.S. Catholic feminist theologian Mary E. Hunt;[78] the U.S. Methodist ethicist Stanley Hauerwas;[79] the feminist theologian Barbara Lee Kerney;[80] the U.S. Lutheran ethicist

---

73. This I take up in chapter 5 regarding responding to the results of the research.

74. Lynch, *Ecclesial Leadership as Friendship*, 186–87; quoting Wadell, "Itinerary to Glory," 443.

75. Lynch, *Ecclesial Leadership as Friendship*, 218.

76. Carmichael, *Friendship: Interpreting Christian Love*.

77. Edgar, *God is Friendship*.

78. Hunt, *Fierce Tenderness*. Although I do not reference her work again in this study, her book was useful in the initial stages of my work in understanding the breadth of the theological discussion around friendship.

79. Hauerwas, "Virtue, Description and Friendship," 170–84; Hauerwas and Pinches, *Christians Among the Virtues*.

80. Kerney, *Theology of Friendship*.

Gilbert Meilaender;[81] the German Lutheran systematic theologian Jürgen Moltmann[82] and the Roman Catholic theologian Paul Wadell.[83]

Liz Carmichael writes in summary at the end of her book, *Friendship: Interpreting Christian love*,

> The love of friendship . . . is love that sets people free to be and to become in their own individual uniqueness, and which is essentially directed towards, hopes for and invites, reciprocal love and the joy of fulfilment in mutual relationship: but without possessively demanding it.[84]

Part of the aim of this research, through gaining understanding around the dynamics of friendship through the interviews and my analysis and reflection thereon, using the hermeneutic phenomenological method, is to discuss the possible meaning of such statements as this within the pastoral setting.

Having thus in this first chapter delineated my field of research through identifying an issue in my experience which I think needs to be critically challenged, it will be necessary now for me to give myself consciously to the phenomenological attitude characterized both by a state of wonder and by the attempt to bracket as much as possible my own prejudices and prejudgements while listening closely to the rich descriptions of experiences and the verbalised thought of the interviewees around the phenomenon of friendship within their parishes. This is undertaken reflexively, always with an awareness that my own interpretations of terms and concepts influence not only my thought but also my way of listening and attending to what is happening in the interviews. With this mind, I turn now to my inquiry into specific lived experiences of friendship amongst ordained pastors within their congregations in the Swiss Reformed Church.

---

81. Meilaender, *Friendship*.

82. Moltmann, *Open Church*; Moltmann, *Church in the Power of the Holy Spirit*; Moltmann, "Open Friendship."

83. Wadell, *Becoming Friends*.

84. Carmichael, *Friendship*, 200.

2

Inquiring into Lived Experiences of Friendship Amongst Ordained Pastors

INTERVIEWS WITH ORDAINED PASTORS IN THE SWISS REFORMED CHURCH

HAVING INTRODUCED THE SCOPE, theme, and situation of this study, and having taken a look at the literature surrounding the theme of the lived experience of ordained Christian pastors around friendship, we are now ready to apply a qualitative research method. The aim here, in what Swinton and Mowat call the "excavation of the complex matrix of meanings within the situation,"[1] is to develop a deep, nuanced, and rich understanding of the dynamics underlying the practice into which I am inquiring.

Suitable Methods

The research method I have chosen for this study in practical theology is that of hermeneutic phenomenology within qualitative research. Having briefly laid out the reasons for this in the first chapter, in this section I take a further look into the method and why it is suitable in the context of this study.

---

1. Swinton and Mowat, *Practical Theology and Qualitative Research*, 95.

Qualitative Research

One of the challenges of studying the subject of friendship within the pastoral ministry is that each person's predication and view of their relationships within their congregations is highly subjective. Whereas kinship relationships, such as those of father and mother, or brother and sister, have genetic and legal definitions, and while certain professional relationships, such as those of doctor and patient in the hospital setting, or teacher and student in the school setting, or indeed that of pastor and parishioner in the setting of established churches, are also held together in a legal framework, there is no legal definition of a friend. Friends are defined solely through a person deciding to call someone a friend and understand them as such. Why they choose to do that is specific to that person's experience, cultural background and life-world. Thus, a method for research into such a question as what it means for pastors in the Swiss Reformed Church to have friends in their congregations and how they experience such friendships, must be able to work constructively with the complexity involved in studying such subjective experience without prematurely falling into generalizations. Here, qualitative research seems to be the most useful tool for gaining understanding. The sociologist Jennifer Mason writes about the qualities of qualitative research:

> Through qualitative research we can explore a wide array of dimensions of the social world, including the texture and weave of everyday life, the understandings, experiences and imaginings of our research participants, the ways that social processes, institutions, discourses or relationships work, and the significance of the meanings that they generate. We can do all of this qualitatively by using methodologies that celebrate richness, depth, nuance, context, multi-dimensionality and complexity rather than being embarrassed or inconvenienced by them.[2]

Qualitative research in general then, according to Mason, is not inconvenienced by the highly subjective experience and predications of a person, but indeed celebrates such context, complexity, and nuance. It is interested in a type of knowledge known as idiographic knowledge.[3] Different from the type of knowledge built on the three criteria of the "scientific method"—falsifiability, replicability, and generalizability—which

---

2. Mason, *Qualitative Researching*, 1
3. Compare Swinton and Mowat, *Practical Theology and Qualitative Research*, 32–51.

is known as nomothetic knowledge, idiographic knowledge is understood as meaningful knowledge which has to do with unique life experience, which is not replicable. The psychologist Richard L. Gorsuch in describing idiographic knowledge uses the example of stepping into a stream.[4] It is not possible to step into the same stream twice in precisely the same way. Although much may have stayed the same, something will always have changed between the two steps; the particles of water will have moved and be in different places and perhaps leaves or dirt will have fallen into the water in the meantime. Even the consequences of the first step mean that the stream has changed a little, and thus by the time of the second step, it is, in some ways, not exactly the same stream into which one is stepping. In the same way, people's experiences, although outwardly comparable, are always different from each other, and even the same person will not experience something in precisely the same way twice, although the experience will in all probability be similar and thus allow for an associative form of generalization in persons' reflections on it. Comparing idiographic and nomothetic knowledge Gorsuch writes, "although we may theorize or even dream in a nomothetic world, we never live in it."[5] A nomothetic approach to knowledge using the three criteria of the "scientific method" appears to work well in theory and in certain parts of the scientific endeavour, yet even natural scientists who are convinced of the value of the nomothetic method approach the task of experimenting idiographically, bound as they are to their own unique narrative, working within their own specific historical and sociological settings, and sometimes only partially aware of their own precommitments. Gorsuch puts it in the following manner: "Science is never done without being affected by both the scientist's and the discipline's idiographic perspective."[6]

Swinton and Mowat take this up and contend that this is of significance for practical theology, and for theology in general, as

> idiographic truth . . . is integral to the language of Scripture and tradition . . . The major events of the Christian narrative—incarnation, cross, resurrection—are clearly idiographic.[7]

---

4. Gorsuch, "Pyramids of Sciences and of Humanities," 1830.

5. Gorsuch, "Pyramids of Sciences and of Humanities," 1831.

6. Gorsuch, "Pyramids of Sciences and of Humanities" 1831; Gorsuch refers here to Kuhn, *Structure of Scientific Revolutions*; compare also Polanyi, *Personal Knowledge*.

7. Swinton and Mowat, *Practical Theology and Qualitative Research*, 43.

Within practical theology, it therefore makes a lot of sense to be familiar with and use research methods which are not bound only to nomothetic knowledge but take idiographic truth seriously, being aware that much useful and relevant research can be and indeed has been done using both approaches.

Any process within research, whether it is based on nomothetic or on idiographic knowledge, must however be a systematically and rigorously conducted one. Within qualitative research, it will have a dynamic focused on the specific and the particular, looking at reality in a reflexive manner, searching for situated knowledge and centring around description, interpretation, and understanding. Such understanding will be necessary to allow researchers to judge whether the results of their research should lead to ways of acting differently in the world.[8] In this context, the question of generalizability is important to consider.

If the task of the practical theologian, after having worked on the "excavation of the complex matrix of meanings" within a situation, is "to test the authenticity of the praxis of the Church against the vision of the coming kingdom,"[9] how then can researchers use the findings of qualitative research, which focus on the particular context of a particular situation, to illuminate other contexts and situations? Swinton and Mowat, questioning the idea posited by Lincoln and Guba[10] that the qualitative researcher only provides thick descriptions of inquiries and has no responsibility to look for generalizations, suggest that the terms identification and resonance will be helpful:

> While the findings of qualitative research studies may not be immediately transferable to other contexts, there is a sense in which qualitative research should resonate with the experiences of others in similar circumstances. This resonance should invoke a sense of identification with those who share something of the experience.[11]

While generalizability is not something for which qualitative researchers are bound to look, as the specific context of a situation is their focus, the idea and experience of "transformative resonance" means that

---

8. Compare Swinton and Mowat, *Practical Theology and Qualitative Research*, 45–46.
9. Swinton, *Resurrecting the Person*, 12.
10. Lincoln and Guba, *Naturalist Enquiry*, 316.
11. Swinton and Mowat, *Practical Theology and Qualitative Research*, 47.

data resulting from qualitative research frequently has implications beyond the immediacy of the research context. With regard to this, Swinton and Mowat point out that in two of the qualitative studies presented in their work, such "transformative resonance" was experienced. In a study, for instance, involving chaplains, during a feedback session with other chaplains several chaplains recounted "that they felt a resonance with the results of the study. That is to say, they identified with what we found and resonated with the perspectives that our study raised."[12]

Further, Swinton and Mowat point to the term "theoretical generalization" used, for instance by Julius Sim,[13] which takes into account that the researcher, along with being interested in thick descriptions of experience by the people involved in a particular situation, also hopes that the study "will contribute to theory development with wider implications for other individuals and groups."[14] The German psychologist and sociologist Philipp Mayring similarly suggests that moderate generalization is necessary and usually also the aim of qualitative research, and that it can be helpful as long as the results are regarded not as laws but as possible rules which may have any number of exceptions.[15]

Within this study specific to the context of ordained pastors in the Swiss Reformed Church, it will be a search for possible transformative resonance around the question of what it could mean for pastors to have friendships within their congregations which will be the focus of the fourth stage. That fourth stage involves the envisioning and formulation of a possible revised practice, or in terms of the pastoral cycle, of action or responding, in chapter five.

Hermeneutic Phenomenology

As noted before, my research question, exploring what it could mean for pastors to have friends in their congregations places high value on subjective understanding. The term "friend," as we have already seen, does not lend itself to any easy extrinsic definition and is dependent in its use on the psychological reality of those involved. Regarding research into situations such as this, a phenomenological approach within qualitative research

---

12. Swinton and Mowat, *Practical Theology and Qualitative Research*, 47.
13. Sim, "Collecting and Analyzing Qualitative Data," 345–52.
14. Swinton and Mowat, *Practical Theology and Qualitative Research*, 48.
15. Mayring, "On Generalization in Qualitatively Oriented Research."

seems most suited, as such an approach, as already noted in chapter one, "aims to focus on the psychological reality of the lived experience (its givenness) rather than the 'reality' (material or otherwise) itself."[16]

Amongst the various approaches to phenomenological research, already referred to,[17] hermeneutic phenomenology focuses on the meanings and interpretations which make the lived experience accessible. It assumes that our very approach towards discovering the phenomena of life is already drenched in interpretations we have learnt. Of some of these we already have an awareness, and others are more intuitive; some of them we may like and some of them we may not like; and although we may attempt to lay these interpretations aside, they will inevitably play a role in the manner in which we are able to grasp the phenomenon being studied. With this awareness that there is always an interpretive, and thus hermeneutical, dimension to all our understanding, the phenomenological dimension remains important for the method. In terms of the method, it is necessary to go beyond our own theories and assumptions in order to begin to understand the phenomenon as lived. Interpretation, although always present and acknowledged, should, in a sense, be seen as a second-order activity that emerges from the phenomenological attitude, which allows one to dwell in the material. Finlay refers here to what she calls a "kind of dance," which involves sliding between attempting to bracket pre-understandings and then through reflexivity exploiting them as a source of insight.[18] Constant reflexivity and self-awareness regarding one's own interpretations, language, and motives while giving oneself to the phenomenological attitude therefore remain essential within the research process. Such reflexivity enables the hermeneutical circle to become more of a hermeneutical spiral as the iterative dynamic of the process of interpretation helps deepen and widen an understanding of the phenomenon being studied. It allows the researcher to become increasingly situated in an appropriate and self-conscious manner in relation to their research project.

In engaging in such reflexivity, questions I constantly need to have in mind in my research are those concerning my own influences on the topic of friendship in the pastoral ministry. How am I myself entangled? What precommitments are guiding my value judgements within the inquiry? What about my bodily and emotional responses during the

16. Finlay, *Phenomenology for Therapists*, 75.
17. Compare Gill, "Phenomenology as Qualitative Methodology," 73–94.
18. Finlay, *Phenomenology for Therapists*, 74.

interviews and in the course of thinking about and working on the project? And in what way does my own social location affect my understanding, and the research?[19]

Key Terms Within This Study

In the context of the questions mentioned above, it will be useful to explain some of the key terms I am using. For the specific confines of this study, the immediate context of the term "pastor" as used in the title of this study, "The pastor as friend?," refers in the first instance to ordained, or soon to be ordained, theologians within the Swiss Reformed Church, which is the denomination to which I myself currently belong and in which I was ordained. In the German-speaking environment in which I work, ordained theologians serving in a Church community and usually having been voted into their ministry by an assembly of Church members, are called *Pfarrpersonen*,[20] which I have translated as "pastor." I am aware that along with the term "friend," that of "pastor," could in some ways be understood as part of the exploration in this research. Unlike "friend," however, the term "pastor" is used as a title within a legal framework within the church, and is only given to those who fulfill certain professional qualifications and are given a mandate to be such a person. How each individual with that title understands what it means to be a pastor, or what it should mean to be a good pastor, will vary. My research question exploring what it could mean for pastors in the Swiss Reformed Church to have friends in their congregations will necessarily involve not just excavation around the meaning of friendship, but also around what it might mean for each of those interviewed to be a good pastor. However, I have chosen to focus my research on exploring how the participants understand and experience relationships they designate as friendships, which then in turn may itself shape the understanding of pastoring that emerges.

The setting within which I work and in which this study is carried out is the Swiss Reformed Church. On an official level, there is a body which could be translated in this way, in German the EKS *Evangelische Kirche der Schweiz*. However, the actual church bodies are organized according to varying forms of Presbyterianism in the separate *Kantons*

---

19. Bennett et al., *Invitation to Research in Practical Theology*, 42.

20. *Pfarrperson* is the gender-neutral form. The individuals themselves are called *Pfarrerin* if they are female or *Pfarrer* if they are male.

or counties of Switzerland. They are connected, but only loosely, in the national "Swiss Reformed Church," and within that body the Methodist Church in Switzerland and the Evangelical Free Church of Geneva are also included. The Swiss Reformed Church represents, according to their website, around two million Christians within Switzerland, which amounts to a little less than a quarter of the population.[21] All of the interviewees work within one of the various Swiss Reformed Churches within a specific *Kanton* but the ordination process after theological exams at a university is the same in all the Reformed churches in which the interviewees work or have worked.

The churches within the body of the Swiss Reformed Church emerged from the Reformation and theologically were originally moulded by Huldrych Zwingli and later Heinrich Bullinger in Zürich, Johannes Oekolampad in Basel, and John Calvin in Geneva. Put very succinctly, Reformed churches in general place emphasis on the faith of the individual, their own study of the Bible, their personal discipleship of Christ, and on all of these being done soberly and rationally to the glory of God. Because of that emphasis, they have historically also laid more emphasis than other churches (such as the Lutheran churches) on the ethical outworking of Christian faith through the individual in the public sphere. The Encyclopedia Britannica writes of the historic proponents of Reformed piety in its classic form: "Living under God's mercy, they showed little fear of the powers of this world and were ready to make choices on a pragmatic basis."[22] This has often meant that Reformed people and congregations highly value their independence and a degree of autonomy, sometimes preferring to split off from existing churches and start a new congregation rather than submit to the authority of others.

Regarding my own social location, as mentioned in chapter one, I grew up in an evangelical free church setting in England, oriented to Reformed theology, in what would have been regarded as a middle-class family. When I was thirteen years old, I moved with my parents to Switzerland, and my life changed fairly dramatically as I learnt to cope as a foreigner and learned a foreign language. The experience of being foreign in a society, and for a while of being inhibited by neither understanding the main language spoken nor being capable of expressing myself adequately in it and similarly not understanding any number of cultural

---

21. https://www.evref.ch/organisation/mitgliedkirchen/.
22. See the article "Reformed and Presbyterian Churches" in www.britannica.com.

particularities, I think heightened my awareness for others who may feel foreign in a social setting. This has, I think, in turn affected the way I view issues such as benevolence, hospitality, and compassion as I often experienced benevolent, hospitable, and compassionate people as being important for my own development, both in terms of social competence and spiritually.

A number of years ago I gained Swiss nationality, and presently have dual nationality, having both British and Swiss citizenship. In 1993, I married Martina, who grew up behind the iron curtain in the German Democratic Republic and who came to Switzerland when she was sixteen years old, thus also knowing what it is like to be in a foreign culture, and we have since had four children. My relationship to my wife, Martina, has probably affected my own understanding and experience of friendship the most, as I regard her as, amongst other designations, my best friend.

Research Design

There are four main components to the design of this study, which are centred around the four stages of the pastoral cycle outlined in chapter one:

- an introduction to the situation concerning the subject of friendship within the ordained, pastoral relationship;
- data collection and data analysis;
- theological reflection, as a process within the hermeneutical circle, on the results of the research findings; and
- suggestions concerning how the results of my research might be useful for the envisioning and formulation of revised forms of practice around the subject of friendship within the pastoral relationship.

After chapter one of the study, the following section looks briefly at issues around data collection. This is followed by a description of the interpretive steps used for data analysis, and then the bulk of the chapter is concerned with my analysis of the data collected.

Data Collection

To interview people around a sensitive personal subject, such as their experience around their friendships, needs a certain amount of critical consideration. For my research project, it was clear to me that individuals have interests and integrity of a personal kind, which cannot simply be set aside in research in order to achieve greater understanding in practical theology or to benefit the Church in other ways. A researcher has a responsibility to protect the personal integrity of those interviewed and thus to preserve their individual freedom and self-determination as much as possible. Respect for each interviewee as regards how they choose to answer a question or not and the protection of a participant's confidentiality is of importance. Thus, I have used pseudonyms for names and abbreviations for places to protect the identity of participants.

Phenomenological research requires that participants in a study be capable of providing rich and detailed accounts of their specific experience. For the research to be relevant, they also need to have experience around the actual issue being studied. Sampling in qualitative research is thus often not random but what is called purposive. This means that samples are selected using the judgement of the researcher about where the processes being studied are most likely to occur and that, due to the nature and purpose of the question under research, it is usually limited as only a likewise limited number of people can serve as a source of data.

For my purpose of gaining understanding about what it might mean for ordained pastors in the Swiss Reformed Church to have friendships in their congregations, I considered that purposive sampling would be most suitable as there are indeed only a limited number of people ordained into ministry as pastors in the Swiss Reformed Church.[23] Regarding where the processes being studied were most likely to occur, I considered that working with ordained theologians, each with a university education and experience in public speaking and counselling, should mean that they were able to give rich accounts of their experience and should also have experience around relationships within their congregations. Thus, the sample of participants should centre around ordained pastors with a number of years of experience with the different type of people and situations involved in a pastorate, ideally those with responsibility for entire congregations.

---

23. According to the *Schweizerisches Pastoralsoziologisches Institut* in St. Gallen, there are around 2,300 ordained Swiss Reformed pastors, of whom around 1,800 are working in parishes and around 500 are working in specialised fields, as chaplains in hospitals or counsellors in other institutions, for example. See: https://kirchenstatistik.spi-sg.ch/die-situation-in-den-evangelisch-reformierten-kirchen/#close.

The psychologists Nigel King and Christine Horrocks note in their textbook *Interviews in Qualitative Research* that it can also be useful to look for diversity as a criterion for purposive sampling in qualitative research, and that thus researchers might "seek to recruit participants who represent a variety of positions in relation to the research topic, of a kind that might be expected to throw light on meaningful differences in experience."[24] Having judged, as mentioned above, that my purposive sample of participants should centre around ordained pastors with a number of years of experience with responsibility for whole congregations, I considered it could also be useful for throwing light on "meaningful differences in experience" to include in my sample other pastors with less experience in whole congregations and with more focused ministries to particular groups within the Church.

Further, regarding the possible number of participants in my study, I decided that 8 to 10 interviews would most likely be a good provisional number for my investigation, and if necessary (as posited for instance by the sociologist David Silverman[25]), I could change that during the research, depending on my appraisal of the richness of the experiences described during the interviews.

Aware of my own status as an ordained pastor in the Swiss Reformed Church myself, I considered whether it might be difficult to find interview partners around the subject of friendship in pastoral work amongst colleagues, as they may find it strange or uncomfortable to talk about such a theme with a colleague. As it turned out, this was not the case and over the next months I was able to carry out nine interviews. Of the nine participants, six had responsibility for entire congregations, and five of these had a number of years of experience in ordained pastoral ministry, while one of them had only just begun their ministry as an ordained pastor. Regarding the three other participants, one was a soon to be ordained pastor with experience in another professional field, one a recently ordained pastor with a specific function within their congregation surrounding mainly work around church growth, and one an ordained pastor with many years of experience in the leadership of a large Christian community.

Having planned the interviews carefully, I made sure that I arrived for them punctually, which is important within the Swiss context as a sign

---

24. King and Horrocks, *Interviews in Qualitative Research*, 29.
25. Silvermann, *Doing Qualitative Research*, 146.

of courtesy and respect. I took time beforehand to consider the questions for the interviews afresh and prepared myself to listen attentively and to adopt a phenomenological attitude. I used two pieces of electronic equipment to record the interviews, thus being certain I would have a backup should one of the pieces of equipment not work for some reason. Language is an interesting phenomenon in a place like Switzerland, which has four official languages (German, French, Italian, and Romansch) and where English is also used frequently amongst professional people, and my interviews were also held in different languages. Four of the interviews were held in English, three of the interviews were in Swiss German dialect, which is the native language of the Swiss Reformed Church in the Basel area, and two of the interviews were in high German. This was possible for me as I am familiar in my everyday life with switching between Swiss German dialect, high German, and English. I transcribed the recorded interviews, English into English, German into German, and Swiss Dialect into high German. For an initial cycle of analysis looking for rich and thick descriptions of experience, I used the original languages. This made sense in the context of my study as it is not always easy to translate adequately the sensibilities and subtleties of a language. The translation of the relevant passages into English for the purposes of this study then took place in the writing up of the analysis.

The nine participants who agreed to take part in my study I have given pseudonyms. They are Beat, Clare, Denise, Markus, Nicole, Olivia, Stephanie, Theo, and Ueli. The qualitative interviews I conducted with them were semi-structured interviews, which means they were held as a loosely structured form of in-depth interviewing using a relatively informal style. This allowed the interviewees a lot of space to communicate their experience and develop their formulations but with the intention of keeping the conversation centred around the theme of the research.[26] The interviews were based around the following four areas of questioning which, in keeping with the hermeneutic phenomenological method, concerned the lived experience and self-reflection thereof by pastors

---

26. Compare, for instance, Mason, *Qualitative Researching*, 62–63. Mason quotes from the sociologist Robert G. Burgess, who she thinks fittingly calls such interviews "conversations with a purpose." Burgess, *In the Field*, 102. Critically, however, Swinton and Mowat contend that although interviews contain elements of similarity to conversations, "their focused nature, the necessary power dynamics and their non-clinical focus make them markedly different," and they reemphasize the importance of reflexivity for the entire qualitative research process. Compare Swinton and Mowat, *Practical Theology and Qualitative Research*, 66.

of relationships within their congregations, and which were oriented towards the questions already noted in chapter one as the focus of this study. Each of the areas allowed room for me to ask the interviewees to elaborate or expand on their description of experiences or thoughts where I considered this could be fruitful:

1. How do you think Christian pastors should act or speak within their relationships both professionally and personally? (Possible elaboration: Can you give me examples of your own experiences with such obligations?)

2. How would you describe your approach to friendship with others within your Church community? (Possible elaboration: Do you have relationships you would regard as friendships? Could you describe an example?)

3. How in your experience would you describe the difference between friendliness and friendship? (Possible elaboration: What do you think transforms a relationship of some kind into a friendship? What sort of role might issues of hierarchy and dependence play?)

4. What type of relationships do you think hold the body of Christ together? (Possible elaboration: In your experience is there a connection between the discipleship of Jesus and friendship? Or between friendship and Church worship?)

Data Analysis

The method of data analysis for this study was adapted from different researchers including Swinton and Mowat, van Manen, Finlay, and Mason.[27] Data analysis is defined helpfully by Swinton and Mowat as

> the process of bringing order, structure and meaning to the complicated mass of qualitative data that the researcher generates during the research process. . . . Analysis is a process of breaking down the data and thematizing it in ways which draw out the meanings hidden within the text.[28]

---

27. Swinton and Mowat, *Practical Theology and Qualitative Research*, 57–58; Van Manen, *Phenomenology of Practice*, 311–25; Finlay, *Phenomenology for Therapists*, 227–45; Jennifer Mason, *Qualitative Researching*, 147–204.

28. Swinton and Mowat, *Practical Theology and Qualitative Research*, 57.

The goal of data analysis in hermeneutical phenomenology is to respect and maintain the uniqueness of each interviewed person's lived experience, while at the same time allowing for an overall understanding of the meaning of the phenomenon itself. "Theoretical sensitivity," an ability to be aware of historical, cultural, political and contextual issues which could have a bearing on the research, is a quality which needs to be pursued by the researcher, indeed such sensitivity is "an important dimension of the rigour of a piece of qualitative research."[29] Next to pursuit of this sensitivity, Osmer, for instance, reminds the researcher in practical theology that to interview Christians about their experiences also demands a spirituality of presence. He describes this attitude as "openness, attentiveness and prayerfulness."[30] This attitude, coupled with reflexivity, is relevant in the process of data analysis within qualitative research, for the main tool for analysis is the researcher's own self-awareness, as well as their own experience and body of knowledge in approaching the data.

The procedure of data analysis is not a linear process. The focus with all phenomenological analysis is on pulling out explicit and hidden meanings by iteratively examining the data. It is this iterative character of the hermeneutic circle, or spiral, which means that the analysis can in many ways never be completely finished, as there is always more that could be explored when revisiting the data. Engaging this process involves the researcher "dwelling" with the data, examining it, and progressively deepening different aspects of understanding and meaning. This is challenging for every researcher. I found the vastness and complexity of the reflexive process at the beginning of the analysis both exciting and overwhelming, and Finlay's way of putting this resonated with my own experience:

> the analysis process can be a messy one, involving both imaginative leaps of intuition as well as a systematic working through of many iterative versions.[31]

Although van Manen, for instance, warns against what he calls a seductive reduction to a methodical schema or an interpretive set of procedures while doing phenomenology,[32] in approaching this "messy" process I found certain steps for the analysis helpful and fruitful and I have

---

29. Swinton and Mowat, *Practical Theology and Qualitative Research*, 57.
30. Osmer, *Practical Theology*, 34.
31. Finlay, *Phenomenology for Therapists*, 228.
32. Van Manen, *Phenomenology of Practice*, 22.

listed them below, although once again the iterative nature of a number of these steps must be emphasized.

1. *Transcription*—The interviews were digitally recorded and transcribed. As noted above, those interviews held in English were transcribed into English, those held in Swiss German dialect or German into German. I used the transcribed texts as the material for the analysis. I also took reflective, analytical, and personal memos throughout the entire research process and wrote them down in my research diary.

2. *"Dwelling" in the data*—I read through the texts several times in order to become familiar with and reconnect with the participants' narratives and experiences and the dynamics of the interviews. In doing this, the process of analysis became what Finlay terms an "embodied lived experience in itself"[33] as the immersion in the data nurtured my conscious awareness and understanding of a person and their experiences[34] as well as a renewed awareness of my own contribution to the interview process and the resulting data.

3. *Coding, the first cycle*—The first cycle of coding entailed me marking with a colored pencil whatever I initially regarded as important texts, in other words, whatever seemed obviously relevant to my research question and contained rich and thick descriptions of the phenomenon of the experience of friendship under study. The markings were accompanied by short notes I made in the margin.

4. *Coding, the following cycles*—The second cycle required a more analytical and conceptual interaction with the data. By revisiting the data and sorting and ordering the texts by noting the various themes about friendship that emerged, a deeper understanding began to surface. The following cycles then entailed a process of going back and forth between the various texts and comparing the statements and rich descriptions given therein and the context of the questions in which they were given.

---

33. Finlay, *Phenomenology for Therapists*, 229.

34. In Lindseth and Norberg's threefold method of analysis, this is the part which they call "naïve understanding." See Lindseth, and Norberg, "Phenomenological Hermeneutical Method for Researching Lived Experience," 145–53.

5. *Analysis of each transcript*—Using the results of the coding, I constructed a thematic analysis for each transcript, which I made visible by the use of further colored pencils and further notes in the margins.

6. *Categorizing*—This step involved further deep reflection on the codes and thematic analyses of the transcripts. The transcripts were compared with each other, what I regarded as related themes were clustered together, and an attempt at categorization was made according to the similarities, differences, and relationships apparent in the texts. This was a complex process, as many of the texts fit into multiple categories simultaneously.

7. *Fusion of horizons*—The interaction between the interviewees' descriptions of their experience and my own perception and understanding in the emergence of the different themes and categories which sprang from my dwelling in the data needed to be reflected upon continuously. This reflexivity was an integral and essential part of the whole research process.

8. *Validation of data*—None of the participants in the interviews withdrew their consent for the use of their interviews, which, as was stipulated on a consent form agreed upon before the interviews, they could have done. Also, none actively asked about the use of the data after the interviews. I decided not to discuss the interview data again with the interviewees within the process of the research as that would have amounted to the collection of further data, which would require further interpretative steps within a research process which I judged was already sufficiently complex.

RESEARCH FINDINGS FROM THE INTERVIEWS

We turn now to the research findings. Having conducted nine interviews using the hermeneutic phenomenological method, a breadth of data was produced concerning the interviewees' experiences around friendship within the congregations in which they minister. Such qualitative research, as we have seen, takes seriously the particular situation of the individual and gives weight to the experiences and thought of that individual in their own setting and context. Attempting to preserve the interviewees' unique experience and working with the method described earlier in this chapter, I suggest that four attributes within relationships described by the participants in their answers to the questions in the interviews appear essential in their experience of what friendship is. By essential attributes, I mean those without which the interviewed pastors would no longer regard the relationship as a friendship, however interesting or otherwise friendly the relationship might be.

The four elements which I suggest from the analysis of the interviews are essential to the experience of friendship for the participating pastors are:

- Mutuality as an experience of reciprocal give and take in very personal areas of life;
- Affection as an experience of liking the presence and character of the other specific person;
- Freedom as an experience of choosing to want to be with and trust the other person; and
- Openness as an experience of honest communication of personal thoughts and feelings that would otherwise be held back and a willingness to become vulnerable.

The rest of this chapter deals with the research findings from the interviews. In it I will first demonstrate the importance of these four elements within the interviews for the experience of friendship described by the interviewed pastors. However, essential though these attributes appear, I found none of them alone to be sufficient for an adequate phenomenological construction of how the participating pastors experience friendship. Rather than conceiving of each of these attributes exclusively, it seemed necessary to picture them as interconnected. It is the multi-layered interplay of these four elements which leads to an experience and a rich description of that which the interviewed pastors regard as friendship—a relationship characterized by mutuality, openness, freedom, and affection. After having demonstrated the essential quality of the four elements in four separate sections, I will then further show how each of these elements interplays in the complex experiences of friendship described by the interviewed pastors.

Part of the reflection process involved in the interviews was concerned with differentiating between friendly relationships and friendships. This differentiation was necessary to attempt to get at that which is pivotal in the participants' experience of friendship. And yet, within the complexity of human relations as experienced by the pastors within their congregations it would be misleading to divorce qualities of friendliness from an overall interpretation of what friendship means as described by the interview participants. Such qualities of friendliness are helpful in describing the breadth of experience involved in reflection on friendship. In some cases, relationships enabled and enriched by friendliness develop into ones the participants understand as friendships, and in many cases, they remained relationships characterized by a friendliness moulded by the Christian and professional expectations the pastors have of themselves. Including phenomenological inquiry into the attributes of friendliness within this data analysis is also insightful in bringing into focus how in some cases the interviewed participants' deliberate desire for qualities of friendliness hinders the development of relationships into something they would regard as friendships. This can, for instance, be the case when the theme of equality and benevolence towards each and every person (which pastors feel is required of them as ministers of the friendliness of God) hinders them from choosing to become what they would understand as partial and develop particular relationships, especially when they are unsure of what their reasons are for wanting to do so.

Thus, I have subsequently included within the data analysis five sections which deal specifically with elements of friendliness described by the interviewed pastors in their relationships. These are:

- Benevolence as general goodwill and kindness to everyone with whom the pastors come into contact;
- Closeness as offered situational companionship to those who ask for it;
- Equality as the discipline of consciously and self-reflectively avoiding letting prejudices cloud the professional and Christian treatment of people in the congregation;
- Faithfulness as loyalty to Christ leading to trustworthiness and reliability in other relationships; and
- Hospitality as the spirit of welcoming all who wish to be welcomed and inviting them into community.

As noted in the previous chapter, the questions in the semi-structured interviews were centred around four themes, which in concordance with the goals of phenomenology, were formulated to lead the interviewees towards the subject being studied without introducing words or concepts which would prematurely influence the direction of the conversation.

Before moving on to the actual findings of the data analysis, I shall repeat the questions I asked in the interviews and briefly discuss my reasons for posing them.

- How in your experience should pastors act or speak within their relationships both professionally and personally?

This question opened up the general field of relationships within the pastoral setting to hear and understand how the interviewees understand and judge their own behavior and attitudes as Christian pastors and what motives they are aware of in the formation and development of their relationships.

- How would you describe your approach to friendship with others within your Church community?

This question introduced the main subject of the study but left space open for the participants to bring in the elements and themes which were important and of vital interest to them within their vocation.

- How in your experience would you describe the difference between friendliness and friendship?

Here the question introduced a focus which allowed the interviewees to delve deeper into their own experience with people and describe something of the attributes which they regard as pivotal for their own perception of friendship.

- What type of relationships do you think hold the body of Christ together?

This question opened up space for the interviewees, who are all academically trained theologians, to bring their own experience around the theme of relationships within the Church into a reflective, theological dimension.

All of the interviewees were describing and reflecting experiences at different levels, and most mentioned that the interview itself was an interesting and stimulating experience both in regard to their thought and their ministry. As is always the case in using hermeneutic phenomenology, in recognition of the co-creation of meaning I chose to give voice to certain core patterns in the data material regarding what I found to be particularly insightful and essential to a phenomenological construction of how pastors experience relationships they would understand as friendships within their congregations. Some statements the participants made were clear, others less so, and some gave hints to important intuitive experiences they were not able to define but nonetheless tried to share. Sometimes I extracted and put together data from across an interviewee's transcript in order to form a longer quotation. This was done carefully to enhance the readability of the data and to illustrate the breadth with which a person discussed an element or aspect over the course of the semi-structured interview. Sometimes, for the sake of precision, I have included in a footnote the German word or phrase used by the interviewee, if it was an interview conducted in German or Swiss dialect. As mentioned previously, each person was quoted or referred to with a pseudonym.

The Essential Elements of Friendship Within the Experience of the Interviewed Pastors

I now turn to the findings of my analysis and show how the four elements I suggest are essential to the experience of friendship for the participating pastors emerged, namely those of mutuality, affection, freedom, and openness.

Mutuality as an Experience of Reciprocal Give and Take in Very Personal Areas of Life

I have divided the first element, regarding what I have described as mutuality as an experience of reciprocal give and take in very personal areas of life, into four areas which the participants talked about, namely: mutuality and the difficulty of this in the professional pastoral role; mutuality in shared personal experiences; mutuality and reciprocity; and mutuality and personal trust.

Mutuality and the Difficulty of This in the Professional Pastoral Role

Each of the interviewed pastors has a professional role to play within their communities. This professional role is bound up with them as people and their vocation, and within their congregations they are very aware of this. Clare, for instance, in the context of a question I ask her about the way she thinks pastors should act or think in their relationships, describes situations she experiences and puts it straightforwardly:

> when I am invited to a house of a person who is a member of my congregation, even if it's not a pastoral situation . . . I am in a way seen as a private person, but I also act as and am also seen, and I am very aware of it, as the minister of this church . . . I am very aware that this is how they see me even if they don't speak about it.

The dynamics of such a pastoral role, bound up with any number of often nebulous issues such as those around spiritual authority and social status immediately make an easy, unencumbered mutuality within such encounters tricky. Sometimes, however, the people involved do not need the pastoral relationship to be mutual in any deep sense in regard to friendship. Stephanie, recently ordained, describes her experience in the parish she is in:

> My orientation is to emulate how Jesus lived . . . his whole ministry was to establish relationships with people. That would also be a wish of mine that I would have the ability to establish relationships with people and to accompany them on a part of their path. . . . But I realize now . . . that it is also a professional expectation. . . . most people like to talk about themselves and to communicate . . . sometimes difficult stories, but also everyday stories . . . I have noticed this in my new role as a pastor, people perceive you as the pastor and . . . you are often "grasped" or "taken hold of". . . I have felt that very strongly . . . they want you to listen and perhaps give good advice . . . or they want you to take time . . . but I don't have the impression that people expect me to become their friend.

Being "grasped" or "taken hold of" is something other pastors experience as well. It seems to be part of the expectation some people have regarding the role of pastors. And yet the expectations can be different from situation to situation.

Whereas Stephanie had the impression that people in her parish in the city did not expect her to become their friend, when I asked Denise about her approach to friendship with others in her experience of Christian communities, she replied:

there are individuals who expect me to be their friend. That means that they feel they can come to me at any time, day or night, and complain about their suffering, and I should understand everything . . . and I have to say, no, I can't be a part of that. Here there are many expectations, . . . Sometimes there is a symbiotic element, . . ., that's something I really have a hard time with. I'm not that type of person. . . . I don't like it, when there is a one-sided expectation, a one-sided pressure too, . . . friendship is something mutual for me,[35] and within the community it is something quite possible, but it is not something exclusive. . .

Here Denise uses the word *mutual* to define how she would describe a friendship in contrast with a relationship of one-sided expectations or one-sided pressure.

Similarly Theo, in contrasting the friendliness which he sees as a "deserved expectation of pastors" says: "friendship I see as something different, as there is a mutuality, obviously, to friendship." When asked what this obvious mutuality might look like, he answers, "in shared experiences, honesty, openness, humour." The role accorded to Theo as the pastor, then, in his experience allows only a little room for the kind of sharing and openness which he terms mutuality.

Mutuality in Shared Personal Experiences

When I ask her if she has experienced relationships within Christian communities she would regard as friendships and if she can describe them, Denise responds along the same lines as did Theo regarding shared experiences:

> Yes, I would say so, especially those with whom I have been on holiday. . . you can pray together, you can exchange ideas together, you can be happy together, you can be sad together, you can experience pain, even cry.

Doing things together such as praying, exchanging ideas, being happy, being sad, experiencing pain and crying, describes what Denise understands by the mutuality she associates with friendship. These are things of a personal nature. Later, while reflecting further about the relationships she has had within communities, the subject of her experience of perceived

---

35. "...während Freundschaft schon für mich etwas Gegenseitiges ist..."

dependencies and the impact of hierarchies arises, and here she differentiates between types of mutuality and what they imply for friendship:

> with a senior administrator . . . that's absolutely mutual[36] . . . I wouldn't say that we were friends, but I would say that these were friendly expressions of how we were on the same path together. . . . I think mutuality plays a role everywhere, when you have responsibility and leadership, you do things with regard to each other . . .

"Doing things with regard to each other" describes a form of mutuality which would seem to be healthy in any relationship, but which of itself is not yet constitutive of friendship.

Stephanie, in describing further her approach to relationships in her congregation, describes how she invites team members of a project she has started to dinner at her home and conveys to them that she understands herself as a "team person" and that she thinks, "it would be nice if we got to know each other a little better, if we want to serve other people together." This form of friendly mutuality, doing things with regard to each other, perhaps with the goal of wanting to serve other people together, can lead to the deepening of relationships. But Stephanie herself points out that it is different from the mutuality she experiences in friendship. When I ask her what in her experience the characteristics of friendship are that stand out from friendliness, she answers:

> I think friendship is clearly mutual, I give and I take.[37] I show myself in friendships with sides, which I do not share in my field of vocation. . . . I share my fears, worries and needs . . . it is a give and take . . . you experience something and have fun together. . . . I can also speak about my doubts. . . . and I can expect the other person to help me . . . also with very practical things. . . . life sharing, that's what makes up friendship for me . . . praying for each other . . . you can think aloud with each other, you can also say, that annoyed me, or I need concrete help, moral support. And I think friendship also means, I feel like I'm doing the same for the other person . . .

Sharing fears, worries, and needs, speaking about doubts, thinking aloud with each other and speaking out when the other has annoyed her are all aspects of friendship for Stephanie. Once again, however, these

---

36. ". . .absolut auf Gegenseitigkeit. . ."
37. "Freundschaft ist für mich ganz klar gegenseitig, ich gebe und ich nehme."

are things of a personal nature, "sides which I do not share in my field of vocation." And as Stephanie puts it, the mutuality of friendship means there is a reciprocal give and take, "I feel like I'm doing the same for the other person . . ." She elaborates on this reciprocity in an aside while responding to a question I ask her about whether she has people in the congregation she would regard as friends and whether she can describe some attributes of those friendships:

> Mutuality is important, especially when in a friendship one side ceases to cultivate taking and giving . . . then a friendship also somehow ceases. I have experienced that in my life . . . with a friend. . . . there was suddenly no more interest in the life of the other and something then becomes unbalanced. . . . some things you feel first before you can say them. . . . I was uncomfortable for a long time with this person and didn't even know why. But then I noticed that the mutuality had been lost.

What Stephanie here calls a feeling of imbalance and which led to a perception of being uncomfortable with the other person points to a difficulty in defining how reciprocal give and take can be measured and how it actually works. How much "interest in the life of the other," how much cultivation of taking and giving does there need to be for both sides to feel that the mutuality of the relationship is still alive?

Mutuality and reciprocity

Beat also takes up the topic of there being a variety of grades of mutuality in his relationships, and then points to the same problem of imbalance, which Stephanie also notes:

> Within mutuality . . . I think there is the possibility of having friendships with a sort of gradient in them, that's possible where age plays a role . . . or friends being professional people . . . yet it has to be mutual. I always think that in a friendship if you are always the one who cares, who gives, who takes initiative, the friendship will dry out.

Without a living understanding and practice of mutuality, which expresses itself in reciprocal interest in each other, a "friendship will dry out." This type of reciprocity does not, however, have to be something shown or demonstrated all the time. When I ask him what elements are important for him in friendship, Beat recalls the relationship he has with a good friend, whom he had not seen for many years, and yet when they met recently "it was as if no time had passed." In this he recognizes a mutual faithfulness to each other which is not dependent on a quickly changing time-frame. This mutual faithfulness, a reciprocal give and take of personal trust in friendship, is of great importance to him. He mentions at this point in the interview how a ballad written by the German poet Friedrich Schiller, "The Pledge" (*Die Bürgschaft*) influenced him as a young boy:

> someone is condemned, but . . . I don't remember the story exactly, . . . he needs to visit his family before he is killed, and then his friend stands in for him, as a guarantee, and the emperor says if you don't come back on time then I'll kill him. And then he comes back at the last possible moment . . . and the king is so overwhelmed by this friendship, and this faithfulness, that he wants to be part of it. . . . That impressed me hugely as a boy, and it gives you an idea of some of the values, friendship means standing up for . . .

The idea of mutual reliability and trust within friendship, even to the point of endangering one's life, made a huge impression on Beat.

Mutuality and personal trust

In reflecting on the relationships within her congregation which she would in some sense regard as a friendship, Clare likewise takes up the theme of reciprocity and applies it to levels of trust and reliability:

> it's a trust level that is very deep . . . I think reliability is important . . . I think that reliability is also a very important part of the work relationship. In friendship, though, it means a little bit more than that. Where there's a friendship, it's the reciprocal relationship of reliability, whereas in a work relationship, I think that I expect to be reliable for the other person but I don't necessarily expect them to be reliable towards me . . . I think reciprocity is very deep in human nature, deeply anchored in our desire for friendship. It is also something we cannot deny, however professional we might be . . .

This deeply anchored desire for mutuality in friendship, a type of reciprocity which "we cannot deny however professional we might be," points to the tension within the pastor's ministry surrounding friendship.

Part of the professionality of the pastoral ministry is seen as being independent of reciprocal personal trust relationships, which could be seen to create unhealthy dependencies within the congregation.

In describing his approach to friendship in his congregation, Ueli critiques such an understanding of professional ministry which would, in its desire to avoid the dependency of mutual personal trust, also avoid friendships altogether. He describes two concrete friendships he has within his congregation as gifts:

> I hadn't consciously thought about it, with whom I wanted to be friends, but I believe that such a thing is a gift. I think friendship is a gift, and it is not only something I give, but also something I receive. And of course, I don't offer it to everybody, because then you are overextended. . . . discipleship together . . . as a church does not mean that we are all friends, even though I am familiar with the passage in John (he laughs). . . . My understanding of being a friend is where you share your heart . . . where it is protected, where there is security . . . that is a rare gift. . . . when you have found such people, a lot of friendship can grow. I take advantage of that for myself, and I think in doing that I am also a role model for the church . . . I believe that in the church you can find a lot of friendship . . . but you can't do it with everyone.

This gift of friendship should be received and thus become a mutual, reciprocal give and take of personal trust, according to Ueli, and in doing that he understands himself, as a pastor, as "a role model for the church." But he is also aware of the tensions and possible detrimental consequences involved. He describes what he understands as mutuality:

> I think it has something to do with the experience of respecting each other, . . . like me they draw from the same Bible, we can pray together, there I feel a mutuality, that not only I pray, because I am a pastor . . . and not only do they tell me when they have problems, but I can also tell them . . . there the scales should always be roughly in balance . . . but you don't have to be with each other all the time . . . you also have to keep a mutual independence. I find it quite difficult, if the one person absolutely needs me, and I don't need them in that way, then it's not mutual . . . it's not an emotional reciprocity. . . . Esteem is important, . . . that both manage to remain themselves.

Ueli sees the balance of a reciprocal relationship in mutual sharing, where both sides give and take equivalently but where emotional dependence is treated with caution and mutual independence is kept.

Olivia, not yet in a parish of her own but in her practical year as a curate, cannot imagine friendships working for pastors within their congregations because of this balance which would be necessary:

> For me, the concept of friendship for what happens at church is difficult, because what I personally have as friendship otherwise is something completely different from the kind of friendship you probably mean in the community. . . . Friendship is not one-sided, friendship is an interaction, something that happens. . . friendship is not a one-way street. . . . It should be a respectful interaction with each other . . . balanced . . . it's a receiving but also a giving. . . . Perhaps the term is a bit different for the relationship with the church, because there you actually give a bit more. . . . That's why I find the concept of friendship in the congregation difficult to deal with, because . . . the account can't be balanced . . . because we as professionals have the task . . . that we are ready and should give, but we will . . . possibly . . . never get it back.

In summary, in the interviews the essential necessity within a relationship understood as a friendship of some form of reciprocal give and take on a personal level is something that is shared by all the pastors. Yet whether such a mutuality is possible or liveable within the pastoral setting of their congregations is something about which they disagree, at least initially.

Affection as an Experience of Liking the Presence and Character of the Other Specific Person

I have divided the second element, regarding what I have described as affection as an experience of liking the presence and character of the other specific person, into three areas which the participants talked about: consciously caring for another person; loving to be with someone; and affection for others and God's love.

Consciously Caring for Another Person

The question of liking people is one that is fraught with tension in the lives and experiences of pastors. On a professional level, I think most pastors would agree with what, for instance, Nicole answers when I ask her about the difference between friendliness and friendship:

> I have a certain joy in people, curiosity about what drives them in their lives, . . . also an interest in very different ways of living . . . And that is for me an important attitude . . . not only in the pastoral role but also for life in general. . . . When friendliness is not just an attitude I adopt, but when friendliness starts to become something I consciously care for, or when I start investing in a relationship, then the attitude becomes an activity and then it becomes friendship-like.

"A certain joy in people," a liking of people in general, would seem to be a good characteristic for pastors, as they spend much of their time working and speaking with people and it would surely be detrimental to their integrity if they basically did not like other people! But Nicole notices within her own motives different degrees of liking people, as when a general joy in people in certain instances develops and "friendliness starts to become something I consciously care for," rather than just a pastoral, professional attitude. Why does this development start happening though? What it is that causes pastors to start caring for actively and consciously, and in that sense also liking specific people rather than people in general?

Markus points out, "On a natural level people would look for people with similar interests, age etc., those are natural elements." Clare explains this in more detail, but does so more critically:

> friendship is very much a matter of sympathy. . . . I think it comes from speaking the same language . . . I mean she (my friend) remembers the same sayings which I remember from my childhood. We come from a very similar social milieu and therefore we recognize each other as having something in common even though we haven't known each other for more than a few years and there's an immediate click which is not made by decision but it . . . just happens. Sometimes I think some reasons why people can react to each other in a very personal friendly, open, trusting way are also grounded in factors which we would be ashamed of if we really knew them. . . .

The reasons for affection for actual specific people are often grounded in what Clare calls sympathy. Here she is using the word in a German sense; if you find someone *sympathisch* it basically means that you like them. You often like people for reasons of similarity in thought and upbringing, but also for more nebulous reasons, which Clare contends may be "grounded in factors which we would be ashamed of if we really knew them."

Part of the aforementioned tension in pastoral "liking" of people has to do with a sort of battle on a primeval level between what the pastors experience as their often intuitive instincts with people, which are not always clear to them and of which they may be ashamed, and their conscious attempt to be professionally friendly as Christians. Olivia puts this in an interesting way when I ask her about her experience around the difference between friendliness and friendship: "Friendliness . . . as a concept is actually something outward. . . . I am friendly, but that has nothing to do with affection. Real caring comes from within." That is the reason she then gives for not having friendships in the Church. The task of the pastor, as she sees it, is one in which one's affections and emotions need to be tightly controlled:

> So, like perhaps with singing, you are the medium through which the music goes, music as sound, as word, but you cannot bring your own emotions into it, . . . I wouldn't strive for friendship in the church, I would look for it outside.

Here it is clear for Olivia that friendship must involve the emotions and affections toward specific people and if, because of the nature of the pastoral task, such emotions and affections should not be involved and would even be regarded as an unfitting gratification of one's own needs, then friendship should not be sought within the Church.

Loving to be with someone

For Beat, friendship must similarly involve the affections. It is clear for him that,

> a friend is someone with whom I just love to be, . . . it's just loving to be together, for no purpose, not because we want to achieve something, or we have to fulfil a task . . . it is unintentional.

This unintentional "loving to be with" or liking the presence of someone with no ulterior motive other than simply enjoying their company is the reason Beat finds the idea of friendships within the church as "a sort of grey zone." Such affection is naturally limited and involves a closeness which cannot be experienced with too many people:

> you cannot be friends to thousands of people . . ., then it becomes demagoguery . . . that is false friendship when you give the impression that we are very close and half an hour later you feel he has forgotten my name.

There can, however, be gradients of this affection, even in situations which are not merely unintentional. We see this when Beat describes his experience of and feelings toward a person who regularly comes to morning prayer at his church:

> we have a man who lives here and joins us for morning prayer at least once a week. . . . I don't know him, we know very little about each other and yet I feel that we, to a certain extent, are friends, just because for a number of years now at least once a week we pray together. I suppose there is an almost eschatological level in that.

Nicole, as well, takes up the idea of affection and the enjoyment of each other developing over a period of time through sharing regularly in the Lord's Supper. The embodiment of spiritual things she regards as fundamentally important and eating and drinking together, she says, "can also be constitutive for friendship." And the "experience of participating in a table community, especially with people who are a bit difficult . . . can at the end mean that you might even enjoy each other."

Affection toward Others and God's Love

Ueli believes it is part of his calling as a pastor to be friendly to people "who are a bit difficult," even if he does not presently like them, because "the gospel creates a ground to appreciate each other on." He has no problem in having friends within the church whose presence he enjoys and with whom "it's like an oasis that opens up." With such friends (and he mentions two of them in particular), he

> can really be happy . . . where I am not perceived as a pastor or anything else . . . where you don't have to have an agenda, you can meet just like that . . . there does not have to be a reason to meet, you just look forward to [being with] each other.

As well as liking the presence of his friends, Ueli mentions how he also likes their characters and tries to describe what it is that he likes. "There is something about them that fascinates me or does me good... the other can somehow manage his life in such a way that a lot of peace is created around him." Viewed critically this might be understood as an example of the pastor gratifying his own needs rather than caring for the other, but Ueli believes that the living out of such a friendship where there exists a form of actual mutual esteem and affection can be a role model for others within the Church.

Denise likewise addresses the emotional element involved in considering the qualities of friendship: "friendship means that I let myself be affected by emotional, sometimes powerful situations, in which there are also irritations, ... I am not just indifferent." Denise, though wary of what she calls "symbiotic" emotional elements in relationships, sees the possibility of "pieces of friendship" happening as a pastor and leader within a Christian community. Whereas with friendliness, "maybe my heart does not need to be necessarily totally involved," she suggests that certain aspects of friendship are different where they actually involve love and affection felt for a specific person at a specific time:

> friendship ... I feel is something precious, which I think is very important to me. The aspect of friendship can be there, when I realise, especially according to the first epistle of John, that we have the love that God is. He not only has love, he is love ..., we can share in love, and if I have trouble with someone, then I can say ‚Lord, for this person, I need a lot of love now', ..., and I don't just sit with them for a conversation and think, hopefully it will be over soon, but I say, ‚Jesus, I need a lot of love for this person' and I have experienced conversations where tears have come to my eyes, just out of compassion ... and there I also feel something ..., the whole person is there ..., it is like a piece of friendship that happens. It's also something that God gives, through his love for someone.

In situations such as those described by Denise, the affection felt is experienced as something real and directed towards the specific person, not as unfitting or gratifying for a pastor, but as a participation in God's love for that specific person. But it is only felt after the pastor consciously endeavours to overcome their own baser instincts of whether they like someone or "have trouble with someone" by praying that the love of Jesus might be present in the encounter. Also, from Denise's account it is not clear how often this affection for someone might be given, and, although a "piece of friendship" might happen, it is unclear whether the relationship after such an encounter would be regarded as a friendship, either by the pastor or the other person.

Nicole sums up well the tension involved in the pastoral question of affection (or lack of it) for others within the Church, as well as the longing that the love of Christ might make a difference:

> if it would be possible to define something like friendship as a constitutive element of a church, and then also try to live it, this could have a huge potential for the church. . . . but obviously there is a tension in it . . . how do I live together amicably with someone I don't really like? . . . But I believe . . . the discipleship of Christ plays a completely essential role . . . only in this way can you get involved with each other somehow, even if you actually don't yet like each other.

It is discipleship to Christ which "plays a completely essential role" in Nicole's estimation of how she can "somehow" get involved with people for whom she does not currently feel affection.

Freedom as an Experience of Choosing to Want to Be With and Trust the Other Person

I have divided the third essential element for friendship, described in terms of freedom as an experience of choosing to want to be with and trust the other person, into four areas which the participants talked about: freedom not to have to play a role; freedom to let go; freedom in the context of age and experience; and freedom and one's motives for choice.

Freedom Not to Have to Play a Role

> I think it is just a duty of civility to be friendly with everyone . . . but we don't have a duty to be friends with everyone. It is something we can choose, or they can choose.

Markus, in answering a question around the difference between friendliness and friendship, succinctly states what he regards as fundamental in his experience of friendship. There is and can be no obligation "to be friends with everyone" if there is to remain an authenticity around the word friendship. There has to be a freedom involved, "something we can choose, or they can choose." In a similar context, Denise uses the metaphor of an open drawbridge, such as those used over canals, where only when both sides have been lowered can the bridge function as a bridge:

> You can lower your bridge and the other side is free to lower it too. Or they can also leave it up . . . but the freedom of both parts, that is essential . . . When pressure comes or something like that, then I realize that I am someone who likes to live in relationships with freedom, not that I only do what I want, but I don't want to be emotionally captured . . . or if you always have to account for everything you do or don't do. That seems like dictation to me.

On the part of the pastor, freedom here, according to Denise, is about not letting oneself be hemmed in by the expectations and dictates of the other person, not being "emotionally captured," and not always having "to account for everything you do or don't do." Denise calls such a feeling of having to account for your actions all the time "playing a role," and states that in her experience, "if I have to play a role, friendship, or friendly forms of togetherness, are somehow rather excluded."

Theo likewise mentions something similar. He says, "there is an understanding in friendship, which is not tethered to a certain social role or professional function." Friendship then, as he experiences it, has to be something which goes beyond the professional expectations associated with the pastoral role, and which can only thrive and develop in a climate where the free choices of those involved in the friendship are respected. Nicole talks about this freedom in describing to me in her interview why she does not have friendships within her Church community.

> Having no friendships in the church itself is a decision. I have had past experiences with friendships in church . . . I simply experienced that friendship was abused, . . . that people were also somehow overwhelmed with the fact that they were friends with the pastor . . . that experience has very much shaped me . . . I'm someone . . . who is reasonably transparent, and I think that by being someone like that I also have to pay a lot more attention to how I define the relationships for myself. I can live quite a lot of closeness with a lot of people, but real closeness with very few people.

Freedom to let go

The aforementioned freedom to "define the relationships for myself" is important to Nicole. Through her experience of a friendship which she describes as abusive, she has learnt what levels of "closeness" she is willing to allow with different people and at what point she would choose to call a relationship a friendship. She also is willing consciously to leave the other person that same freedom. In elaborating what she understands by freedom, she uses the term "indifference":

> it also has to do with indifference for me, . . . in a true friendship I can also live with it, if someone chooses to end the friendship . . . I am reconciled . . . to let the other move on . . . that is for me the highest form of freedom that you can give yourself in a relationship.

Initially I was irritated by the word "indifference" as it seemed to imply a conscious attempt not really to care, and it struck me as strange to be indifferent about whether friendships were flourishing or coming to an end. Later, on reflection, I realised Nicole was approaching the topic from the perspective of Ignatian spirituality, to which she referred to on a number of occasions, where indifference is seen as an internal freedom which is strong enough to let things and people go in order to grow in relationship with God and to share more in God's redemptive work.

Beat also talks about his need to let go and that this is a vital part of freedom for him. He mentions how important he has found the book *Exclusion and Embrace* by Miroslav Volf and says, "embrace consists of accepting the invitation of closing your arms and then letting go."

Freedom in the context of age and experience

Theo brings up an interesting aspect of freedom in the pastoral role that has to do with age and pastoral experience. I ask him if he himself would feel free to have or not have friendships with people in his congregation, to which he replies,

> I think fundamentally I feel free to establish friendships. I don't feel constrained that I have to, but I guess I'm at a stage of life and career at which I don't feel that at this particular moment in time I have to do either the one or the other.

The freedom here is one in not feeling "constrained" either to search for and live friendship in the congregation or to avoid such friendships at all costs.

Beat makes another comment about freedom and age. He refers to a volume of Karl Barth's early sermons, which had just been published at the time of the interview. In that, Barth refers to his congregation at the beginning of the sermons as "My friends." He recalls,

> Barth was twenty-four years old when he was preaching in Geneva, and when you read his sermon you think this is an elderly friend talking to, "My friends". I mean he was twenty-four years old, he was still a boy . . . But that was his role and the role carried him and the congregation. They all agreed that he had this authority to speak.

Beat finds fascinating the idea that a young preacher might call the congregation his friends and that the congregation does not seem to find that unusual or unfitting, but he immediately points out that he has a different understanding of his congregation: "I am used to addressing [the members of] my congregations as brother and sister when I preach. I think it's important that our relationship is a given, it's not something we choose." Later in the interview he elaborates on this:

> I love the term of brother and sister, because we are just given to each other . . . and then you have the grand commandment, of course, love and everything . . . But I think . . . this deep unquestioned knowledge that we belong to each other is good. . . . we have obligations towards each other, but we do not have to enjoy each other's company all the time, sometimes we just have to function . . . we should not set the goal too high as a general rule because then within this freedom and this open space then you can have friendships.

Friendship for Beat can grow out of the freedom which is afforded a pastor in knowing that the people in his congregation are not necessarily people he might otherwise choose as friends but are what he calls brothers and sisters, people given to each other, whether they like it or not. In such a relationship, the idea of obligations to each other seems to be not so much a question of free choice but of a common responsibility to God.

Freedom and one's motives for choice

Clare, in thinking along similar lines, does not use the terms of brother or sister in this context but takes up thoughts by Bonhoeffer about the relationship that people within the church have to each other: "as Dietrich Bonhoeffer said, we are related to each other not just by our earthly nature. This is not just natural intimacy which we feel, a sympathy which we feel to one another." Initially in the interview it is obvious to her, "that developing friendships within the congregation means to select, or to be selected by individual members of the church with whom I can . . . deal on a deep personal level and those are few." But later, towards the end of my interview with her, the idea of being given to each other, even as friends, starts to grow in her mind as she considers the themes we have talked about.

> I mean God's work with us, God's providential work with us is . . . beyond our recognition. I don't know how people can befriend each other easily and what the reasons are . . . it's a miracle to me. . . . I think the more I think about it the more I come to the conclusion that friendship is something given which I cannot control, I can't decide to be your friend. I can decide to stick with a friend when it becomes difficult, but I cannot decide to be a friend . . . The reason why I can be friends with this person, and I cannot really be friends with this other person does not mean that this other person is less worthy: it just means that somehow this gift of friendship is given to me with this person and not with the other one, and I think . . . that is beyond decision, beyond freewill.

In Clare's interview, as in the others as well, the conversation is constantly developing as the participants think out loud with me over the course of the interview about a subject with which they have experience but about which they have often not previously reflected deeply on that experience. Clare, it seems to me, is not so much denying that friendship has to do with choice, but is asking, perhaps in classic Reformed fashion, where the motives for our choices come from, what they have to do with God, and in what sense can they be regarded as free.

Ueli also regards the friendships he has in his church as a gift. He had not consciously thought about with whom he wanted to be friends, but friendship was something he was happy to receive as a gift and then to give himself. But as he says, "Of course I don't offer it to everybody, because then you are overextended." He then explains something of what he means by being overextended by defining what he understands by friendship:

> My understanding of being a friend is where you share your heart . . . where it is protected, where there is security . . . that is a rare gift, and you have to cultivate it again and again by going out of your way to be a friend.

As Ueli describes it, part of the freedom involved in friendship is choosing whom to trust, with whom to "share your heart," and then choosing to "cultivate it again and again." Such a sharing of one's heart takes emotional energy and time. It is for this reason that being "overextended" can happen quickly if a person really tries to be friends with numerous people.

Openness as an Experience of Honest Communication of Otherwise Held Back Personal Thoughts and Feelings and a Willingness to Become Vulnerable

I have divided the fourth essential element for friendship which I have described as openness as an experience of honest communication of personal thoughts and feelings that would otherwise be held back and a willingness to become vulnerable, into three areas mentioned by the participants: openness and pastoral responsibility; openness and vulnerability; and openness and authenticity.

Openness and pastoral responsibility

All of the participants in the interviews mention openness both as a quality of the friendliness they regard as pertinent in their role as pastors and also of deeper actual friendship. For instance, in describing the way she thinks a pastor should speak or act, Clare says, "I am curious, I am open, I think I am friendly." This is part of her integrity as a pastor, that she "cannot but be myself," as she says. Then she qualifies what she means by this: "I would not hide myself, even though I would not like to reveal everything about my personality or life." It is the degree of openness which causes her to regard a relationship as moving from being a friendly one into being a friendship. In considering at what point this might occur, she conjectures:

> I think . . . at the point where you can open yourself without thinking what will this do to this person in terms of his or her relationship to me as a pastor, then friendliness turns into friendship.

Here she seems to be saying that while she is open on a pastoral, friendly level, she feels responsible for the effect her openness has on the other person and will therefore choose her words of openness carefully. But when she no longer feels this responsibility but considers the trust level with the other person to be great enough not to worry about the effects of her openness, then the relationship has developed from a friendly, professionally pastoral one to a friendship. When Clare describes an actual friendship she has, she says: "I can be silly with her, I can laugh and giggle and tell jokes without thinking that one of us may be hurt . . . it's a trust level that is very deep."

Beat as well feels it is part of his professional pastoral role to communicate "openly, politely." But it is only with close friends that there is a "sort of very deep trust." In recalling how he relates to one of his oldest friends after they caught up with each other again after a long period, he notes, "I know that I could tell him things that I would tell very few other people." In elaborating on his thoughts about trust, he says:

> there is a vulnerability which has to do with trust . . . As you trust someone you make yourself vulnerable because she or he knows things about you which might destroy you, if he or she would use them against you, which is often the terrible tragedy of divorces.

Beat states the risks of vulnerability quite drastically: you might be destroyed if the other person chooses to abuse your trust. He offers the case of divorce, as he sees it, as an example of a type of friendship, in marriage, which has ceased to be a friendship and just leaves both sides knowing they are vulnerable because the other person knows so much about them.

Openness and vulnerability

Nicole takes up the theme of openness and vulnerability in her experiences of relationships and says:

> openness is a prerequisite for friendship, that I'm willing to show my vulnerable side . . . For me, that is also an aspect of integrity, . . . I stand by my downsides, but I don't always have to open them up to everyone, . . . even in a friendly relationship they have to play a role, but above all friendship has to be able to bear them. Perhaps the willingness . . . to communicate my injuries, my wounds, my soul wounds, is important, . . . in the awareness that core injuries and core competences are two sides of the same coin. . .

Communication of core injuries is here seen not merely as a risk, but also as a recognition that "core competences" may only have been able to develop because of the wounds that one has suffered. Nicole has chosen not to have friendships within her congregation because she has experience of abused friendship. She likes to be "reasonably transparent" and says of herself that she "can live quite a lot of closeness with a lot of people, but real closeness with very few people." But while reflecting on the relationship between the discipleship of Jesus and friendship, she does consider the possibility that "following Jesus together" could, in a "kind of triangular relationship," make friendships in the congregation possible.

> If you as a pastor manage to move consciously with your congregation into discipleship, with all your gifts and limitations, then I believe that friendship could be possible.

Such a development would only be possible in an atmosphere of trust and openness in which the "gifts and limitations" of the pastor are accepted and in confidence that the trust will not be abused.

Markus references discipleship to Jesus on numerous occasions in his description of his experience around friendship and openness. He sees different levels of openness in the life of Jesus himself with his disciples, and works with a concept of what he calls "concentric circles." He conjectures, "it's a bit like Jesus and the twelve apostles . . . you have to be open to anyone, but there is a group which is closer." This being open to anyone as a pastor he sees as accessibility, being "open and frank and sharing life to an extent which is feasible." In response to my ensuing question about what he regards as feasible, he reflects that in parishes where pastors are responsible for "over a thousand people," there needs to be a form of delegation, where others involved in the church can also be encouraged to live open, accessible Christian lives, and as he mentions perhaps there are those in the congregation who have had pastoral or counselling training. Markus is convinced, "At church . . . you have to be open and accessible" and through this trust, in both directions, can grow.

Regarding friendships within the congregation, he states:

> There are definitively relationships which I would regard as friendships within the church. In those relationships I am very open . . . It could be a friendship on a purely personal level . . . but it is also a friendship in the service for the church community; because for me as a pastor, there is only so much I can do, but there are others who are in a sense ministers, not ordained but acting as ministers. I want to be friends with them, I want to get to know them. . . . I suppose I might understand some of my friendships . . . in the church, within the context of "something good for the church."

Markus' experience of what he regards as friendships seems to encompass a broader spectrum than most of those described by the other interviewees. He appears to have fewer problems calling relationships friendships after a degree of openness has been shown, and he is happy if the friendships he can thus develop are "something good for the church." Yet somewhat later in the interview, while reflecting on vulnerability, he does make a difference between closer and more distant friends; "opening up makes you vulnerable . . . I think it is very important to have a kind of 'closest circle' of friends where you can talk about everything." In this context, he refers to a place for "confession," such as that about which Bonhoeffer talks in *Life Together*. Such a "closest circle" of friends could be the place where the pastor regularly goes and can be open, without worrying about the effect his openness will have on them. From the way he talks about this circle of friends, Markus appears to assume that they will not be people within his own congregation, but he does not expressly rule this out.

OPENNESS AND AUTHENTICITY

Similar to Markus, Ueli refers to Jesus having some of the apostles as closer friends, but in contrast to Markus he says that he has a fairly narrow understanding of friendship and that he himself cannot "manage more than two friends." With these he can "share his heart," and he uses the metaphor of "being naked" to describe the degree of openness he attempts to live with them. This "being naked" he calls vulnerability and points out that one's capacity for doing this can only grow slowly, but that it is "only natural" in real friendships. It is the giving of something of oneself which could be abused in the hope that "despite all my quirks" the other person will be happy to accept and esteem me. Interestingly, he describes his own need in friendship as needing "good mirrors":

> I need to have people who dare to be critical of me . . . where it's not just dissatisfied barking because that is too exhausting for my soul . . . I need people who can formulate criticism properly.

This criticism, which he regards as necessary for his growth as a person and a pastor can only properly take place within a solid framework of trusting friendship.

Ueli, like all the other interviewees, regards a degree of openness as essential for the role of a pastor, and he brings this openness into the context of authenticity. Recalling his turning to faith as a young man, he remembers his experience of what he calls "God turning his face to me," and how he saw this as the beginning of an open door for his life. And having experienced God's openness towards him, he is convinced that the pastor must attempt to show God's openness to others through his own authentic openness to them, however difficult this might be.

Theo also believes that a friendly openness as a "willingness to evidence the friendship of God" is a "deserved expectation" of pastors. This should be kept up even in places where there appears to be little openness to the pastor. Theo recounts that in his present congregation, where he has been for about a year and half, that in all the time he and his wife have been in the parish "we've never been invited to dinner, or over for a coffee or something." He puts this into the context of a high turnover of clergy in the parish, where none of them have stayed very long, and thus he suspects the congregation is weary of opening up to ever new pastors. In describing the qualities of friendship, however, he immediately lists honesty and openness as essential, and brings this, in a similar manner as Ueli, into the context of authenticity:

> when people sense authenticity, and authenticity happens through openness and vulnerability, when they sense that, that can be the beginning of a relationship that could go towards

friendship . . . I think, you have to try and create situations in which you are accessible and I think many clergy people try very hard not to do that, because when you open yourself up in situations where people can have some accessibility to who you really are, then that leaves room open not just to experience something together but also for being wounded, for being rejected, . . . but, what is the alternative? The alternative is that you do your job like an accountant would, you tick off all the boxes, you make sure that you said the right words, in the right sequence and then the file is closed and then forgotten.

Theo states here that the cost of openness can be rejection, and that because of that risk pastors are wary of opening themselves up to people. But the cost of not being open and allowing the possibility of friendships to develop is also high. In describing a pastor doing his job much as an accountant might, his implication is that that cannot be a realistic option for any pastor who has a "willingness to evidence the friendship of God."

The idea of doing her job as an accountant might is far from what Olivia thinks is right for a pastor. Olivia is in her curacy year before ordination. Describing how she thinks a pastor should act or speak, she says, "What about 100% approachable . . . Through her something else should be visible, and that is the gospel, that is Jesus, that is God." In this transparent way, she hopes to be a pastor who opens the door to the gospel, and she believes, "the more I can adopt this attitude, the easier communication becomes." For her, friendship is all about honesty, openness, and authenticity, but within the congregation she is wary and says,

I think that there are relationships that are called friendships by the other side . . . but I never really am in friendship, because I don't reveal everything about myself . . .

Not revealing everything is her way of not becoming too vulnerable, because if she became a "much more vulnerable person," she imagines it would then become difficult for her to keep up her "100% approachable" attitude. Within the church, she strives for authenticity and a degree of openness, even a degree of vulnerability. But only in a real friendship is "everything visible," which might remind us of Ueli's metaphor of "being naked."

In summary, all the pastors regard openness as a core quality of both their calling as pastors and of friendship. The openness of friendship, however, is more personal and trusting than that of mere friendliness. Most are wary of having such openness with people in their congregations, as they feel the risk of becoming too vulnerable is detrimental to their pastoral work. Others feel that the exemplary role a pastor can have is also applicable in the way they live in friendship with a very small number of members of their parish.

Essential But Not of Themselves Sufficient: The Necessity of the Interplay of the Essential Elements in the Way the Pastors Describe Their Experiences of Friendship

Each of the elements emerging from the interviews that I have suggested are essential to the participants' understanding of friendship if taken by themselves do not appear to be sufficient to describe their experiences of friendship. Or to put it another way, only through the interplay of the elements do the descriptions of friendship really make sense. This becomes apparent when looking at the forms and degrees of the four elements as they are involved in the process of developing relationships.

I have formulated the participants' descriptions of mutuality as "an experience of reciprocal give and take in very personal areas of life." This only works when the participants are open to communicating on a personal level and choose to do so with whomever they like.

The affection described as "an experience of liking the presence and character of the other specific person" can only be reached through gradual and usually iterative choices to respond to the sometimes nebulous and intuitive mutuality felt and to the openness exhibited by the other person.

The freedom the participants experience as one "of choosing to want to be with and trust the other person" once again seems to be an iterative process in which trust is built up through liking what is openly communicated and then, by one's own choice, responding by sending signals of mutuality.

Openness, described "as an experience of honest communication of personal thoughts and feelings which would otherwise be held back and a willingness to become vulnerable," has to do with constantly choosing what to reveal of oneself, a choice which itself is influenced by the degree of affection and mutuality felt and perceived as coming from the other person.

These are just a few ways of trying to describe how these elements relate to each other. There appear to be many and various other ways in which these elements intertwine with each other. Over the next few paragraphs, I shall highlight three of these, each connected to the experience of one of the participants, ways that I think demonstrate the interplay and are relevant to the theme of this research as to how pastors understand and experience friendship and how they relate that to the context of their ministry and the people within their congregations and communities.

Example One—Denise

Denise, as noted before, in elaborating on what she understands by mutuality, mentions in the interview her relationship with a person in the community, and calls it "absolutely mutual," and then immediately qualifies that she would not call it a friendship, but a "friendly expression" of "being on the same path together." Those relationships that she herself would consider as friendships she says have come about through spending times of relaxation and refreshment together, such as going on holiday with people, and have led to relationships in which there is mutual openness in "praying together . . . and exchanging ideas together" and a type of mutual affection in "being happy or sad together." Obviously, the fact of going on holiday with someone, something done in one's free time and not as a part of a pastoral responsibility of organizing a community event, already means that a choice was made about with whom one could go. Freedom as "an experience of choosing to want to be with and trust the other person" is very evident in such an act, and a mutuality is involved in the other person also choosing to go on holiday with Denise. The choice to spend time together in a context not immediately connected to one's ministry seems already to be setting up opportunities to be open with each other, which could potentially lead to a friendship relationship. But the reasons and motives for such a choice are less evident, and Denise does not describe them in her account. She says herself that she would "not want to be friends with everyone," but also points out that it would "not be good in a Christian community" if she always went on holiday with the same people, as the others would get the impression that someone is "somehow preferred" and might have "more privileges." She is aware that she has a responsibility within her role, a responsibility that restricts her freedom simply to choose with whom she would like to be, without taking into consideration how that might affect the community at large. But she also regards "not having to play a role" as a pastor as fundamental to her experience of how friendship can even begin to develop, and that involves the freedom to lay aside expectations and to be open about thoughts and ideas she has which might not fit into the category "pastoral" and indeed be personal. This openness and her willingness to become vulnerable she describes as letting herself "be affected by emotional and powerful situations," which she likes to regard as a choice: "I let myself be wounded and am not just indifferent." This affection comes about because she experiences concern for the other person; she cares about them.

Example Two—Nicole

As noted before, Nicole also uses the word "indifference," but differently from Denise and in the way often associated with Ignatian spirituality, where it refers to the freedom one feels—and indeed trains oneself to feel—that is capable of letting others go if they wish to be let go. She does not see this freedom, which she regards as "the highest form of freedom that you can give yourself in a relationship," as a sign that one does not care deeply about the other person. On the contrary, in true friendship the choice to leave the other the room to leave the friendship if they want to is an indication of deep mutual affection, which is concerned for real openness, for honesty, and for authenticity within the relationship. Nicole talks about openness as "a prerequisite for friendship" and sees this as a mutual openness "where you are on a comparable level to each other, but where you can also encourage criticism in the best sense of the word." Similarly, she sees signs of mutual affection as indicative of friendship, where "you have the feeling that there is a dynamic, something lively in the flow of it." In considering the role the Lord's Supper might play in encouraging friendship within the church, she talks about the fundamental role that embodiment of spiritual things plays. Eating and drinking together can be constitutive for friendships in general, and in the church "sharing life" and "participating in a table community, especially with people who are a bit difficult" could lead to the possibility that "you might even enjoy each other." In other words, the choice to partake mutually in a form of openness before God and each other in the Lord's Supper, with people whom we might not initially like, may mean that an affection for them grows. Here the interplay of some of the elements of friendship allows other elements to develop and blossom.

Example Three—Markus

In Markus' experience around friendship, the interplay of the elements can also be seen in the way he reflects on the development and maintenance of relationships. He regards an openness with friends as a form of accountability, which he puts into the context of a "concept of confession," as something "you have to have" to remain spiritually and mentally healthy. This he sees as a mutual sharing of feelings and thoughts with a friend or "a group of close friends," and not just as a one-sided exercise with a spiritual director or in the frame of professional supervision or intervision. With a close friend or friends, if you are willing to regard them as such, "there must be a lot of openness in that friendship, and if there isn't you have a problem." A "lot of openness" will mean honest communication about very personal things. Interestingly, however, Markus then qualifies this openness and considers how his freedom to choose how much he wants to communicate is also important:

> Now, if you do have friends to share with, you always reflect how much sharing would be helpful, how much would be destructive . . . it is a complicated process to find out what is right and helpful and what would be too much . . . in a sense you always try to protect people . . . but you have to protect yourself as well . . . too much information can be destructive.

Within his mutual and open relationships with his friends, he is constantly exercising his freedom of choice regarding the quantity and intimacy of his communication, and he does this within a process of reflection of how much vulnerability is useful and good both for himself and the other person. It is not obvious from the interview which concrete criteria he would use to work out how much vulnerability is useful and good, but his desire that the community within the church be strengthened is something he mentions as being important to him. Here he points out that friendships can flourish where "things are not understood as only on the level of nature but also seen as the work of the Holy Spirit," and that the Holy Spirit may work in such a way that "your motives can be changed by God." Thus, the affection he feels or does not feel for specific people is dynamic and may change as the community is "moulded together" through mutual experiences of faith in Jesus when "if you move towards the centre, you get closer . . . to each other."

The Elements of Friendliness Which the Interviewed Pastors Expect From Themselves and Which Lead to and Enrich Their Friendships

As noted previously, some qualities of what the participants described as friendliness are helpful in describing the breadth of experience involved in reflection on friendship. Part of this chapter has dealt with what, in my analysis of the data, I have shown to be the essence of friendship relationships as described by the participants of the interviews, namely mutuality, affection, freedom, and openness. Yet other attributes in their relationships were also important to them and were referred to often in the context of their reflection on how they viewed the dynamic of those relationships. These were: benevolence as general goodwill and kindness to everyone with whom the pastors come into contact; closeness as situational companionship to those who ask for it; equality as the discipline consciously and self-reflectively to avoid letting prejudices cloud the professional and Christian treatment of people in the congregation; faithfulness as loyalty to Christ, leading to trustworthiness and reliability in other relationships; and hospitality as the spirit of welcoming all who wish to be welcomed and inviting them into community.

Sometimes the interviewees themselves struggled to articulate the point at which they might regard a relationship as developing into a friendship. But they all described the type of relationships they considered as good for a pastor to be seeking in terms of friendliness. In the following chapter sections, I shall show from the interviews how these elements of friendliness were described and how, within relationships, they both lead to and enrich the development of friendships and also, in some cases, hinder a further development as the tension becomes apparent, for instance around the attribute of equality, between the preference necessary in developing a specific friendship and the ideal of non-preferential treatment for all.

Benevolence as General Goodwill and Kindness to Everyone with Whom the Pastors Come into Contact

The first question I asked the participants in the semi-structured interviews involved how they thought a pastor should speak or act within their relationships. In her response, Nicole talks about "basic goodwill," which she hopes to achieve by striving "for a purified existence in the sense of being in harmony with oneself." This, she says, is a "demand that I make, especially of a pastor." It helps her "to have patience, to be able to wait for the right time and ... not just to be exhausted and disinterested." Such an attempt at being in harmony with oneself is "like a prerequisite for any kind of friendly relationship, whether it's professional friendly relationships or other friendly relationships." "In all benevolence," however, she believes it is necessary to "keep the relationship structure in a clear framework." This means that she regards the relationship first and foremost as a professional one. Within this framework she attempts to have an attitude that is

> basically well-meaning ... to the other person ... so that I don't expect you to want to just fool me somehow, ... trust plays a role, but also a certain joy in people, curiosity about what drives them in their lives, also an interest in very different ways of living.

Similarly, Ueli talks about interest in other people. In relating his own conversion experience while a young man, he describes the effect of his realization of God's friendliness to him, in that it changed him and he "came out of his loneliness" and "learned to approach other people" and be "interested in them." This development of an attitude of goodwill he attributes to coming to understand that "God is our father, also yours ... and you are not just a sparring partner in this world, but the love of the father is also with you." His attempt to be benevolent stems directly from his faith, that God has been and is a loving father not just to him, but to others as well.

Theo describes what he calls friendliness as a "deserved expectation of office-holders, of pastors," and in a similar line of thought to Ueli, he says that they should "be willing to evidence the friendship of God" and thus be "friendly in their demeanour." This friendliness evidences itself in basic goodwill and kindness. Later on in the interview, in response to a question regarding what type of relationships he sees as integral to the life of the Church, he speaks about authentic relationships which "leave room for disagreement" and "which also have a respect and a willingness to acknowledge the worth of another person who may have a very different set of experiences or background." Such a goodwill approach to others opens up room for the development of good and healthy relationships amongst people, which although not necessarily leading to something he would call friendship, "really help define a Christian community that is living and real."

Denise formulates a similar approach, "I always try to see the other person . . . as far as that is possible . . . from the perspective of how God might see them." She elaborates further and describes this as feeling "in a sensitive and empathetic way what concerns the other person." Later in the interview she brings this basic goodwill towards the other into context with a Bible verse reflecting on the Church as the body of Christ. Ephesians 4:15 speaks about the whole body being joined together, "whereby each member supports the other according to the measure of his strength." The idea that everyone has to bring the same amount of competence or strength into a relationship is here reappraised: through the lens of the love of Christ, "everyone can contribute in the way that suits them." This allows for a benevolent attitude to people, an attitude that is defined not only by the pastor's perception of their strengths and weaknesses

Clare recalls that at her ordination as a pastor, one of the sentences which has remained with her was, "Don't give up on anyone." This sentiment she describes further: "it is grace which we experience, and it is grace which we owe the people to whom we are connected." She understands this grace as being basically goodwilled toward all whom she meets, because she has experienced God's goodwill toward her. When I ask her to elaborate on what this benevolence might look like in not giving up on anybody, she replies that it means not breaking off communication. If no "meaningful conversation" is possible anymore, then she would regard that as having given up on the person. Her goal, she says, would be "to have open communications with everybody." This is, she admits, given the numerous scenarios of relationships with which she has to deal, a difficult goal, as a number of such scenarios may involve struggles around important issues. These can involve verbal and emotional attacks by others, be they deliberate or not. But she uses the metaphor of armour to try to describe what she means.

> I wouldn't say friendliness is when you put down your weapons, but you at least don't hold your sword in your hand anymore. But you can have your shield and sometimes you wear your helmet.

Benevolent, open communication involves laying one's offensive weapons aside, so as to be seen not to be threatening to the other person, whilst however keeping oneself protected.

Closeness as Offered Situational Companionship to Those Who Ask for It

Within pastoral work, many pastors experience people's trust, which is associated with their office and which allows for a form of closeness which in other circumstances would be unusual outside of a recognized close relationship, such as a familial one or a friendship. Olivia, in reflecting on relationships within the congregation, says that she thinks some of her relationships would be "called friendship by the other side," but she herself would not regard them as such, "I never . . . really am in friendship, because I don't reveal everything about myself." The lack of mutuality in the openness of the relationship means that the closeness involved remains part of a professional friendliness, a situational companionship which pastors can offer to those who wish to talk to them and share with them. Olivia describes it as "a good encounter, a togetherness" which might be felt as a form of friendship by the other person, "because they have the feeling of being able to say everything, they have the feeling that someone is there." Here a professional attitude and training on the part of the pastor will mean that they need to be sufficiently self-reflective or self-aware to realise what type of response is fitting and suitable in such circumstances.

Depending on the emotional and personal intensity of the encounter, it may be absolutely essential for pastors to keep a professional distance, and this should help them to avoid manipulation, be that from the other person, or be it their own. The closeness which can occur when a pastor offers situational companionship, be that in a counselling situation or while visiting someone at home or in a hospital, makes the other person become vulnerable. Needless to say, pastors must never abuse such vulnerability for their own ends and their own satisfaction. Olivia puts this in quite strong and forthright words: "you cannot bring your own emotions into it. That would be like a form of self-gratification."

There are, however, situations in which a form of mutual closeness can occur through situational companionship, where such closeness is not necessarily manipulative. This does not necessarily mean that the relationship will turn into a friendship, but it shows that professional friendliness and professional distance do not have to involve a total avoidance of anything personal. Markus relates an experience he had with a couple who came to him as the pastor. The couple had been battling "financial problems for decades." In talking to them, Markus practiced what he called "openness as a kind of sharing" and spoke about the financial challenges he and his wife had experienced. He felt this helped the couple to realise that "all of us have to deal with this and that" and that through this personal response they were encouraged and did not feel quite as lonely with their perception of their struggles. In the interview, Markus himself points out that pastors must be aware of how personal their replies are, as "too much information can be destructive" but that there is room for a certain type of personal response in situational companionship, if this opens up space for trust and for people "to be themselves."

Theo and Beat both talk about a type of closeness as situational companionship, which they experience in their more "priestly" duties, such as at baptisms and while taking the Lord's Supper. This closeness Beat associates with people intuitively regarding a pastor, even within a Reformed setting, as a "mediator of the sacred." And thus, the closeness some people allow with the pastor is in one sense a search and desire for closeness to God. Theo describes the baptism of a baby, a situation in which the family entrusts the little child to him for a short while and he briefly becomes a close companion to the family members.

> I've sensed it . . . with baptisms where people come harried and stressed and worrying about, you know, is it all going to go alright and then the moment when I take the baby in my arms and I baptise it and then I always walk with the baby through the church and show them who it is, then you can sense that. It started out as a ritual, but it ended up something completely different and here is this little person who is part of this community.

In that setting he knows that the closeness afforded is not a personal one, but that he represents the friendliness of God, and if things go well, then something of God's friendliness will be felt and experienced by the family of the child.

Equality as the Discipline to Consciously and Self-Reflectively Avoid Letting Prejudices Cloud the Professional and Christian Treatment of People in the Congregation

The initial response of all the participants in the interviews around the theme of friendliness was that there should be no preferential treatment of some members of the congregation. Stephanie formulates this quality of equality in the following manner: "Friendliness for me is an attitude that I want to show everyone, no matter how close to or far away from me they are." It is an attitude that she consciously adopts, being aware that a pastor is a "public person" and "people quickly perceive if you are friendly and accessible" to some and "grumpy and in a bad mood" with others. Further she speaks about it being important to her to have "an open ear for all people," and "I communicate and live such that everyone is welcome, ... I do not only have my favourite faces."

Olivia similarly expresses this attempt at equality by stating that God "does not exclude, he connects, he is for everyone...," and reminds herself and us that

> the Church is a body ... in which we try not to distinguish between higher, lower, worse, better, rich, poor, stupid, with psychological problems or something like that.

Following this she then immediately mentions that this attempt not to distinguish between people makes it difficult for her use the term "friendship" sensibly within the framework of her pastoral work in the Church. Later in the interview around a question concerning the role of dependencies and hierarchies in the Church, she states:

> there could be negative dependencies if you ... cultivate a level of friendship with church members ... that they make a certain claim on the pastor, want certain privileges, get given special tasks ..."I am a friend of the pastor, and you are not" ... the feeling somehow, I am better ... I think that this comes automatically ... because one then gets biased ... you prefer the one to the other. ... I think a pastor may have their own opinion or represent it, but I think they shouldn't be biased.

To Olivia, the equality required in the friendliness expected from a pastor seems to be in tension with pastors living out actual friendships within the congregation. Clare also voices something of this tension when she says that she likes to relate to people in a friendly way, and is open to friendships but "has the difficulty ... that as the pastor of this church ... I encounter the expectation that I treat people similarly." And Nicole expresses a similar thought when talking about the situation in her congregation.

> I know that my predecessor had friends here and that it was very difficult, ... it divides a community, with the chosen ones and the not chosen ones ...

In further reflection upon those friendships, she conjectures that perhaps they would not have been as divisive within the community if they had been with other people, possibly some of whom were not as active in the church, or who did not "play a role in the core area," or if they were perhaps with people who were not popular.

In describing the difference in his experience between friendliness and friendship, Ueli points to the responsibility he understands as being embedded in his role as a pastor, namely that he is "called to this congregation and I think that all those who wish to be in the congregation should be allowed to talk to me." He cites an example of a recent counselling session, and although he admits that he does not like the person involved and finds them difficult, he is convinced that the gospel of Christ "creates a common ground to appreciate each other on." Through this common ground for appreciation, Ueli endeavors to maintain a sense of equality in the way he approaches others. This I have described as the discipline consciously and self-reflectively to avoid letting prejudices cloud the professional and Christian treatment of people in the congregation. Towards the end of the interview, Ueli even went so far as to say that this type of equality as friendliness "may not create friendships like the ones I have described," but that there is a sense in which "the friends of Jesus are also my friends." Such an understanding leads us to the next attribute of friendliness to which the interviewees referred often.

Faithfulness as Loyalty to Christ Leading to Trustworthiness and Reliability in Other Relationships

Theo's response to my first question of the interview regarding the way he feels a pastor is obliged to think and speak in his relationships is one which brings this theme of faithfulness to Christ into focus. The pastor, says Theo, should be able and willing

> to reference Jesus Christ in that conversation, it does not have to be explicit, but the pastor should be aware that everything he or she says or does will be interpreted against that framework of whom we represent in our ministry.

This framework of representing Christ in the pastor's ministry is one which he then describes in terms of friendliness as a "deserved expectation of office holders, of pastors," one in which they should "be willing to evidence the friendship of God" and "willing to search people out, rather than just to wait for them."

Stephanie puts this in a similar manner:

> My orientation is to emulate how Jesus lived . . . his whole ministry was to establish relationships with people. That would also be a wish of mine—that I would have the ability to establish relationships with people and to accompany them on part of their path.

Later in the interview in regard to a question concerning the connection between discipleship and friendship, she reiterates this:

> I want to follow Jesus . . . that is exciting, Jesus as a model for my relationships . . . for my standards in relationships; to forgive, to address things, to be friendly, to have patience.

Her discipleship of Christ she sees as leading her into relationships characterized by trustworthiness and reliability, described by concepts such as forgiveness, honesty ("to address things"), friendliness, and patience.

Clare's recalling of an exhortation given to her at her ordination—"Don't give up on anyone," which I already mentioned around thoughts on friendliness as benevolence, also fits well into this theme of faithfulness. She sees this as the "centre of both my professional and friendship role" and as "the connection between discipleship of Jesus and friendship." Indeed, reliability in relationships she regards as one area where pastors can take on an exemplary role, "I think I have the resources to go through deep valleys in relationships and to come out of them and . . . still have a relationship." And further, she says, "one of my strengths . . . is to stick with a relationship."

Such faithfulness is something Beat also prizes highly within his thoughts around friendliness amongst Christians. Reflecting on aspects of community in the church in a stage of relationship which is not yet what he would call friendship, he states, "with some . . . we are just brothers and sisters, we are given to each other, we are friendly, we are loyal." This type of loyal friendliness he regards as the duty of a pastor. Indeed, he understands friendliness "as one of the highest virtues," and expresses the hope that when he dies, his legacy will be such that when people talk about him, they say, "he was friendly." This friendliness, which is so important to him, is grounded in his faithfulness to Christ. Regarding the way he thinks a pastor should act or speak within his relationships he says,

> usually in relationships I just communicate openly, politely, . . . always bearing in mind, . . . like Peter you know, that I should all the time be able to give an answer to the question regarding my hope, when they ask me.

The reference is from 1 Peter 3:15, which states (NIV), "in your hearts revere Christ as Lord. Always be prepared to give an answer to everyone who asks you to give the reason for the hope that you have. But do this with gentleness and respect."

Olivia is convinced that the pastor, through their faithfulness to Christ, should be a person through whom God and the gospel should be visible. Thus, the mutuality, which we have seen is an essential attribute of friendship, is something she feels cannot be lived out well in a congregation by the pastor. In the setting of the congregation, the pastor's faithfulness to Christ and the gospel means that they should not look for mutuality but "give a bit more." Being trustworthy and reliable as witnesses to Christ means, "we as professionals have the task . . . that we are ready and should give, but we will possibly . . . never get something back."

Hospitality as the Spirit of Welcoming All Who Wish to Be Welcomed and Inviting Them into Community

Finally, one further element of friendliness which the interview participants regard as important in their relationships within the church is hospitality. This can be seen partly in personal invitations for meals and such, but also in their understanding of the role communal worship and taking part in the Lord's Supper plays within a community. Regarding the first, Markus regards an accessible hospitality as of vital importance in his work as a pastor. He wants to be someone who "shares life" and is "not a distant pastor," who is happy to invite people to meals or a coffee together. He understands this as an attitude which "creates open doors" and "open avenues." These hospitable encounters with people he sees as a way to create trust and enhance forms of community, which make it easier for degrees of friendliness and then perhaps friendship to grow. If people experience the pastor as a "normal person," someone "with whom you can have a beer," then they are probably more willing to share with and listen to them regarding other areas of their lives, such as that of their spirituality or in areas where they might welcome some form of counselling. He understands his relationships within a framework of concentric circles with permeable boundaries as relationships develop, either becoming closer or more distant. He also sees a certain amount of hospitality within the church as the "work of the Holy Spirit," and where such hospitality is seldom seen, "it would not be a good sign."

As noted previously Theo, recounting his experience in a parish, where he had not been for very long, mentions that a certain lack of hospitality made his work fostering relationships within the parish difficult, for "in a year and a half that we've been here, we've never been invited to dinner, or over for coffee or something." He does not think this is necessarily "that people don't like us, but I think that's just the way it is." He mentions that there had been a "great succession" of clergy in the parish, which he interprets as meaning that members of the congregation are reluctant to "enter into new relationships," and so they regard the pastor "in a separate category." Stephanie, similarly to Markus, regards hospitality as part of the way she likes to work with people. "I am a 'team person', . . . I like to invest in relationships . . . when I manage projects, I like to eat with people." She describes a project which she has just started, and notes that she did not know the team members well, "so I invited them to dinner at my home." This form of hospitality she understands in the context of a friendliness connected with her work, which she declares as such. She does not necessarily regard people she eats with at her home as friends, but is convinced that it is good to get to know other people a little better "if we want to serve other people" in the community together. This getting to know people better is a complex process which must be able to adjust to people's desires to be close or remain distant. A little later in the interview, Stephanie takes up the metaphor of the "body" used in the New Testament to describe relations in the Church, and points out that to remain functional the body needs both those parts which are close and those which are further away: "I think sometimes we put wrong values on relationships . . . when we only put importance on those which are close." Hospitality which respects people's wishes to be close or distant is welcoming and inviting and yet free. It allows for community to be functional and healthy with friendly relationships which may or may not develop into closer friendships. Reflecting on the type of relationships she thinks are important within her church, Stephanie states that they should be hospitable ones, embedded in a welcoming community, noting that "this has to do with openness . . . where others are welcome . . . no matter where I come from, what I believe, how I live," and that what "God wants with us" then happens "through relationships."

For other participants in the interviews, sharing the Lord's Supper likewise expresses something of the hospitality that the pastors wish for their Churches. One dramatic example of this is narrated by Beat, who relates an experience about which a colleague told him from his time in the mission field in Africa:

> all the independence leaders were in prison and [being] tortured . . . and the prisons were overfilled, so they used the stadiums . . . And then M. [*Beat's colleague*] asked if he could hold a service there as a missionary and a pastor, and the secret police allowed it, but told him he was not allowed to preach, but he could hold the liturgy . . . So he had a service, and the service was with Holy Communion, and then one of the prison guards who was a torturer . . . he didn't understand that it was a protestant service . . . for him it was mass, so he joined for mass, and then M. the pastor who afterwards died in prison as a consequence of the torture, . . . he got up and he went to that guard and told him, "You are my torturer, you hold me in prison, but we have shared the bread, and from now on our relationship is a different one."

This remarkable example of the hospitality offered in the sharing of bread and wine in the Lord's Supper by pastors to those who wish to partake in it, which even extends to those who are actively hostile to them, has led Beat to an attitude of patient expectation when he celebrates the Lord's Supper with his congregation: "Often introducing Holy Communion . . . I like to say, it's very ordinary in some ways what we do . . . and yet do not expect nothing to happen!"

For Nicole, celebrating the Lord's Supper together is part of the necessary embodiment of something spiritual, which as a form of hospitality welcomes people and offers a type of closeness by the communal participation in eating and drinking with each other. Such hospitality can foster friendliness and even friendship. Interestingly Denise points out that she has often experienced that those who have been close within a community but, for whatever reasons, are in the process of distancing themselves, will choose not to participate in the Lord's Supper. Regularly missing Communion has often been a type of early warning sign for her that people are possibly moving to other places and communities in their lives. And yet the hospitality is still there and offered if they decide to take part again.

Summary of the Research Findings from the Interviews

In the research findings after having analyzed the data collected in the interviews using the steps outlined at the beginning of the chapter I have attempted to get close to the phenomenon of friendship as described by the participating pastors in regard to their experiences within their congregations. The findings as I have described them I suggest emerge from the interviews. This I have demonstrated by citing what the participants said around the themes I located as essential for friendship and as insightful regarding friendliness. Yet the findings remain bound to my own specific interpretative framework, which I have approached with a reflexive awareness, but beyond which I cannot move. The findings then, in accordance with the hermeneutic phenomenological method, are to be understood as the product of the fusion of horizons between the interviewees' descriptions of their experiences of friendships within their congregations and my own perception and understanding in interpreting those descriptions towards the emergence of those themes which I have deemed essential for friendship and insightful regarding friendliness.

The four themes which thus emerged as essential to the experience of friendship for the participating pastors were:

- Mutuality as an experience of reciprocal give and take in very personal areas of life;
- Affection as an experience of liking the presence and character of the other specific person;
- Freedom as an experience of choosing to want to be with and trust the other person; and
- Openness as an experience of honest communication of personal thoughts and feelings which would otherwise be held back and a willingness to become vulnerable.

A further five themes which emerged as insightful in understanding the participants experience around friendliness, as differentiated from friendship, within their ordained ministry as Christian pastors were:

- Benevolence as general goodwill and kindness to everyone with whom the pastors come into contact;
- Closeness as proffered situational companionship to those who ask for it;

- Equality as the discipline to consciously and self-reflectively avoid letting prejudices cloud the professional and Christian treatment of people in the congregation;
- Faithfulness as loyalty to Christ leading to trustworthiness and reliability in other relationships; and
- Hospitality as the spirit of welcoming all who wish to be welcomed and inviting them into community.

The next stage in this study is that which involves theological reflection on the findings of the research. It is to this stage that I turn in the following two chapters.

3

Theological Reflection Around Friendship in Scripture and the Elements of Friendliness as Found Within the Experience of the Interviewed Pastors

THE PROCESS OF THEOLOGICAL REFLECTION WITHIN THIS STUDY IN PRACTICAL THEOLOGY

My understanding of the task of the practical theologian, as Swinton writes, and as I quote in chapter one of my study, is "to excavate the hidden layers of meaning that indwell the praxis of Christian communities and to test the authenticity of the praxis of the Church against the vision of the coming kingdom."[1] This leads to observation and study of the real lives and communal context of those endeavouring to perform the faith, intertwined with critical appraisal regarding the faithfulness of that praxis to the message and calling of Jesus Christ and the witness of the Scriptures.

The research findings in chapter two of this book using the hermeneutic phenomenological method are part of stage two in the pastoral cycle, that of exploration around an issue that has, in my experience, been identified as needing to be critically challenged. These findings are a contribution to the "excavation of the complex matrix of meanings within the situation." The essence of how the interviewed participants

---

1. Swinton, *Resurrecting the Person*, 12.

experience and understand friendship within their congregations as I have reflexively interpreted it I have described under the four intersecting themes of mutuality, affection, freedom, and openness.

The task of theological reflection is that of the next two chapters. Regarding the way theological reflection can be approached, Elaine Graham, Heather Walton, and Frances Ward in their helpful, contemporary book *Theological Reflection: Methods* emphasize the shift in the identity of practical theology from "applied theology"[2] to "theological reflection" over the last forty years since around 1980. They crystalize the key tasks of theological reflection as located around the following three themes: the formation and nurture of a Christian; understanding what it means to be the body of Christ; and bringing the good news of the gospel into a relationship with wider culture and society.[3] This formulation of the themes which guide theological reflection I have found to be useful, for it gives the necessary room to the witness of Scripture, to the place and voice of those practicing their Christian faith together and to the relevance of discussion with other approaches to understanding, such as those of philosophy or psychology.

Within theological reflection, what is needed is *phronesis* or what Thomas Aquinas identified as *prudentia*. This *phronesis* refers to a way of practical moral reasoning and it works with what Dorothy Bass and others describe as

> a kind of knowing, which resides at the core of the Christian life that is closer to practical than to abstract reason—closer, that is, to embodied, situated knowing-in-action than to disembodied theoretical knowledge.[4]

Practical wisdom, they contend, emerges in the interplay between the knowledge formed and interpreted within concrete, particular situations, and that gained from abstract generalized theories. This "back and forth dialogue between analytical thought and the ongoing constitution of meaning" is "necessary for responsive engagement in projects in the world."[5] Using this type of "back and forth dialogue" seems to me an

---

2. For a helpful account of what is mostly understood under applied theology, see Ballard and Pritchard, *Practical Theology in Action*, 58–61.

3. See Graham et al., *Theological Reflection*, 17.

4. Bass, *Christian Practical Wisdom*, 2.

5. Bass, *Christian Practical Wisdom*, 7; quoting from Sullivan and Rosin, *New Agenda for Higher Education*, 100.

appropriate way of approaching theological reflection around a complex theme such as that of this study.

I shall divide my theological reflection in this study into two chapters. In this third chapter, I shall look at the witness of the Hebrew Bible and the New Testament on friendship and bring that into an initial relationship with the findings. I shall then briefly reflect theologically on the elements of friendliness which emerged from my analysis of the interviews. In chapter four, I shall turn in detail to theological reflection around the essential attributes of friendship as found in the hermeneutic phenomenological analysis of the interviews.

THE WITNESS OF SCRIPTURE AROUND FRIENDSHIP

The emphasis in this subchapter will be an attempt to crystalize the main attributes of relationships associated with or designated as friendships, as they are referred to and discussed in the Hebrew Bible and the New Testament. Part of the process of reflexivity within the hermeneutical circle or spiral involves making transparent those things which have influenced, and have an ongoing influence, on one's own views, concepts and intuitions. As I wrote in the first chapter, each of the participants in the interviews and I myself as the researcher are ordained pastors (or, in one case, a soon to be ordained pastor) in the particular setting of the Swiss Reformed Church. Although each has their own particular context and their own specific lifeworld, what is common to each of them is that they have been trained at the theological faculty of a university in the exegesis of Scripture, are familiar with the texts, have agreed in their ordination vows to give witness to the Scripture,[6] and are involved in that task in and with their congregations and in the wider context of their communities. A search for understanding around the theme of friendship and its characteristics from Scripture is therefore both necessary and fitting for theological reflection in this study.

The terms in Hebrew and Greek that are translated as "friend" are used sparingly in the Bible. Relationships described in familial terms—father, mother, brother, sister, even when there is no blood relationship or relationship through marriage—are much more common. In exploring this further in the following, I shall concentrate on the words for

---

6. See chapter 5 regarding pastoral expectations of those ordained in the context of the Swiss Reformed Church.

friendship and friend used in the original languages in the biblical texts but include discussion of characteristics of relationships which point to associations of people with each other often regarded as a form of friendship, such as, for instance, the relationship between Jonathan and David, that between Ruth and Naomi, and that between Job and his comforters.

Friendship in the Hebrew Bible

Friendship, as such, if measured by the literature on the terms involved, is a topic that Hebrew Bible scholars have largely ignored. There are a few dictionary articles[7] and a chapter on "Friendship in the Old Testament" in the Hebrew scholar and Christian ethicist Patricia Vesely's recent book, *Friendship and Virtue Ethics in the Book of Job*[8] as well as a couple of texts dealing with friendship in the Wisdom Literature of the Hebrew Bible.[9] But the first monograph to be published on the subject seems to be that of Saul M. Olyan, Professor of Judaic Studies at Brown University. In his study, *Friendship in the Hebrew Bible*,[10] he ascribes this paucity to the topic's complexity and elusiveness, calling the vocabulary of biblical friendship "frequently ambiguous."[11]

The biblical text has no actual word for friendship, but there are several words for friend.[12] The most common word is *rea* (along with its related nouns), which means something along the lines of "to associate with" or "to affiliate with" and suggests, according to Olyan, a voluntary dimension to friendship.[13] *Rea* and *merea* but also the word *oheb*, coming from *heb*, the verb to love, sometimes translated as "lover," are also used in the rhetoric of friendship, but they can be ambiguous, sometimes

---

7. See, for instance, Fischer, "Freundschaft (AT),"; Dietrich, "Von der Freundschaft im Alten Testament und Alten Orient," 37–56.

8. Vesely, "Friendship in the Old Testament," 74–104.

9. Davies, "Ethics of Friendship in Wisdom Literature," 135–50; Corley, "Friendship in the Hebrew Wisdom Literature," 27–51.

10. Olyan himself notes that the six-volume Anchor Bible Dictionary lacks an entry on friendship; Olyan, *Friendship in the Hebrew Bible*, 118.

11. Olyan, *Friendship in the Hebrew Bible*, 2.

12. Olyan contrasts this to the rich vocabulary of Akkadian, in which he finds at least four words which in some contexts can be translated as friendship. "The lack of an extant word meaning 'friendship' in biblical Hebrew is most likely the result of the limited vocabulary of the Hebrew Bible and nothing more given the various words that can be translated 'friendship' in Akkadian"; Olyan, *Friendship in the Hebrew Bible*, 120.

13. Olyan, *Friendship in the Hebrew Bible*, 120.

being used to denote treaty partners in political relationships who would most likely not be personal friends. This is, for instance, the case in 1 Kgs 5:15, where we read that Hiram, King of Tyre, had always been a "friend" (*oheb*) of David. In a treaty context, this would denote Hiram's loyalty to his parity treaty. Both Olyan and Vesely note that all of these ambiguous words must be examined carefully in their context to determine their relevance in any search to understand what friendship might be.[14] One such example is Exod 33:11, which describes *Yhwh* speaking to Moses face to face, "as a man speaks to his friend." Olyan writes, "it is evident from the comparison that *rea* must mean 'friend' rather than 'neighbour', 'peer', 'fellow, or 'another', given the text's emphasis on intimacy and singularity of communication between two individuals."[15] Similarly in Isa 41:8, God refers to Abraham as "my friend" (*ohabi*). Interesting in the context of Abraham's friendship with God is that obedience is at first the *condition* for divine friendship, but then becomes consequential upon it.[16] In Job 2:11, the word *rea* is used of the three "friends" of Job. And in 1 Kgs 4:5, Zabud, son of Nathan, is described as the *re eh* of the king, and the word appears to designate a specific political role, possibly with an Egyptian origin.[17]

Brian Edgar takes up this theme of the "king's friend,"[18] referring also to 1 Chr 27:33 where Hushai the Archite is translated as the king's friend. Designating a relationship in which intimacy, loyalty, and frank speech are of the essence, the concept of the king's friend appears interesting in this study on friendship and pastoring. One assumes there would have to be trust that the "friend" has the best interests of the king at heart, but the relationship need not necessarily be overly affectionate and only to a degree mutual. Besides that, a reciprocity of status is not mentioned as the king is obviously above the "friend" in status and power.

14. Vesely, *Friendship and Virtue Ethics in the Book of Job*, 76.

15. Olyan, *Friendship in the Hebrew Bible*, 7. This does, however, appear to be a type of circular argument, as one assumes a certain understanding of what a "friend" will be, before asserting that the word means "friend." Vesely points out that the text could just as well be translated as "a man speaks to another human being." Vesely, *Friendship and Virtue Ethics in the Book of Job*, 76. For further discussion, see Lapsley, "Friends with God?," 117–29.

16. Carmichael, *Friendship*, 49; quoting from Ambrose. Jesus also makes the connection between obedience and friendship in the statement in John 15:14: "You are my friends, if you do what I command you."

17. Here, Olyan refers to Donner, "Der Freund des Königs."

18. Edgar, *God Is Friendship*, loc. 581.

On this point Olyan counters Jan Dietrich,[19] who claims that friendship in the Hebrew Bible is normally assumed to be between peers. Olyan however finds nothing in the vocabulary of friendship to suggest that equality of wealth, social status, life stage, or other personal characteristics is required or even desirable in a friendship. Here he points out that Jonathan, prince and heir to Saul's throne, can be David's friend, although David does not share his rank and is represented as Jonathan's vassal, who bows down before him three times in 1. Sam 20:41. Similarly, an asymmetrical friendship develops between Naomi and Ruth, as Naomi is Ruth's mother-in-law and a generation older than her. Hence, says Olyan, Old Testament vocabulary on friendship is not primarily interested in personal equality or inequality but foregrounds the expectation of behavioral parity.[20] This emphasis on behavioral parity, something required from family members and friends alike, may not appear surprising,

> given the importance of reciprocity in the larger context of social and even cultic relations according to biblical texts. Not only are friends, family members, and treaty partners expected to reciprocate good treatment; *Yhwh* himself states that his *modus operandi* is characterised by reciprocity: "Those who honour me I will honour and those who despise me will be diminished."[21]

Interestingly, most texts do not seem to distinguish between the expectations of family members and friends.[22] And in his conclusion Olyan suggests that for the Hebrew Bible close family members are implicitly regarded as paradigmatic intimates and the intimate friend can be comparable to them, as is exemplified in Prov 18:24, "there is a friend who clings more closely than a brother." Contrasting this to our contemporary setting, he writes,

> comparison of family members to friends (as paradigmatic intimates), a commonplace among some groups in contemporary Western societies, is unknown in biblical materials.[23]

Here once again the narrative of Ruth and Naomi might be helpful. The author continues to use the familial language of mother-in-law and

---

19. Dietrich, "Von der Freundschaft im Alten Testament und Alten Orient," 53 54.
20. Olyan, *Friendship in the Hebrew Bible*, 122.
21. Olyan, *Friendship in the Hebrew Bible*, 106.
22. Compare for instance Exod 32:27, Deut 13:7, Jer 9:3, Mic 7:5–6, Ps 38:12, Ps 15:2, Prov 17:17.
23. Olyan, *Friendship in the Hebrew Bible*, 105.

daughter-in-law, even though the two "cling to" each other, in what Olyan calls a "new, voluntary and reciprocal relationship not shaped by familial expectations."[24]

Likewise, within the narrative around the relationship between Jonathan and David, familial and emotional as well as treaty language is used. The two are brothers-in-law through David's marriage to Michal.[25] More importantly, the vocabulary used to indicate the intensity of the relationship, namely of the "self" or "life" of Jonathan being "bound" to the "self" or "life" of David, is found only in one other place in the Hebrew Bible:

> In Gen 44:30–31, it describes the relationship of Jacob to his youngest son Benjamin, whom he is elsewhere said to love (44:20): The "self" or "life" of Jacob is said to be "bound" to that of Benjamin, and were Benjamin to die, Jacob would die of grief. In contrast to the idiom to love someone else as oneself, the binding of selves/lives is not otherwise used in treaty settings and appears to be highly charged emotionally.[26]

This bond, compared to father-son love, means that Jonathan takes delight in David, so much so that his loyalty to David becomes greater than that to his own father. In 1 Sam 20:41 they kiss each other and weep together, which reciprocal act suggests "a personal, emotional bond between the two men, a bond best described as a friendship."[27]

In the narrative of Job and his experiences of calamity and death, Eliphaz, Bildad, and Zophar are referred to as his friends, but different parts of the Job text portray the three friends in different lights. In the prologue they are introduced as Job's friends and act as is expected of friends in that they join him and mourn with him. The middle or core section—the poetic dialogues—however refer to them as "troubling" or "mischievous" comforters, and in Job 13:4 even as "worthless healers" as they are incapable of offering the consolation comforters are expected to provide. And in the epilogue, they are

> rebuked by Yhwh for their lack of understanding with respect to him, but not for any failure of loyalty or sensitivity to Job.[28]

---

24. Olyan, *Friendship in the Hebrew Bible*, 67; for a critical interpretation of the "voluntary" and "reciprocal" relationship, see Lusungu Moyo, "Traffic Violations," 83–94.

25. 1 Sam 18:27.

26. Olyan, *Friendship in the Hebrew Bible*, 71.

27. Olyan, *Friendship in the Hebrew Bible*, 73.

28. Olyan, *Friendship in the Hebrew Bible*, 80.

Thus, according to Olyan, the friends fulfill the formal and social qualifications deemed necessary for friendship, but the relationship is not idealized for, on the level of the content of their conversations with Job, they fail to help him in the way God intends. And interestingly in Job 42:10 of the epilogue, it is only after Job's intercession before God for his friends that his fortunes are restored, which would seem to point to a type of reciprocity in the relationship between the friends and Job.

Another friendship narrative, albeit a short one, is found at the end of Judg 11, where the friends of Jephthah's daughter accompany her for the two months she is given to weep because she will never marry or have children. Olyan contends that the text appears to suggest that the friends are playing the role of comforter, although the word is not used, as they behave in the way comforters do, namely,

> They are present with Jephthah's daughter, separating themselves from quotidian life with her; they embrace her mourning rites— they weep with her according to v.37—not unlike comforters in any number of other texts. Yet these comforters are women comforting a woman who is experiencing a calamity, and this sets them apart from the male comforters of men mentioned elsewhere in the biblical text . . . It may be that the text's authors and audience assume that a woman mourning a personal calamity expects the company and consolation of friends as much as any man does.[29]

Thus, both in the Job narrative and that of Jephthah, friendship involves comforting the other, and it is in this role (in the case of Job) that his friends appear to fail him.

Of interest in the context of this study is that there also appear to be gradations of friendship within the Old Testament texts. The knowledge of an exceptional friend—for instance, the one in the latter part of Prov 18:24 who clings more closely than a brother—suggests that there are others who can be called friends, but who are not "exceptional." These are the ones in the first part of the verse—"friends for friendly exchanges," as Olyan translates the text.[30] Also the term *meyudda* is used occasionally to denote "one who is known to me" and the term *allupi* an 'intimate' would seem to point to a special friendly intimacy or personal knowledge,[31]

---

29. Olyan, *Friendship in the Hebrew Bible*, 81.

30. Olyan, *Friendship in the Hebrew Bible*, 106.

31. See for instance Ps 55:13 where the NIV translates, "my companion, my close friend."

which not all friends would necessarily have. And in Prov 19:4, friends are described as being attracted by wealth. These could perhaps be ranked lower than the "friends for friendly exchanges."[32]

In summary, the picture given in the Hebrew Bible of friendship is of a relationship between people who choose to associate freely with one another, a relationship characterized by positive feelings and affection which the texts describe as love. Further, a degree of personal knowledge or intimacy is assumed, as is mutual goodwill and gentleness of interaction or kindness. Thus, the essential attributes of friendship which emerged from the interviews—namely, freedom, affection, openness, and mutuality—appear also to be important in the context of the Hebrew Bible. Furthermore, a number of the elements of friendliness which emerged from the interviews are also present there. The friend is loyal, hospitable, trustworthy, a comforter, and the friendship is assumed to be reciprocal in that beneficence is expected to be repaid in comparable treatment.[33] Abraham and Moses are depicted as having entered friendship with God; and the examples of Ruth and Naomi, David and Jonathan, as well as Job and his "comforters" have been handed down through the generations as those of paradigmatic friends.

In the context of this study around friendship in the pastoral setting, many of these attributes of friendship in the Hebrew Bible are of interest for reflection: positive feelings and affection described as love, benevolence, gentleness of interaction or kindness, being hospitable, faithful, and comforting. Also noteworthy, as Olyan contends,[34] is that friends need not be of equal status, equal wealth, and equal life stage or personality, and with this in mind, perhaps the term might be appropriate for use on occasion in pastoral situations, something which I shall take up in chapter four. Also, the combination, at times, of familial and friendship

32. Such gradations one could perhaps compare in certain ways with those classically formulated by Aristotle in the *Nicomachean Ethics* 8.3–4. Aristotle identifies and ranks three types of friendship: friendship in virtue towards the good; friendship motivated by utility; and friendship for pleasure. The highest form of friendship, exhibited by the exceptional friend, in the Hebrew text, is that exhibited by loyalty, intimacy, and possibly by proximity, as he "clings more closely than a brother." This seems difficult to compare directly with Aristotle's preeminent form of friendship as shared virtue or excellence. The "friends for friendly exchanges," however, could well be compared to the friends for pleasure and the friends attracted by wealth with the friends motivated by utility. Through such a reading, similarities as well as differences can be made out between classical Greek and Hebrew or biblical models of friendship.

33. See Olyan, *Friendship in the Hebrew Bible*, 5.
34. Olyan, *Friendship in the Hebrew Bible*, 122.

language points to an understanding which allows both kinship and friendship a place of importance alongside each other, such that Ruth's friend is also her mother-in-law and David's brother-in-law is also his friend. Such a place of importance for both kinship and friendship might be seen as helpful in the context of a church congregation, where both the language of kinship and that of friendship are used. And yet a certain tension may remain in regard to the context of the pastoral setting, for instance around the question of to what degree the parties involved in a pastoral setting can be chosen associates, and around areas such as mutuality and the reciprocity and parity of behavior and beneficence. These tensions I shall also address further and reflect upon theologically in chapter four.

The New Testament

Central to Christianity is the conviction that the love shown by *Yhwh*, the God of Abraham, Isaac, and Jacob, is revealed in a new and fresh way and most fully through Jesus the Christ, Israel's messiah. The same God with whom Abraham and Moses entered into friendship in the Hebrew Bible is incarnated in Jesus of Nazareth. Through his life, his death on the cross, and his resurrection from the dead, Jesus embodies the new commandment given to his disciples, "to love one another as I have loved you."[35] This commandment is in the same chapter in the Gospel of John in which Jesus talks about no longer calling his disciples servants but friends if they keep his commandment. Liz Carmichael writes with regard to John 15:13–15, "John's Gospel gives the love of friendship an explicitly central place."[36] Werner G. Jeanrond takes this up, but points out critically with a view to other texts in the New Testament that

> The Gospel of Mark paints a rather dark picture of the quality of the friendship that exists between the disciples of Jesus and their master. At crucial moments in Mark's story, Jesus' friends either misunderstand him or betray him. Christian friendship thus is not as original or prevalent a theme as an isolated reading of the Johannine texts in the New Testament might suggest.[37]

---

35. John 15:12 (ESV).

36. Carmichael, *Friendship*, 39.

37. Jeanrond, *Theology of Love*, 208. Eldho Puthenkandathil points out that among the synoptists, Mark does not use the term *philos* at all. Puthenkandathil, "*Philos*," 23.

Aware of such different priorities given to friendship within the scriptural texts, I shall now take a closer look at the *topos* of friendship in the New Testament and consider what significance it might have in the context of this study.

The actual word "friendship" (*philia*) appears only once in the New Testament, in Jas 4:4, and there in the negative as friendship with the world: "don't you know that friendship with the world is hatred toward God? Anyone who chooses to be a friend (*philos*) of the world becomes an enemy of God" (NIV). Here the world "is not God's good creation but a pattern of perceiving, evaluating, and acting on things as if God did not exist. It reflects a politics—a way of ordering a common life—opposed to God."[38] In contrast, Abraham is cited in Jas 2:23, taking up the Hebrew Bible, as the friend of God (*philos*), who believed God and then acted in obedience upon this faith and it was credited to him as righteousness. Here the attribute of Abraham's faithfulness to God is foremost.

In the Gospel of John, the word friend (*philos*) is used a number of times. In explaining how he understood his role and position in relation to Jesus, in John 3:29 John the Baptist compares himself to the friend of the bridegroom.[39] The bride belongs to the bridegroom, but the friend attends the bridegroom and waits and listens for him and then rejoices when he hears the bridegroom's voice, "He must become greater, I must become less."[40] The attribute of joy in the friendship relationship is significant here and the text might be seen to be relevant in the context of pastoral vocation and identity. One of the main reasons for Christian pastoring is that pastors desire that those who journey with them might encounter the presence of Jesus, "the bridegroom," for themselves and experience anew what it means to be part of the "bride of Christ." In that sense pastors might themselves take on the role of "friends of the bridegroom," those waiting and listening with others in their life situations for Christ to arrive. And when they experience that Christ is present, then, ideally, they rejoice and direct to Jesus the attention of those with them, and away from themselves.[41]

38. See Fowl, *Philippians*, 218; quoting from Johnson "Friendship with the world / Friendship with God," 166–83.

39. For a detailed analysis of the figure of the friend of the bridegroom, see Puthenkandathil, *Philos*, 60–86.

40. John 3:30.

41. For pastors and theologians to compare themselves to John the Baptist as those "preparing the way" is not something new. Karl Barth, the Swiss Reformed theologian of the twentieth century, had a print of the scene from the Isenheimer Altar,

Further, in John's Gospel in 11:11 Jesus calls Lazarus, the one whom he is about to raise from the dead, "our friend." The word "our" would seem to be an extension of the friendship between Jesus and Lazarus, and to encompass a common friendship with Jesus' disciples as well. The Roman Catholic priest and New Testament scholar Eldho Puthenkandathil writes on this topic,

> In the NT writings the term *philos* (friend/beloved) is used as a designation for a Christian believer besides the terms *adelphos* and *agapetos* (cf. 3 John 15; Lk 12:4; Acts 27:3; esp. John 15:13–15). The members of the early Church were friends of Jesus and friends among themselves. This mutual love among the baptized and for Jesus provides them the status of discipleship. Lazarus was a disciple, not in the sense of "one among the twelve" but as one who was a real believer in Jesus, who closely followed Jesus' teaching and who was beloved of Jesus.[42]

Thus, the term friendship is here brought to our attention through association, the friend of Jesus as a disciple being by association also a friend of mine.

John 15:15, to which I have already referred in chapter one, is the main text in the New Testament in which Jesus defines his disciples as "my friends" if they do as he commands. As I wrote there, friendship in this text is not portrayed as an early stage of spiritual relations with Jesus, one which will gradually be superseded by a higher form of love as his disciples grow and mature in their faith. Indeed, it is servanthood which is overcome as Jesus practices a kind of love, shown for instance in the way he is affected by the presence of his friends such as Lazarus or Peter, which exhibits the characteristic of openness and frankness of speech associated with the equality, mutuality, and vulnerability of the way in which friends relate to each other. The sign here that the disciples participate in the friendship of Christ is that they keep his commandments, and as Thomas Aquinas astutely writes this not out of "servile

---

(presently in Colmar in France) just above his desk, more centrally positioned than his prints of Mozart or Calvin, which depicts the crucified Christ. Next to the cross stands John the Baptist, pointing to Christ with an unusually elongated finger, and saying, "Behold, the lamb of God." This print can still be seen in the house in which Karl Barth and his family lived in in Basel, at Bruderholzallee 26, where the University of Basel's Karl Barth Archives are also kept: https://karlbarth.unibas.ch/de/barths-basel/letzter-wohnort-last-residence/.

42. Puthenkandathil, *Philos*, 101.

fear" but out of "filial love."[43] Thus the obedience involved in this keeping of Christ's commandment is "not the cause of divine friendship, but the sign,"[44] which demonstrates that God loves us and we him.

In John 19:12 there is another instance of the term friend being used when the Jews shout at Pilate that if he chooses to let Jesus go, he will no longer be called a friend of Caesar. Referencing this verse, Liz Carmichael writes that it is "a clear case of political client-patron friendship with perhaps the ironic implication that Pilate must choose between friendship with Caesar or Jesus."[45] In this context of political friendship, Luke 23:12 is also of interest as Luke writes that by agreeing to Jesus' death, Herod and Pilate became "friends."

There are further instances of the word "friend" in the gospels. In Matt 11:19 and Luke 7:34, in explaining to his disciples the role of John the Baptist, Jesus says that he came "neither eating nor drinking, and they (i.e. this generation) say he has a demon. The Son of Man came eating and drinking and they say, here is a glutton and a drunkard, a friend of tax collectors and sinners." Here once again friendship as association is significant. The implication is that given by accusing Jesus that he is a friend of such people, he must in a sense be similar to them and condone their behavior in some sort of way. Liz Carmichael comments,

> the conventional limits of love and friendship were being transcended through the life and actions of Jesus. Friendship found itself transformed by grace. God in Christ extended friendship to all human beings, and to be a "friend of sinners," hitherto a genuine insult or impossible paradox, now becomes thinkable and possible.[46]

Perhaps becoming a "friend of sinners" is in one sense part of pastoring and pastoral care, as the role of pastor may well involve association with and possibly counselling of those denoted in society as being at the margins because of certain actions in which they are involved. This may at first sound condescending, as if pastors look down on the "sinners" with whom they have to interact, and then from a position of superiority attempt to befriend them. It may also sound like a type of arrogant and insensitive pastoring, which many working in the Church are thankful

---

43. Aquinas, *Sup. Ev. Ioh. Lect.* 15, lect.3.ii; quoted by Carmichael, *Friendship*, 109.
44. Aquinas, *Sup. Ev. Ioh. Lect.* 15, lect.3.i.
45. Carmichael, *Friendship*, 38.
46. Carmichael, *Friendship*, 39.

has in general been overcome. This is however not what is meant. Having experienced the comforting, transforming, and healing power of Jesus coming alongside them in their own brokenness, need and sinfulness, usually by means of others pastoring them, Christian pastors, ideally, desire that others, regardless of their societal status, may experience such comfort and transformation. This involves coming alongside all types of people with a desire to be of help in situations of brokenness, despair, and guilt. While doing this they respect the individual person with whom they are interacting as having insight into his or her own situation. Christian pastoral care also recognizes the value of the availability of the pastor just being present and listening and hopes that the person will come to an understanding of what is best for them in their own situation, without the pastor necessarily having to know what that is.[47] This would seem to be sensible and good practice, and it takes seriously the dignity of each human being, wherever they may situate themselves or be put by others on the moral spectrum of a society. Yet I believe this does not however leave the Christian pastor merely as a neutral observer or counsellor. The accusation thrown at Jesus, of being a "friend of sinners," referred to the fact that he associated and shared something of himself with those whom "good" society did not deem to be suitable as companions or associates. If the concept of friendship with reference to Jesus as the "friend of sinners" is to have any meaning in the pastoral setting, surely it would involve a certain amount of companionship and sharing, a type of mutuality.

Such a form of coming alongside all types of people, with humility rather than superiority and even a feeling of awe at the possibility of doing so, might open up the idea of friendship as a gift. A type of mutuality in the pastoral setting could take the form of both parties sharing something which is of importance to them. In my own experience, many people have an intuitive feeling about whether something said in a counselling situation is advice from an aloof standpoint or shared with a degree of honesty and caring for the person. Pastors sharing something of themselves with a degree of honesty are choosing not to be totally "neutral." Those with a faith in Christ will be humble, hoping that what is ultimately best for the other person will have something to do with an encounter with Christ through the Holy Spirit, an encounter with the divine "friend of sinners," whatever shape this encounter might take and whatever the consequences might be. Once again this may sound

---

47. See, for instance, Patton, *Pastoral Care in Context*, 213–35.

condescending or even arrogant, as if pastors know what is best for those who come to them for pastoral care. But once again this is not what is meant. If "friendship with God" is a valid way of describing ultimate good for human beings, as has been put forward through the ages by such figures as Augustine,[48] Thomas Aquinas,[49] and mystics such as Julian of Norwich[50] and others,[51] then goodwill and benevolence in wishing others ultimate good is also a way of wishing for them to have an experience of such friendship with God.

A further text in the New Testament takes up the *topos* of friendship without using the word itself. In a description of the early Church in Jerusalem in Acts 4:32 we read: "All the believers were one in heart and mind. No one claimed that any of his possessions was his own, but they shared everything they had" (NIV). This being "one in heart and mind," in accord in all things, is regarded as a classical Greco-Roman attribute of friendship,[52] and it seems reasonable to assume that Luke, the author of Acts, was familiar with this type of classic thought. Alan C. Mitchell, associate professor of New Testament in the Theology Department at Georgetown University, proposes that Luke is here redefining the classic friendship *topos* along the lines of social equality in the *koinonia* of the early Christian community. He writes:

> Friendship was doubtless a vehicle for wealth, status, and power for the ruling elite of Luke's day. Normally, it was formed within social orders, and its benefits were shared by people of the same status. Luke, however, uses friendship to equalize relationships in his own community. He portrays the early Jerusalem community in Acts as a community of friends to show how friendship can continue across status lines and the poor can be benefited by the rich. Redefining friendship this way helps Luke to achieve his social objective: encouraging the rich to provide relief for the poor of his own community. . . . Thus, Luke appeals to the Greco-Roman friendship tradition to help his constituents

---

48. See, for instance, Augustine, *De civ. Dei* I.35.
49. See, for instance, Aquinas, *Summa Theologica* II-II 27.8; I-II 65.5.
50. See, for instance, Julian of Norwich, *Showings*, (Long text c.1393) ch. 76, 329.
51. Carmichael mentions in this context figures such as John Tauler and Mechthild of Magdeburg. Carmichael, *Friendship*, 129-30.
52. See, for instance, Cicero, *De amicitia*, paragraph 20, "For friendship is nothing else than an accord in all things, human and divine, conjoined with mutual goodwill and affection."

reimagine the relationship between rich and poor within their own koinonia.[53]

Here although the theme of equality is emphasized, it is done in a way that contrasts with the classic assumption that only equals can be friends. It is an equality which is sought after among friends as a consequence of their being disciples of Jesus. The idea of the sharing of goods was later taken up in monasticism, as an ideal of unity, but there and in the early Church in general the familial language of kinship, brother or sister, father or mother, was prevalent and the language of friendship was used much less.[54]

Furthermore, in the New Testament, the apostle Paul describes in various places the type of life Christians should be communally living but does not use the word friendship. Paul Wadell lists in the epistles of Paul the kind of attitudes, dispositions and practices Christians ought to show to one another in their life together. Christians are to honour one another (Rom 12:10), live in harmony with one another (Rom 12:18), accept one another (Rom 15:7), care for one another (1 Cor 12:25), be servants of one another (Gal 5:13), bear one another's burdens (Gal 6:2), comfort one another (1 Thess 5:11), be at peace with one another (1 Thess 5:13), bear with one another lovingly (Eph 4:2), and forgive one another (Col 3:13).[55] Here a form of mutuality (an attribute which emerged from my analysis of the interviews as being essential to friendship) is expected of those living the Christian life, as they honour, accept, and care for each other, while bearing each other's burdens and forgiving each other.

Perhaps another hint of the classic Greco-Roman friendship tradition can be found in Rom 5:6–8.[56] Paul takes up the idea of a good per-

---

53. Mitchell, "Social Function of Friendship," 272.

54. With reference to A. Harnack, G. Stählin, M. Paeslack, and J. N. Sevenster, Hans Josef Klauck suggests that the early Church was perhaps especially wary of friendship language due to its elitist use in certain gnostic circles, and was much more at home in the kinship language of the Hebrew Bible. Klauck, *Gemeinde zwischen Haus und Stadt*, 115–16.

55. Wadell, *Becoming Friends*, 30–31.

56. "[A]t just the right time, when we were still powerless, Christ died for the ungodly. Very rarely will anyone die for a righteous person, though for a good person someone might possibly dare to die. But God demonstrates his own love for us in this: While we were still sinners, Christ died for us." Rom 5: 6–8 NIV. Compare, for instance, Aristotle's formulation of the possible consequences of the classical ideal of friendship. Aristotle, Nicomachean Ethics IX.8 (1169a18–25): "But it is also true the virtuous man's conduct is often guided by the interests of his friends and of his country, and that he will if necessary lay down his life in their behalf. . . And this is doubtless the case with those who give their lives for others; thus they choose great nobility for themselves."

son possibly being willing to die for another good person, and shows how Christ is different, in that he is willing, through the love of God, to die for the ungodly. Here the classical form of reciprocity within friendship is transformed by the grace of Christ, who gives himself for those who have not been his friends in the magnanimous way otherwise reserved for only those friends held in the highest regard.

In another significant passage, Paul uses the concept of equality in Gal 3:28 when writing about being a child of God. Here the factor which leads to equality is not equal wealth or virtue or worldly status, but Christ himself and the believer's association with him, for "There is neither Jew nor Gentile, neither slave nor free, nor is there male and female, for you are all one in Christ Jesus" (NIV). As Gregory Sterling, professor of New Testament at Yale Divinity School, writes, this is in keeping with the writings of the contemporary Jewish scholar Philo of Alexandria (20–10 BC until 40–50 AD) who, in developing the classical tradition, had redefined the boundaries of kinship and friendship along religious lines in shared faith in God rather than in human virtue.[57] Because of the passage in Gal 3:28 it now can be understood to be axiomatic that friendship between Christians has its basis in each one's common commitment to Christ. Liz Carmichael refers to this text as a "paradigm shift that widens the community of friendship from the select few to the entire committed Church, including women."[58]

Although once again the actual word friendship is not used, Paul's epistle to the Philippians is variously seen as a letter of friendship, meaning that Philippians fits well within an ancient epistolary genre characterized by the letters friends sent to each other.[59] Stephen Fowl, Professor of Theology at Loyola College in Maryland, especially in his commentary on Philippians, suggests the particular ways in which the epistle might display the nature and practices of friendship in Christ. He discusses four topics which sketch the contours of such "a rich theology of friendship." These topics are of particular interest in the context of this study as Fowl shows that Paul, within his apostolic and pastoral role, regards the Philippians as friends in Christ. He grounds his thought firstly on the character of the triune God, which he sees displayed (referencing Phil 2:6–11) in the life, death, and resurrection of Jesus. His second topic is related to

57. Sterling, "Bond of Humanity," 217–18.
58. Carmichael, *Friendship*, 41.
59. See Fowl, *Philippians*, 207; Fitzgerald, *Friendship, Flattery, and Frankness of Speech*, 141–60. Compare also Fitzgerald, "Christian Friendship," 284–96.

the first, with reference to Phil 2:6–11, and here he focuses on the idea of "seeking the benefit of others as a decisive way in which Christ displays the form and glory of God to us. I take the mutual cultivation of this disposition to be one of the primary practices of Christian friendship."[60] The third topic he addresses relates to an examination of the practices which are constitutive of friendships in Christ. Here he contends that one of the primary practices of Christian friends is their helping each other understand their lives within the larger picture of God's working of salvation, something which he sees Paul clearly exemplifying for the Philippians. This is "a practice that requires the formation of Christ-focused patterns of thinking, feeling, and acting (i.e., practical reasoning) if it is to be done well."[61] And the final topic he takes up is that of joy, as within the epistle to the Philippians, that is something which is given an extraordinary emphasis. He suggests that in Paul's world, "even the best sorts of friends were engaged in a 'friendly' competition for honour" and that, "for Paul and all Christians the result of the proper working of Christian friendship is joy."[62] Regarding the attributes of friendship Fowl thus emphasizes, through topics from Philippians, that the theme of equality, once again, is taken up and transformed in that Christ in Phil 2:6–11, who is equal with the Father, does not use this equality to his own advantage but empties himself. This emptying, or *kenosis* to use the Greek term, reflects God's benevolence and kindness, in the seeking of benefit for others, and can be seen as a key element of Christian friendship in its desire for the mutual good:

> Benevolence implies not only that the friend is loved for herself, but also because she is loved, the active seeking of her good is the sustaining project of the lover's life. This is what friendship is, mutual devotion to the good of the other because it is a good both share.[63]

Further, the attributes of hospitality and companionship are regarded as important for friendship in the practices of the Christian community,[64] and then the attributes of joy and affection, which are so

---

60. Fowl, *Philippians*, 208.
61. Fowl, *Philippians*, 208.
62. Fowl, *Philippians*, 208.
63. Fowl, *Philippians*, 215; quoting Wadell, *Friendship and the Moral Life*, 131–32.
64. Fowl, *Philippians*, 216.

apparent in the epistle.[65] All of these are bound up in the form of love which constitutes the common life of God, Father, Son, and Holy Spirit; "friendship with God is our ultimate end because friendships of love are constitutive of the very life of the triune God."[66]

In summary, we see again in the New Testament a number of the attributes associated with friendship in the Hebrew Bible, namely faithfulness, benevolence, kindness and being hospitable. There are, however, also new emphases. Joy is given a prominent place by Jesus himself as well as by the apostle Paul. Equality is a theme, where it is assumed that those who belong to Christ are equal. Thus, the rich should support the poor and the sharing of goods is portrayed as a model for Christian community. Friendship by free association with Jesus is accompanied by the expectation of a mutuality in love. Openness in speech and intimacy are the reasons Jesus gives in John 15 for now calling his disciples friends rather than servants, as he has revealed to them everything he has received from the Father. And trinitarian language points to a communion of love within God which in its mutuality is vibrant with what we might call intimate friendship.

These attributes around friendship found in the Scriptures correspond well on an initial level with those which emerged from my analysis of the interviews in this study. The four themes of mutuality, affection, freedom, and openness which emerged from the descriptions given by the interviewees as being essential to their experience of friendship are all brought into a context of friendship in Scripture as well in various ways. I shall take up further those four essential elements and their interwovenness in chapter four. Those attributes which I have identified from the interviews as being part of the friendliness which pastors expect from themselves, and which, indeed, others expect of them as well, are however also important in the witness of the biblical texts. These are benevolence or kindness, closeness or companionship, equality, faithfulness or loyalty and hospitality. It is to these attributes that I now turn and on which I now reflect theologically.

---

65. Fowl, *Philippians*, 233.
66. Fowl, *Philippians*, 209.

THEOLOGICAL REFLECTION AROUND THE ELEMENTS OF FRIENDLINESS AS FOUND IN THE ANALYSIS OF THE INTERVIEWS.

As I wrote previously some qualities that the participants expressed in their interviews around friendship and which I have differentiated from the essential attributes of friendship I have described as elements of friendliness. These are helpful in describing the breadth of experience involved in reflection on friendship. It was often clear that the point at which the interviewees might regard a relationship as developing into a friendship was difficult to define but they all described the type of relationships they considered good for a pastor to be seeking in terms of friendliness. What I have described as elements of friendliness in this study are ways of acting and being to which the pastors felt a certain obligation and which they felt could be expected of them as professional people. These ways of acting and being could be part of what made up their friendships, but they could also just be part of the way they conducted themselves with people in general within their congregations.

Benevolence or Kindness

Goodwill, benevolence, or kindness is something which I have identified from the interviews as an attribute of friendliness which the participants expect from themselves in their professional capacity as ordained pastors. Nicole, for instance, spoke of a "basic goodwill" which she expected of herself, and Ueli spoke of an interest in other people, which he regarded as important and which he connected to his own experience of the kindness of God as "the love of the father." Such goodwill is also brought, as we have seen in the previous subchapter, both in the Hebrew Bible and the New Testament into a context of friendly relations. In literature it is something about which the Christian writer, Ambrose, Bishop of Milan, wrote, perhaps most famously known as the person behind Augustine's conversion to Christianity. In reference to the Roman thinker Cicero, he produced a three-volume work on the duties of the clergy with the title *De officiis*,[67] toward the end of which, in the first Christian homily on friendship, he writes the following concerning goodwill:

---

67. The title "De officiis" is borrowed from Cicero, in which he, Cicero, writes about the four major virtues for public leadership, prudence, justice, fortitude, and temperance.

There is such a thing as goodwill, though, and it is closely linked to generosity; generosity itself stems from it, for the actual practice of kindness is secondary to the desire to be kind in the first place. But goodwill is also separate and distinct from generosity. For even where generosity is nowhere to be found, goodwill remains, like the common parent of us all, bringing people together and uniting them in friendship. It is always faithful in giving advice, and it is as ready to share people's joy in times of prosperity as it is to share their sadness in times of grief.[68]

For Ambrose goodwill is as necessary for good human behavior and the functioning of society as the sun is for the world, and without it friendliness and actions of kindness would disappear. He also connects it with *caritas*, one of the Latin words for love and from whence the English word charity stems.[69] Liz Carmichael, who takes up Ambrose's writing on goodwill, shows how its connection to love can be regarded as a Christian development of the key Roman concept of justice, or *justitia*.[70] Benevolence and *caritas* which "unites [people] in friendship," as Ambrose writes,[71] should be present in the Church, leading to acts of hospitality and kindness. Further, such friendly behavior should be seen to be exercised by those in leading positions.[72] Ambrose suggests here that if such friendliness by leaders is indeed practiced it will help to create an atmosphere of friendliness and love which encourages people to trust such leaders. He writes, "How could anyone not have loved him (David), seeing how dear he was to his friends?"[73]

Exemplifying what Ambrose calls friendship is of interest for our specific focus on friendship and friendliness in the pastoral setting. In Ambrose's thought, strangers will be willing to entrust themselves to the clergy to the degree that they see, through benevolence leading to concrete acts of love and friendliness, "that you (the clergy) are dear to so

---

68. Ambrose, *De officiis*, I.167.
69. Ambrose, *De officiis*, I.127.
70. Carmichael, *Friendship*, 45. She writes: "Cicero had summarized the requirements of justice in a twofold rule: do no harm, and do good wherever opportunity occurs. For Ambrose, justice directs our natural love first to God, then towards our country, our parents, and finally to all, and from this is born caritas, . . . 'which puts others before itself and does not pursue its own interests; this is where justice has its primary seat' (I.127)."
71. Ambrose, *De officiis*, I.167.
72. Ambrose, *De officiis*, II.36.
73. Ambrose, *De officiis*, II.36. Compare also Carmichael, *Friendship*, 46.

many."[74] Benevolence leading to concrete acts of love interestingly has (at least in the context of the church in North America) led to the use of the word to mean the organized giving of money and financial assistance to those within the community in need, where there may even, in certain Churches be a "benevolence pastor,"[75] thus reaffirming a proximity to generosity and beneficence.

Ambrose's use of the word friendship, both here and in the previous quotation where he refers to goodwill as "bringing people together and uniting them in friendship" points to the difficulty in defining where friendliness might be regarded by some as turning into friendship. None of the interviewees, perhaps with the exception of Markus, who at times had the broadest definition of "friend," refers to those with whom they merely feel a bond of kindness or benevolence as friends. As a relationship characterized by kindness and benevolence develops it may at some stage turn into what one might call a friendship, but initially it is not that and may well never be seen as such. Indeed, that benevolence might lead to friendship has not been obvious in the history of pastoral care in the Church. Benevolence or kindness are often seen to be attitudes pastors should exhibit to everyone, regardless of their relation to them and might thus be thought of in the context of friendliness. But they are not generally brought into the specific, contemporary context of what pastors regard as friendship. This can perhaps be best understood in the context of the tension between the specific relationship of friendship, which in its specificity means it always expresses itself with a degree of exclusivity, and the friendly relations expected of pastors to all characterized by general kindness and compassion.

Robert Dykstra, Professor of Pastoral Theology at Princeton, points to this tension in his article "Subversive Friendship"[76] in which he uses the instructive example of the friendship of the Church Fathers Basil and Gregory. They lived together in their younger years and were good friends and close.[77] When Basil became Bishop of Caesarea, he "not only abandoned his friend for a distant city, but he did not even draw his

---

74. Ambrose, *De officiis*, II.39.

75. In a Google search for the phrase "benevolence in the Church" (accessed on 21st July 2021), at least the first fifty links all had to do with financial giving or taxation around giving.

76. Dykstra, "Subversive Friendship," 585–86.

77. See, for instance, Gregory Nazianzen, *Letters (Division II)*, Epistle 58: ". . .if I get any profit in life it is from your friendship and company."

intimate Gregory into consideration of whether to accept the election."[78] Here Dykstra refers to an essay by the practical theologian Philip L. Culbertson[79] in which Culbertson regards this "crisis between friends as stemming from competing philosophies about the evolution of friendships over time, with Basil representing Plato's approach and Gregory reflecting Aristotle's" with the question at hand being whether friendship should move from the particular to the universal, or the universal to the particular. Gilbert Meilaender explains these "competing philosophies" particularly well:

> For Plato, friendship is a universal love which grows out of more particular, affective attachments. For Aristotle . . . , it is a narrowing down of the many toward whom we have good will to a few friends whom we especially choose. Plato's theory begins with a particular attachment, which then grows toward a more universal love. Aristotle's moves in precisely the opposite direction.[80]

Culbertson points out that Basil, in his "Aescetic Sermon I" on Matt 5:45, claims that perfect love must be impartial in its imitation of God's love for humanity but that, in contrast, Gregory did not just regard his friend Basil "as a steppingstone to universal love"[81] but as a particular individual with whom he had a specific friendship. Dykstra writes here, "Though Culbertson makes clear [that] he favours Gregory's priority of the particular in the sphere of love, Christian orthodoxy over time instead elevated Basil's loftier perspective."[82] Indeed, the idea of a loftier perspective of giving up the partiality of a particular friendship for a "universal love" characterized by benevolence, compassion, and kindness to humanity, or what I have termed friendliness here, is a reminder of the tension to which I have already referred in the first chapter in the context of Craig M. Barnes' essay "Pastor, not Friend," to which some of the interviewees referred. This benevolent friendliness has in general been of more significance in the pastoral setting, as the experience of the interviewees shows.

---

78. Dykstra, "Subversive Friendship," 585–86.
79. Culbertson, "Men and Christian Friendship," 149–80.
80. Meilaender, *Friendship*, 8.
81. Dykstra, "Subversive Friendship," 586.
82. Dykstra, "Subversive Friendship," 586.

Closeness or Companionship

From the analysis of the interviews, I have identified closeness or offered situational companionship to those who ask for it as one of the attributes of friendliness about which the interviewed pastors talked. This attribute can occur in personal encounters in counselling situations, such as described by Olivia, or while administering more "priestly" duties, such as described by Theo in the baptizing of a child. Similarly, we saw from biblical texts that companionship in the community of believers is brought into the context of friendship language. In his book *Befriending the Stranger*, the Canadian Roman Catholic theologian and philosopher Jean Vanier[83] taking up Jesus' words about the *paraclete* in John 14:16, points out that the Greek word *parakletos* comes from *para*, "close to" and *kaleo*, "to call" and thus can be translated as "to call out to someone for help" or even more literally "to call out for someone to be close" and the *parakletos* is the one who answers the call.[84] Vanier does not here see that call as a particular one for those ordained to pastoral ministry, as he lists, for instance, God in the person of the Holy Spirit, a mother, or a community as being *parakletes* for people, but he does link it to friendship. It is in the community that Vanier invests most hope of companionship, and in the introduction of another of his books, *Community and Growth*, Vanier defines the two poles of community as:

> the goal which attracts and unites, the centre of interest which provides the "why" of life together; and the friendship which binds people, the sense of belonging to a group, solidarity and personal relationships.[85]

Here, he uses the term friendship in the context of the binding of people together or the sense of closeness, of belonging together, and indeed he

---

83. I am here aware of the controversy surrounding Jean Vanier and the cases of sexual abuse which have come to light since his death, first in February 2020, *Inquiry: Summary_Report*, www.larche.org/wp-content/uploads/documents/10181/2539004/Inquiry-Summary_Report-Final-2020_02_22-EN.pdf, then in the fuller very recent report from January 2023, *Control and Abuse Investigation on Thomas Philippe, Jean Vanier and L'Arche (1950–2019)*, https//commissiondetude-jeanvanier.org. After careful consideration I decided to leave the references to Jean Vanier and his writing in this thesis. In the context of my study, they are a painful and poignant reminder, especially within a section dealing with companionship and closeness, of how delicate the theme, not least in the pastoral setting, is and how even those with much experience and with an ordered spiritual life may fall into sin and abuse of others' trust in them.

84. Vanier, *Befriending the Stranger*, 126.

85. Vanier, *Community and Growth*, 2.

concludes the introduction by quoting from John's Gospel, chapter 15, that no one has greater love than the one who lays down his life for his friends.[86]

Yet after using the term friendship to define the form of closeness and companionship he envisions within a community, the main metaphor Vanier chooses for relationships within the community is that of family. Thus, for instance in referencing Jesse Jackson and Mother Theresa, he writes, "'My people' are my community . . . my brothers and sisters remain written within me. . . . I cannot be a universal brother unless I first love my people."[87] Indeed, fairly quickly, friendship, seen now as exclusive and private, becomes something dangerous and detrimental to community, something which creates barriers and needs to be overcome, and he posits that "a community is only a community when most of its members have consciously decided to break these barriers and come out of their cocoons."[88] Yet later on, in a short section entitled "The Friend," Vanier emphasizes the necessity of having special trusted companions to whom to talk, which he regards as "an absolutely essential resource"[89] for people within communities, and as a place of security where they may feel uninhibited in expressing their feelings and thoughts.

The tension to which we have referred to a number of times in this study between the experience of the warmth and joy felt in the closeness and companionship of a friend, and the fear of that becoming narrow in scope and detrimental to others, is also found here in Vanier's use of the term of friendship. Sometimes he uses that term broadly, almost as a synonym for the friendliness of companionship in the context of good communal relations, and at other times he uses it in an exclusive manner, which he regards as both necessary for the emotional health of a person and at the same time dangerous for the cohesion of the community as a whole.

C. S. Lewis, in his book *The Four Loves*, helpfully differentiates between the various uses of the terms companionship and friendship. Companionship, he writes, is something the community needs. It is the mutual respect and understanding of people who live and work with each other and have pleasure in cooperation. Some people when they speak of their "friends" mean only their companions, and although, he states, that

86. Vanier, *Community and Growth*, 4.
87. Vanier, *Community and Growth*, 8.
88. Vanier, *Community and Growth*, 13.
89. Vanier, *Community and Growth*, 135.

is not friendship itself, it is the "matrix of friendship."[90] Companionship thus as a form of friendliness can be seen as a matrix which provides a framework in which friendship can arise. That can happen, says Lewis, when within that matrix of companionship a mutual vision and deep interest in something particular is discovered, which creates a bond between those involved.[91]

What, however, of companionship and its relation to friendliness and friendship within the pastoral setting of ordained ministry within a local congregation? The pastoral setting is one where people do (to take up Vanier's reading of *paraclete*) ask for someone to be close to them and, in specific situations, to be a companion to them. Given the importance in the New Testament of the work of the *paraclete*, it is perhaps surprising that in Clebsch and Jaekle's classic summary, *Pastoral Care in Historical Perspective* neither terms like companionship nor closeness as such, or even friendliness or friendship, appear in the index, and it is hard to find references to them. The authors summarize what they call the functions of pastoral care under the four categories of healing, sustaining, guiding, and reconciling, and using historical texts from recognized leaders in the Church and the study of religion they show how these activities have been central to what they regard as authentic and good pastoral care. Within the section on sustaining in the context of offering help and companionship in situations of bereavement the role of a skilful pastor is equated with that of a friend.[92] Yet this mention seems to be more of an aside and is not discussed further. In general, the emphasis is on pastoral modes of what in the context of this study we might call friendly activity for people and not on pastoral modes of being with people.

Regarding pastoral companionship, the work of the Jesuit priest Gerald J. Calhoun in Boston looks specifically at ministry with seriously ill persons and their families and is also helpful in a wider context.[93] Concerning the nature of companionship, his description of the ministry of the young student chaplain Harry is instructive. Harry helps Marie, who has had multiple sclerosis for many years and whose husband has recently died of a heart attack. Harry assists Marie in grieving and then becomes, for a time, what Calhoun calls "a substitute for her dead husband,

---

90. Lewis, *Four Loves*, 96.
91. Lewis, *Four Loves*, 96–97.
92. Clebsch and Jaekle, *Pastoral Care*, 44.
93. Calhoun, *Pastoral Companionship*.

someone to take care of her and 'never abandon her.'"[94] In Vanier's terms, Harry becomes a type of *paraclete* for Marie. Over time he learns to help Marie become more independent and find strength in herself, and his role shifts.

Here, Calhoun is writing about what he sees as vital in sincere pastoral companionship, and how that can facilitate wellbeing in those who are seriously ill.

> Companionship with seriously-ill persons and with their families involves many facets. It begins with and is grounded upon a sincere, sustained interest in the whole person, not just the sick person; . . . ministers who can let themselves be known as persons and not just as chaplains facilitate a companionship that embraces this interest in the whole person. Especially with seriously-ill persons, it is imperative that self-disclosure be a two-way street. Getting to know the pastoral minister as a unique person, with family and outside activities, with opinions and feelings, pleases seriously-ill people because they value a bond that transcends a cool professionalism . . . If the minister can enjoy this mutual interest and caring then trust deepens and their companionship becomes rooted in friendship.[95]

Here the matrix of companionship, going further than just a general friendliness and involving the conscious two-way street of self-disclosure, and the pastor's enjoyment of mutual interest and caring, leads to what Calhoun describes as a companionship rooted in friendship, but he does not discuss the term any further. Yet it is clear that he regards such a relationship as positive and helpful in ministering to those with serious illnesses.

Regarding the relationship between Harry and Marie, Harry's becoming for a time "a substitute for her dead husband" might seem problematic in terms of closeness and intimacy with its possibilities of abuse. Calhoun does not pursue this, but he emphasizes throughout his book the necessity for reflection around helpful and sincere forms of vulnerability and authenticity of those involved in pastoral ministry with those who are seriously ill. Such reflection he sees as a necessary part of spiritual and pastoral formation, which can be encouraged and trained within the scope of the formal education of pastors.

---

94. Calhoun, *Pastoral Companionship*, 10.
95. Calhoun, *Pastoral Companionship*, 10–11.

In this context the American Baptist pastor David Wood writes, in an article taken from a lecture he held at a Princeton Forum on Youth Ministry,[96] that questions surrounding companionship and closeness in the pastoral educational setting tend to be centred around the problems of abuse and misconduct rather than a positive and healthy way of practicing closeness. He cites an article by Martin Marty, an American Lutheran professor of religion, who suggested that a main problem in attempting to combat misconduct amongst clergy was a failure to address what might be one of the leading causes of such behavior, namely "the reality of a friendless clergy."[97] Wood writes:

> Compare the amount of time spent schooling pastors on the hazards of intimacy to the amount of time spent on exhorting them to the practice of friendship. The importance of bonding has been displaced by the necessity of boundaries. We have developed a thoroughgoing hermeneutic of suspicion when it comes to intimacy. This is not an argument against a healthy understanding of the importance of boundaries in the negotiation of the complex relational landscape of ministry. Rather, it is a call for a corresponding emphasis on the importance of friendship to one's capacity to negotiate intimacy.[98]

Wood here laments the lack of formation in pastoral training which might enable ongoing pastors to train themselves in a friendliness which has the capacity to allow them to become good and authentic companions and perhaps indeed friends within the scope of their congregational ministry.[99]

Alan Jones, an Anglican priest and founder of the Centre for Christian Spirituality at General Theological Seminary in New York City, does take this up in his book *Exploring Spiritual Direction*. He believes Christian companionship to be vital and necessary for growth and health as a Christian. His work is focused on the theme of spiritual direction and is thus not specifically directed at pastors of local congregations. But he understands spiritual direction as a form of companionship, and also uses the term "spiritual friendship" to describe what he himself looks for in a spiritual director.[100] In a chapter entitled *The Need for Companionship*,

---

96. Wood, "Recovery and Promise of Friendship," 165–80.
97. Marty, "What Friends Are For," 988.
98. Wood, "Recovery and Promise of Friendship," 170.
99. I return to this theme in the context of the Swiss Reformed Church in chapter 5.
100. Jones, *Exploring Spiritual Direction*, 11.

Jones takes up the imagery of spiritual warfare, as depicted for instance in Christian's battle with Apollyon in Bunyan's *The Pilgrim's Progress*. Although he emphasizes how helpful such imagery can be in an age of instability and uncertainty, he also recognizes that it can lead to a number of problems, namely an oversimplification of who or what the "enemy" might be, and an overconfident arrogance, once that particular "enemy" has been identified and perhaps even initially overcome. "Both problems point to the need for companionship, guidance and direction."[101] It is companionship, he contends, which is needed for Christian discernment, and indeed also a trusted spiritual companion who may have the courage to confront one with truth and wisdom about oneself. And although the tradition of spiritual direction is associated with a type of submission and obedience on the part of the one seeking guidance, for Jones it is important that the type of companionship, or "spiritual friendship," he envisions in spiritual direction is one of mutuality under the Holy Spirit. Thus:

> It is only when a person has a certain amount of self-knowledge that he or she is ready for spiritual direction. The person utterly occupied with himself is not ready for the mutuality of Christian companionship. . . .Directors know that from God's point of view there is very little difference between them and their friend. They, for the time being, and only for the time being, have a word, a healing word. They know that all the time they must be listening for the healing word from those who come to them for guidance.[102]

Jones is evidently well aware that both parties in an encounter of spiritual direction need to be open to the working of the Holy Spirit, and that directors, although theoretically regarded as superior or more practiced, may have just as much need for a healing word from the companion as the companion does for one from the director.

This setting of spiritual direction is of interest for the theme of this study as it is, in certain ways, similar to a specific part of what pastoral duties for ordained ministers entail. People do come voluntarily to pastors for spiritual direction and sometimes they may indeed be looking for companionship or "spiritual friendship." What Jones sees as the difference between friendship as such and "spiritual friendship" is not something on which he elaborates, but in describing what he regards as

---

101. Jones, *Exploring Spiritual Direction*, 14.
102. Jones, *Exploring Spiritual Direction*, 64.

Christian companionship he refers to openness in the sense of frank and honest speech, the courage to confront the other with truth and wisdom, and to a mutuality for which he hopes through the working of the Holy Spirit.[103] Yet these attributes alone would not seem to qualify the relationship as moving from one of friendliness to one of friendship in the terms we have seen emerging from the research in this study. Regarding the essential attributes of friendship, that of affection for the specific person is not mentioned. And regarding the attribute of freedom and the free choice of one's friends, the situation is ambivalent as the person seeking direction, although coming voluntarily, comes to the encounter with a specific purpose in mind and the spiritual director, although likewise voluntarily agreeing to the encounter, has a specific task to fulfill within that. I shall take up this ambivalence and tension in my reflection around freedom in chapter four.

Equality

Each of the participants in the interviews saw the need for the pastor to treat each person in the congregation equally well. Stephanie, for instance, formulated it like this: "Friendliness for me is an attitude that I want to show everyone, no matter how close or far away they are to me," and Olivia grounded such an attitude in her understanding of God as one who "does not exclude, he connects, he is for everyone." As we saw in the discussion around the attributes of friendship in the New Testament, both Luke and Paul regard equality as of importance in the friendships of those within the Christian community. Yet this equality is one which is bestowed on all those who are disciples of Christ. It is not determined by social status, wealth, or power. Friendship, being understood as between equals, was well within the common Greek and Roman *topos* of friendship and yet the way Luke and Paul referred to it was at the same time unusual, with its understanding of equality as something given to people of all walks of life within a fellowship together due to their faith in Christ. Cause and effect were in one sense reversed, in that it was not because of a feeling of sameness or equality in education or class that people became friends. Rather, through their friendship with Jesus they learned that they were equals with other friends of Jesus.

---

103. Jones, *Exploring Spiritual Direction*, 61–64.

The late New Testament and preaching scholar Gail O'Day points out how important such friendship among equals was seen to be in Greco-Roman society. She writes:

> for Aristotle and the classical philosophers who followed him, friendship was not an incidental relationship. It exemplified, rather, the mutual social obligation on which the polis depended. In the democratic ideal of the Athenian polis, the relationship between friends, *philoi*, was a relationship between equals contributing together to the public ethos of citizenship. To be a good friend was by definition also to be a good citizen.[104]

Thus, getting to know others in the community of Jesus' disciples and understanding them as friends led in turn to the classic fruits and responsibilities of friendship within Greco-Roman society such as generosity, the sharing of wealth and commodities, and the nurture of the community as a whole.

The connection between getting to know others and recognizing them as equals with the potential of them becoming friends within a Christian community is something about which Jürgen Moltmann writes in an essay entitled *Knowing and Community*.[105] In Aristotle's concept of the ideal, or what he calls the complete friendship, it is those who are alike in virtue and status who may become friends and discover in the other "another yourself."[106] Moltmann takes this up and connects it to what he calls the Aristotelian principle of knowledge in general that like is known only by like, and to the Greek extension of this principle of analogy that similar is known only by similar. He then offers a critique:

> If only like ones know one another, then I only know in other humans that which corresponds to me in my being. I do not perceive that which is different and alien about the other humans; I block it out. I only know that which is the same in both of us and only that can become the basis of community between us. "True friendship," says Aristotle, "exists on the basis of likeness" (*Nicomachean Ethics* 8.4). Friendship of like ones was the embodiment of the Greek doctrine of society. Although some heroes were called friends of the gods, one cannot actually speak of a friendship of the humans with the god-father Zeus. This is

---

104. O'Day, "Jesus as Friend in the Gospel of John," 146.

105. Moltmann, "Knowing and Community," 162–76.

106. Aristotle, "Nicomachean Ethics," 1156b7–8; 1169b6 in Pakaluk, *Other Selves*, 33; 62.

also the case between men and women, between the free and the slaves. On the basis of likeness, friendship operates in an exclusive manner. From like ones only closed societies arise. In them, the like ones mutually affirm their identity through the exclusion of the others and the repeated assurance of not being like the others. Even in our so-called open society, the like ones come together in exclusive circles. Not only is such behavior painful for the excluded others; it leads those who are in it into a deadly boredom because they have already heard a hundred times all of the stories and jokes with which closed societies usually entertain themselves. The "eternal return of the same" is in fact not an image of eternity, but rather of the dying of the living.[107]

Thus, according to Moltmann, the principle of correspondence, the equal to the equal, the like to the like, or the similar to the similar, does not lead to a gain in knowledge but rather to the constantly repeated self-verification of what is already known. Applied to God, as he writes, "the principle of likeness leads either to the deification of the human or to the humanisation of God,"[108] neither of which represents reality as revealed by Christ.

Against this Moltmann sets what he calls dialectical thinking, which is capable of welcoming what is different. What is different however is only approachable through contradiction and thus, to a degree, through pain. As he points out using the imagery of a different Greek philosopher, Anaxagoras, the darker it is the more we experience what light is, the colder we are, the more we experience warmth. It is in this dialectic approach that a holistic perception of the world and relationships, of community with those who are diverse becomes possible and can even be enjoyed. Moltmann sees this enjoyment becoming possible through the very origin of all knowledge, which he locates, once again in reference to Greek philosophy, in our ability to be amazed.[109]

In the context of this study around friendship in the pastoral setting, Moltmann's critique of a rigid understanding of the relational advantage of sameness, and in that sense equality, is refreshing. He writes:

> People whom we respect in their individuality remain amazing for us, and our amazement opens the freedom for new possibilities of the future of our community with them. . . . Amazement

---

107. Moltmann, "Knowing and Community," 165.
108. Moltmann, "Knowing and Community," 166.
109. Moltmann, "Knowing and Community," 169–74.

is the inexhaustible source of our community with one another, with nature and with God. Amazement is the beginning of each new experience and the source of our expectant creativity.[110]

Learning to approach each new encounter with a person in the church community from a deep sense of belonging together on equal footing before Christ, and yet with an attitude of amazement at the diversity and uniqueness which characterizes that person, even after perhaps many years of knowing them, also sounds like a good way to understand relationships within the congregation. And the mention of the pain involved in coping with contradiction makes the approach closer to real experiences with real people within that community.[111] Yet whether such encounters will necessarily develop from those characterized by a friendliness which seeks equal treatment for each person to a relationship which both would regard as actual friendship, as described by its essential attributes in this study, is something each individual will have to decide for themselves.

Faithfulness or Loyalty

Most of the interviewed pastors viewed faithfulness, trust, and loyalty, first of all to Christ and then through that to those in their congregations, as part of the friendliness which they wanted to uphold within their pastoral vocations. Theo, for instance, talked of friendliness as a "deserved expectation of office holders, of pastors," where they should "be willing to evidence the friendship of God," and Beat made reference to the exhortation from 1 Pet 3:15. As we have seen in Scripture, faithfulness and loyalty are often associated with friendship. Yet they are also contentious issues, and faithfulness and loyalty can often lead to difficulties and conflicts when there are various people vying for them. In writing about friendship at the workplace, the philosopher Mark Vernon points out that such conflicts become difficult for organizations:

> There is . . . an argument that organisations are inherently suspicious of friendship since they set up networks of loyalties that can act against the organisation's best interests: the activities of

---

110. Moltmann, "Knowing and Community," 175–76.
111. I shall take this up further in chapter four in my discussion about openness.

friends can easily be viewed as time wasting at best or nepotistic and subversive behaviour at worst.[112]

That this has been the case within the Church as an organization as well is something Liz Carmichael notes when she refers to the suppression of friendships in monastic life during the Middle Ages. Particular friendships were understood to have a seditious effect in monastic communities in causing cliques and exclusive groups, such individuals potentially showing more loyalty to each other than to the community. Those in authority feared that such friendships would lead to a distraction from inner calm and possibly to other sins.[113] This fear of the seditious effect of relationships of friendship leading to conflicts of loyalty within communities is not hard to understand. As I wrote in the first chapter my own experience as a pastor in contact with other ordained colleagues has been that they have often avoided actual friendships within congregations because of such a fear of conflicting loyalties leading to messy and emotionally draining situations of jealousy and disappointment.

Writing about friendship and fidelity, Gilbert Meilaender points out that the question of conflicting loyalties is as old as the discussion around friendship itself and is not just bound to personal relations but also to loyalty to a greater good or to truth. Here, he quotes Aristotle's exhortation that truth must be honoured even above the friendship one has with a friend, and then continues:

> Indeed, in Christian terms one must always presume at least one such qualification to be written into friendship; namely, that loyalty to the friend could not override faithfulness to God if these should seem to conflict.[114]

God's own faithfulness and our faithfulness to God are at the heart of the Christian life. And in the context of this study as research in practical theology within the framework of the pastoral setting, we saw in Swinton and Mowat's description of what practical theology should be how they regard faithfulness to the message and calling of Jesus Christ as witnessed to by the Scriptures as the key to testing the practices of the Church.[115] In the same vein, this faithfulness to Christ can also be understood as a key to understanding and practicing pastoral ministry. In the area of pastoral

---

112. Vernon, *Philosophy of Friendship*, 26.
113. Carmichael, *Friendship*, 3.
114. Meilaender, *Friendship*, 55.
115. Compare Swinton and Mowat, *Practical Theology and Qualitative Research*, 9.

friendliness and friendships, it is perhaps especially poignant in that the primary loyalty of pastors is to Christ.

As John's Gospel documents, Christ himself, who lays down his life for his friends, exhorts his disciples to love one other as he has loved them. In this context Gail O'Day, whom I quoted earlier, putting into perspective the faithfulness of Christ towards his friends with the writings of philosophy and taking up John 15, writes:

> What distinguishes John 15:13 from other teachings on friendship and death is that Jesus does not merely talk about laying down his life for his friends. His life is an incarnation of this teaching. Jesus did what the philosophers only talked about—he laid down his life for his friends. This makes all the difference in appropriating friendship as a theological category. The pattern of Jesus' own life and death moves the teaching of John 15:13 from the realm of abstraction to an embodied promise and gift. . . . Jesus' disciples are urged to live the same way Jesus has lived, to be the kind of friend that Jesus has been. He is not simply asking them to be good citizens or moral exemplars. He is commanding them to embody the very promises that he has embodied for them (15:14, 17).[116]

Faithfulness to Christ thus becomes a reason for Christians, and in the framework of this study, also Christian pastors, to be faithful and loyal friends themselves, embodying in their actions and speech the friendship love of Christ. O'Day elaborates on this:

> The title "friend" becomes something into which Jesus invites his disciples to grow. The name "friend," and with it the relationship of friendship, is a gift from Jesus to them, just as his life is a gift to them. The disciples begin with the explicit appellation, "friend," and the challenge for them is to enact and embody friendship as Jesus has done. The disciples know how Jesus has been a friend, and they are called to see what kind of friends they can become. Jesus' friendship is the model of friendship for the disciples, and it makes any subsequent acts of friendship by them possible because the disciples themselves are already the recipients of Jesus' acts of friendship.[117]

In faithfulness to their calling and by modelling the friendship of Jesus, pastors can, says O'Day, "see what kind of friends they can become,"

---

116. O'Day, "Jesus as Friend in the Gospel of John," 150–52.
117. O'Day, "Jesus as Friend in the Gospel of John," 152.

in the empowering realisation that acts of friendship are possible because they are already living in the faithful friendship love of Christ.

This will not necessarily make the everyday choices involved in living and negotiating relationships within a community much easier, and conflicting loyalties will likely remain. And it also does not easily resolve the tension between faithful, friendly behavior to all in the congregation and specific relationships of friendship to a few. But it puts a promising perspective onto pastoral choices regarding the giving of time and effort. And it helps encourage pastors to become ever more aware that God's faithfulness is at work even when they may feel inadequate themselves.

An instructive example, perhaps, of this faithful friendliness is given by Joan Paddock Maxwell, a hospital chaplain in the middle of her training in CPE. In a short article entitled "Great is Thy Faithfulness,"[118] Maxwell tells about her encounter with a thirty-one year-old patient who did not wish to speak or communicate at all with anyone. On her first visit, he said nothing in response to her introduction or efforts at conversation, although Maxwell noticed that his eyes appeared interested when she talked about the deer in a field outside the window of the hospital. She returned the next day and the patient still did not wish to talk, but he nodded in response to her question of whether he had seen the deer. The next day she went again, and again he did not talk, but again he did nod when asked about the deer. On day four, the nod was accompanied by a "yes," but nothing more. On day five he sat up in his bed, when Maxwell entered the room, asked her to sit down and then talked to her for over an hour, at first about the deer in the field, but then about his life and his failures and disappointments but also about his belief in a loving God who cared for him although he thought no one else did. At the end of the conversation Maxwell prayed to that loving God together with him.

When she returned to visit him after the weekend, he told her about an overwhelming experience he had had during the night, and he recounted having experienced God:

> "There was nobody in the room, nobody in the hall, nobody came in. It was so quiet. But there was such joy." His face glowed. "From three until 4:30 in the morning. Joy. Joy in the room." He paused, remembering. "Oh, I needed that. You don't know how much I needed that. I didn't dare move. I didn't want it to end. I just laid there. Just laid still. No one in the room," he repeated, "just joy."[119]

118. Maxwell, "Great Is Thy faithfulness," 465–66.
119. Maxwell, "Great Is Thy Faithfulness," 466.

He told his story twice to Maxwell and then they prayed together. That afternoon, she heard that he had been moved to a hospice, and three days later he died. Maxwell writes, "As I think of [that patient], I am reminded of the goodness of God, who brought him such joy at the last, and whose deer were so exceedingly faithful."[120]

Both the experienced faithfulness of God in the encounter with the patient and also the faithfulness and friendly perseverance of the chaplain in a relationship which at first seemed not to be taking off, are of interest in the context of this study. Maxwell does not use the word friendship in her article, but through her faithfulness in visiting the patient repeatedly and in opening space for relationship, she acted in a friendly way, as a friend would. Indeed, by referring to Matt 25:40,[121] she clearly understood herself to be acting within the framework of and in loyalty to her relationship with Christ, who becomes just as present to her in the moving encounter as He does to the patient.

Hospitality

From the interviews we saw how the participating pastors regarded hospitality to be an important form of friendliness in the fulfillment of their vocation. Markus and Stephanie, for instance, regarded an accessible hospitality to be of vital importance in their work as pastors, and were consequently happy to invite people to meals or for a coffee together. Similarly, the study of the biblical texts earlier on in this chapter shows that hospitality appears to be closely related to the concept of being a friend. The archaic distinction "friend or foe?" could be understood as a way of determining whether the person or persons met should be shown hospitality and welcomed into the community as guests, or repelled and fought off. Indeed, the German word for hospitality has the word friendship built into it: *Gastfreundschaft* or "guest friendship."[122] The complicated dynamics of Christian hospitality might also be understood to be close to those experienced in pastoral friendliness and friendship, as the

---

120. Maxwell, "Great Is Thy Faithfulness," 466.

121. Matt 25: 40 NIV, "Truly I tell you, whatever you did for one of the least of these brothers and sisters of mine, you did for me"; Maxwell, "Great is Thy Faithfulness," 466.

122. Interestingly for our study, in regard to freedom as one of the essential attributes of friendship, the Dutch word for hospitality has freedom in it, *gastvrijheid* or "guest freedom."

roles of who is host and who is guest are constantly challenged the deeper a relationship becomes.

Elisabeth Newman, Professor of Theology and Ethics at Baptist Theological Seminary in Richmond, Virginia, and Christine Pohl, Professor Emerita of Christian Ethics at Asbury Theological Seminary in Wilmore, Kentucky, have written informed and challenging books on Christian hospitality.[123] Both emphasize the counter-cultural dimension of a hospitality which welcomes the stranger. For instance, Pohl writes:

> Especially when the larger society disregards or dishonours certain persons, small acts of respect and welcome are potent far beyond themselves. They point to a different system of valuing and an alternate model of relationships.[124]

In attempting to get to the core of the concept, Newman distinguishes Christian hospitality from four forms of hospitality, which she calls sentimental hospitality, privatized hospitality, hospitality as a mode of marketing, and hospitality as inclusivity.[125] These distinctions are helpful in the context of this study around friendliness and friendship within the pastoral setting. Newman equates sentimental hospitality with a superficial "being nice," which has little regard for truthful and meaningful communion, and she connects this with a sentimental idea of God:

> The sentimental distortion of hospitality often coincides with a distorted picture of God, who becomes "simply a therapeutic nice guy who asks only that we be nice too." As D. Stephen Long notes, "It is as if God has been reduced to a friendly character with open arms who meets us at the entrance to his magic kingdom, inviting us to come in and find our individual fulfilment." This kind of Disney World hospitality might make us feel good, but such feelings will be short lived. A faithful hospitality will not aim for niceness and frozen smiles but rather for truthful communion with God and others. Long rightly concludes, "Jesus is not a personal Saviour who only seeks to meet my needs. He is the risen crucified Lord of all creation who seeks to guide me back into the truth of the Triune God."[126]

---

123. Newman, *Untamed Hospitality*; Pohl, *Making Room*.
124. Pohl, *Making Room*, 61.
125. Newman, *Untamed Hospitality*, 23.
126. Newman, *Untamed Hospitality*, 24.

Taking this up within the context of a pastoral relationship, the hospitality offered will be challenged not to be content with a bland niceness which, though unthreatening, by its sheer superficiality allows no room for a meaningful encounter with the other. The opposite of such cheap, sentimental hospitality perhaps is more akin to what Beat describes referencing his experience on the mission field, where the hospitality offered and shared by a pastor in the Lord's Supper extends even to those who have been actively involved in oppressing and torturing them.

Privatized hospitality is what Newman calls "entertaining." It is confined to a single sphere of life, namely the home, and is almost always extended to those more or less like oneself in terms of status and class.[127] She criticizes such privatization for moving hospitality out of the public sphere, making hospitality not so much a way of life as a mode of private entertainment. Similar to a sentimental form, this can lead to an emphasis on appearances, which can be driven by a need for approval, and on social expectations and such like, and which lead away from truthful and open encounters. Further, Newman suggests, a privatized hospitality cannot do justice to the calling of followers of Christ, for

> Christian hospitality involves not a private set of beliefs (held in check at the dinner table) but rather having "one's body shaped, one's habits determined, in a manner that makes the worship of God . . . unavoidable." We could say that hospitality as entertainment, or civilized hospitality, trains one to be, at best, self-conscious about Christianity and, at worst, embarrassed such that Christianity becomes interiorized. Yet we are called to practice a hospitality consistent with our self-confident worship of God, a hospitality that is not our achievement (having the home in perfect order, providing entertainment, and the like) but rather is a gift of the Holy Spirit for the sake of the Church and the world.[128]

In a parallel line of thought, friendly, pastoral relationships opening up the possibility of friendship, which are motivated by the discipleship of Jesus, cannot be relegated to a mode of private entertainment with those of one's own status or class. In using the very same words as Newman, it might be possible to understand pastors to be called to practice forms of pastoral friendliness, leading possibly to friendship, which are consistent with our self-confident worship of God, a friendliness, and

127. Newman, *Untamed Hospitality*, 26–27.
128. Newman, *Untamed Hospitality*, 27.

even friendship, that is not our achievement but rather is a gift of the Holy Spirit for the sake of the Church and the world.

Newman's third distinction is that of hospitality as a mode of marketing, a way of selling things. Here she uses an illuminating example of her experience on a cruise ship. The crew were hospitable, but the service was expensive, and although the idea was floated of everyone on the ship being one big family, in reality

> the crew and the rest of us on the boat pretty much remained strangers to each other. In fact, one of the rules for the crew was that they were not to interact for any length of time with the "guests."[129]

Market hospitality is about consumerism, about pandering to the lifestyle desires of the "guests," whether these be materialistic or aesthetic—in exchange for money. It focuses on the satisfaction of personal desire, and has little to do with any real desire for the welfare of the other. One of the lower forms of friendship which Aristoteles posits is that of utility friendships, which can be understood as friendly relationships which are of use to both parties, such as business friendships or the like. Given that a pastor is typically paid to act, the degree to which pastoral friendliness or friendship can be understood like this is a difficult question, and the tensions involved have already been mentioned. And even if a form of friendliness can be expected, professionally, of a paid pastor, yet it seems clear that the idea of friendship bought with money jars with the most central attributes of friendship, freedom, mutuality, openness, and affection which have emerged from the analysis of the interviews and to which Scripture testifies as part of what Christian friendship will be about. The mutual freedom and affectionate openness and honesty required in a friendship as a way of faithfully and authentically living the gospel of Jesus will thus be different from friendship sought as a way of selling the gospel, even when a friendly professional element is involved.

Finally, Newman's fourth distinction is that of hospitality as inclusivity. As she herself notes, at first this may not seem like a distortion of what Christian hospitality is about as Jesus himself welcomes inclusively the outcasts of his society. And yet Jesus' inclusivity is not without expectations, as can be seen well in the story of the woman caught in adultery.[130] The gospel does not embrace every type of diversity, but God gives

---

129. Newman, *Untamed Hospitality*, 28.

130. Newman, *Untamed Hospitality*, 30–31: "Jesus accepts her and reminds those

different people different gifts for the building up of the body of Christ. There is therefore a purpose in hospitality, which is larger than diversity and inclusivity in themselves. Neglecting this purpose makes it difficult

> to discern which differences are truly good and therefore "gifts" and which are more reflective of our fallen world.[131]

Likewise, hospitality offered out of a spirit of pastoral friendliness will entail not only friendly inclusivity of diversity and difference, but will seek the best for the other, aware that in truthfulness and faithfulness to the friendship of Jesus, this may mean both the embrace of differences with which the pastor may not initially be comfortable as well as the challenge to test some forms of diversity in which people wish to live as to whether they reflect a faithful discipleship of Christ and are helpful in the building up of the body of Christ or not.

Summary

This chapter is the first of two concerning theological reflection on the findings of the analysis of my hermeneutic phenomenological study around the theme of how ordained pastors within the Swiss Reformed Church describe and experience friendship within their congregations. I have described my approach to this by making reference to the following three themes described by Graham, Walton, and Ward which can be used as a guide for theological reflection: the formation and nurture of a Christian, understanding what it means to be the body of Christ, and bringing the good news of the gospel into relationship with wider culture and society. I have studied the witness of the Hebrew Bible and the New Testament around the terms and the *topos* of friendship, and have reflected theologically on the results of that alongside the results of the analysis, specifically in this chapter through elements which I have identified from the interviews as being part of the friendliness which pastors expect from themselves. These are benevolence or kindness, closeness or companionship, equality, faithfulness or loyalty, and hospitality.

In the next chapter, I turn to theological reflection concerning the essential attributes of friendship and their interwovenness as they have

---

who would stone her that they too are sinners: "Let him that is without sin cast the first stone." Yet Jesus also says to her, "Go and sin no more." He loves and accepts her but also calls her to a different way of life."

131. Newman, *Untamed Hospitality*, 31.

emerged from my research findings from the interviews; mutuality, affection, freedom, and openness.

4

Theological Reflection on the Essential Elements of Friendship and Their Interwovenness Within the Experience of the Interviewed Pastors

IN THIS CHAPTER, STAYING close to my data analysis and the results which emerged, I take up the four essential elements of friendship experienced by the interviewed pastors and discuss how they interact within a broader theological framework. As we have seen in the analysis, the interviewed pastors' relationships with members of their congregations which they regard as friendships involve the interplay of the following essential elements: mutuality, affection, freedom, and openness. Where some of these elements are present in a relationship but one or more of them is missing, though that relationship may be regarded and described (as does Denise, for instance,) as "a friendly expression of being on the same path together," for her it does not qualify as a friendship. Although each of the interviewed pastors might lay more or less emphasis on the different aspects of their friendships, there appears to be an agreement between the accounts, and this becomes apparent as soon they describe their experiences in any detail. Specifically, certain elements are necessary for them to feel that the relationship is a friendship. The four sections within this second chapter concerning theological reflection respond to this finding:

- Theological reflection on a kind of mutuality within a pastoral relationship, which is affectionate, free, and open
- Theological reflection on a kind of affection within a pastoral relationship, which is free, open, and mutual
- Theological reflection on a kind of freedom within a pastoral relationship, which is open, mutual, and affectionate
- Theological reflection on a kind of openness within a pastoral relationship, which is mutual, affectionate, and free

Although at first each of these sections would seem to be basically the same—in that each takes up all four elements of friendship within a pastoral relationship—the emphasis I have chosen for each section allows for a differentiation and focus on each of the single elements without losing sight of its interwovenness with the other elements within friendship relationships.

THEOLOGICAL REFLECTION ON A KIND OF MUTUALITY WITHIN A PASTORAL RELATIONSHIP, WHICH IS AFFECTIONATE, FREE, AND OPEN

Mutuality is a basic attribute of friendship which we have encountered both in the data analysis and in the study of the scriptural texts around friendship. M. Craig Barnes' reason (as I quoted him in chapter one) that pastors cannot be friends to others given their position in their parishes was that it is necessary to maintain a distinction between relationships of mutuality and those of service as a pastor. Similarly, Seward Hiltner, who was a Presbyterian pastor and professor at the Princeton Theological Seminary, in an essay he wrote called "Friendship in Counseling," differentiated between friendship and the friendliness expected of a pastor, using the term *mutuality*:

> Friendship, personal and intimate, is different [from friendliness]. It is not merely a relationship to which the pastor gives something, but also one from which he gets something. . . Friendship is a personal and mutual relationship.[1]

As he uses the term here, friendship refers to a specific type of mutuality within a relationship, a personal mutuality. Similarly, the data

1. Seward, "Friendship in Counseling," 28–34.

analysis has shown that only in a relationship involving mutuality which is affectionate, free, and open did the interviewed pastors experience that relationship as one which they would regard as a friendship. Mutuality as such, in that it refers to types of reciprocity within a relationship, does not necessitate friendship, as there are various relationships which exhibit (for instance) mutual respect, or mutual empathy, which neither side of the relationship would designate a friendship. The type of mutuality described in friendship terms by the interviewed pastors is one of give and take in very personal areas of life. Embedded in my description of such mutuality is the element of openness as an experience of honest communication of otherwise held back personal thoughts and feelings, which necessarily includes a willingness to risk vulnerability within the relationship.

In a broad theological and also cross-disciplinary framework, research around mutuality and openness often leads to the work of the Jewish philosopher of religion Martin Buber,[2] notably his books *I and Thou* and *The Knowledge of Man*, and to those who took up his thought.[3] Within this theological reflection on a mutuality within a pastoral relationship, which is affectionate, free, and open, I shall first turn to an author who interprets Buber, especially in the area of understanding around mutuality. In his book *Mutuality: The vision of Martin Buber*, Donald L. Berry, an Episcopal priest and Professor of Philosophy and Religion, shows that a core issue in Buber's thought can be understood to be that of mutuality.[4] Berry's work on what he calls the "Helper" is the first matter of

---

2. Buber is widely regarded as a religious existentialist who, amongst others, had a significant influence on the development of pastoral care and counselling in the twentieth century. The existentialists "find the clue to human existence in the depth of human subjectivity, in the individual's finite freedom as that freedom is shaped and distorted by the anxiety it arouses." Emphasizing human freedom, they call for "authentic existence," part of which can be understood as the recovery of an openness and mutuality in human relationships, which has been lost and replaced by "defensiveness, alienation, self-centeredness and hostility." Yet Buber's existentialism cannot be regarded as that of a "solitary, fraught soul in search for meaning." The essence of humankind is not to be found in the individual or in collectivity, "but only in the reality of mutual relations 'between man and man.'" Hunter, *Dictionary of Pastoral Care and Counseling*, 385–86; Soskice, *Kindness of God*, 169; quoting from Buber, *Between Man and Man*, vii.

3. See also the article "Buber, Martin" in Hunter, *Dictionary of Pastoral Care and Counseling*, 111.

4. Berry points out, I think correctly, that a general understanding of Buber's work around the 'I-thou' relationship, and thus around a form of mutuality in human relationships, is familiar to a wide audience, but that there are areas of Buber's thought, to which insufficient notice has been given, one of these areas being that of the "Helper." Berry, *Mutuality*, x–xi.

special interest for this part of my study. There, he investigates "Buber's claim that those human relationships which are constituted or defined by a task to be performed are prevented normatively from achieving full mutuality."[5] In doing this he studies how Buber's comments on degrees of mutuality can be used to understand what type of mutuality professional helpers might experience in their professional relations, if these are not to be termed "normative."

The second area of special interest concerns the work of the German Lutheran pastor Dietrich Bonhoeffer. His theological thought around relationships within the Christian community, and indeed around friendship, specifically the friendship he enjoyed with Eberhard Bethge, are particularly well known. Whereas Berry's thought is more centred around the two elements of mutuality and openness, and later also freedom, in Bonhoeffer's writing around friendship we find all four of the essential elements of friendship—including affection—that we have seen emerging from the interviews in this study. Of special interest for this study is a recent dissertation by Preston David Sunabacka Parsons, *A Friendship for Others: Bonhoeffer and Bethge on the theology and practice of friendship* and a collection of essays edited by Christian Gremmels and Wolfgang Huber, *Theologie und Freundschaft; Wechselwirkungen Eberhard Bethge und Dietrich Bonhoeffer* in which some forty-five years after the death of Bonhoeffer Bethge reflects on his friendship with him. The word *Wechselwirkungen* means interaction, or interplay, something intricately woven into any understanding of what mutuality is.

Mutuality and the "Helper" in Donald L. Berry's Interpretation of Martin Buber

In the context of this study, it is Berry's discussion of the type of mutuality which he regards as possible within a given role in a relationship as a "helper" which is relevant to my reflection. As helpers Berry lists three types of professional persons to whom Buber himself had alluded. These are: physicians in their relationships with their patients; teachers in relationship to their students; and, of paramount interest for this study, what Berry calls priests in relationship with their penitents or those coming to them for religious counsel. To understand why these helpers are given a special position in Berry's work, it is necessary to understand

---

5. Berry, *Mutuality*, xi.

something of how Berry's interpretation of Buber envisages mutuality amongst humans.[6]

Two Levels of Mutuality

In describing his understanding of Buber's work, Berry says that mutuality occurs between humans on two levels. The first level is where two persons simply meet without there being a role to be performed by either one. This is where mutuality is "most fully possible."[7] This type of mutuality is implicitly referenced in the interviews, for example when Theo says, "there is an understanding in friendship, which is not tethered to a certain social role or professional function," or when Denise says "if I have to play a role, friendship, or friendly forms of togetherness, are somehow rather excluded." On an initial level, "fullness" of mutuality, as Buber terms it, can only happen in the kind of relationship in which there is no defining task or role to be played. And even there Buber himself notes that it is by no means something which can be taken for granted. Indeed, he uses the religious language of "grace" to describe the presence of such mutuality, noting that, "It is a grace, for which one must always be ready and which one never gains as an assured possession."[8] Yet in his interpretation of Buber, Berry points out that, "Fundamental to an appreciation of Buber's thought is the recognition that the mutuality of which he speaks admits of degrees."[9] These degrees he describes more as "modes" rather than quantitatively, noting that they need not necessarily be regarded as "less than" but more as a "mutuality that is fitting, or appropriate to the situation."[10]

The second level of mutuality, says Berry, is in the "sphere of the interhuman," where, in contrast to the first level of fullness of mutuality, there is "the presence of a task or a special defining role that is necessarily involved."[11] Here Berry, in quoting Buber from the Postscript to the 1958

---

6. For the purposes of this study, I am referring mostly to Berry's work. For further comprehensive study on Buber, see for instance Schilpp and Friedmann, *Philosophy of Martin Buber*.
7. Berry, *Mutuality*, 41.
8. Buber, *I and Thou*, 131.
9. Berry, *Mutuality*, 41.
10. Berry, *Mutuality*, 41.
11. Berry, *Mutuality*, 40.

edition of *I and Thou*,[12] writes of what Buber calls the "normative limitation" on mutuality, which occurs where there is one-sidedness present, which hinders the practice of what Buber calls "inclusion," namely "experiencing the relation from the other side . . . from the point of view of the life situation of the other person."[13] For there to be mutuality, whether in fullness or a degree of fullness, it is necessary for both sides to distance themselves from each other and then enter into relation. The other person must be affirmed and confirmed as a unique and free person. Berry quotes Buber, "I confirm and further my Thou in the right of his existence and the goal of his becoming, in all his otherness."[14]

In our discussion of friendship this is important for naming the freedom necessary for each person in the relationship to choose how close they want to get to the other person. Berry emphasizes how important this "setting at a distance" is in Buber's thought, as it allows the other to be other and not to be superficially subsumed merely as an object for my observation or for my emotional satisfaction. It also allows one to be wary of an all-too-quick insistence "upon intimacy, closeness, harmony and oneness as marks of authentic relation."[15] The movement of entering into relationship with another is then characterized by one life opening up to the other life "without one incorporating the other," and yet still allowing one to feel, perceive, or think what is "occurring in the mind and body of another individual."[16]

Here it becomes clear why openness (one of the essential elements of friendship as reported in the interviews in this study) is understood to be of such importance. For mutuality with a degree of inclusion, at least as described and understood by Berry, is not possible without such openness. "Inclusion" is close to what is often termed empathy, but Berry, in interpreting Buber, and others who take his line of thought, reject the word "empathy" as too "absorptionist." Maurice Friedmann, for instance, defines empathy as the "transposing of oneself into the dynamic structure of an object, . . . hence the exclusion of one's own concreteness. . ." Yet inclusion is actually the opposite. It is

---

12. Buber, *I and Thou: Second Edition*, 133.
13. Berry, *Mutuality*, 42.
14. Buber, "Interrogation of Martin Buber," 28.
15. Berry, *Mutuality*, 43.
16. Berry, *Mutuality*, 43.

the extension of one's own concreteness... In inclusion one person without forfeiting anything of the felt reality of his activity, at the same time lives through the common event from the standpoint of the other.[17]

This appears to be a form or ideal of mutuality which is hard to attain, and it has been criticized.[18] Yet for our study it is useful, as it is in response to this criticism that Buber most clearly stated that pragmatically lived mutuality must admit of degrees. Berry writes, quoting Pedro Sevilla, that in overcoming the "I-It" divide on the way to an "I-Thou" mutuality, complete reciprocity implied by mutual inclusion may not be necessary:

> The relation with God is not fully reciprocal nor [is] the relation with things and beings in the natural sphere. And it is not uncommon for someone to "stand over against another with less than complete presence and openness and yet not necessarily regard the other as 'It', as a mere object of observation and reflection."[19]

It is to the degree of mutuality possible in a relationship that Berry now turns in his analysis of Buber's thought.

A Mutuality of Degrees in the Pastor-Parishioner Encounter

Of the three relationships—teacher, healer, and pastor—Buber sees the "sacerdotal" character of the relationship involved in the pastor-parishioner encounter as the most obviously problematic.

> The most emphatic example of normative limitation of mutuality could be provided by the pastor with a cure of souls, for, in this instance an inclusion coming from the other side would attack the sacral authenticity of the commission.[20]

The "sacral authenticity" of the task has to do with the priest or pastor being "armed with sacred possessions of divine grace and holy

---

17. Berry, *Mutuality*, 44; quoting Friedmann in his introduction to Buber, *Daniel*, 33; and Buber, *Between Man and Man*, 96–97.

18. Here, Berry mentions criticism by Emmanuel Levinas. For a critical discussion of Buber's thought by Levinas and others, compare Morgan, "Martin Buber and Some of His Critics," 232–41; see also Schilpp and Friedmann, *Philosophy of Martin Buber*.

19. Berry, *Mutuality*, 44; quoting Sevilla, *God as Person in the Writings of Martin Buber*, 45.

20. Buber, *I and Thou*, 133.

word."[21] What type of pastor or priest Buber was thinking of here is of interest for this study. Berry understands Buber to be referring to the priest within what we might call a high Church framework, in which case the dispensing of the "sacred possessions" refers to the giving of absolution, something which, within the coherence and framework of the Roman Catholic, Orthodox, Anglican, or Old Catholic tradition, can only be done by a priest. The priest-penitent relationship is by definition one-sided and thus excluded from the fulness of mutuality, from the practice of "inclusion" from both sides. Yet Walter Kaufmann in his translation of Buber regarded Buber's Jewish heritage as important for understanding what he meant by pastor, and he translated the passages using the words priest or pastor in a more rabbinical, and also more low Church, fashion, to refer to "those charged with the spiritual well-being of their congregation."[22] This has a bearing on the context of the qualitative research done in this research.

All of the interviewed pastors in this study work within the framework of the Swiss Reformed Church, a denomination, which traces its history back to the Reformation of the sixteenth century in Switzerland and which concerning its position on the priesthood would be regarded by all as low Church, upholding the priesthood of all believers. The ordained role of the pastors is one of acknowledged authority and order within the Church, but not one in which they are understood to have special ritual "powers" above and beyond that which any member of the congregation could have. Although now working within a Reformed Church, a number of the interviewees come from other traditions, such as the Anglican or Lutheran traditions, and others have for some time been associated with other traditions, such as that of Ignatian or Benedictine spirituality. To what degree they understand their own pastoral roles within a more high or low Church model was not a question I asked them.

One study by Phillip Hammond, a Professor of Religious Studies and Sociology at the University of Arizona,[23] suggests that those whose understanding of their own role is closer to a high Church model find it easier to have friendships within their congregations, as they in general differentiate the fulfilling of their "sacred" role as a priest from their personal life. A "rational-legal" authority, which is given them

---

21. Berry, *Mutuality*, 50; quoting Buber, "Healing through Meeting," 139.
22. Buber, *I and Thou* (Kaufmann), 179.
23. Hammond et al., "Clergy Authority and Friendship with Parishioners," 185–201.

THEOLOGICAL REFLECTION ON THE ESSENTIAL ELEMENTS OF FRIENDSHIP

through the charisma of their office, means that they do not tend to define themselves in that office by the quality of their relationships or by their exemplary behavior in those relationships. This sets them free to have, or not have, friendships with others within the congregation, as they do not see these friendships as having anything to do with their well-defined "sacerdotal" role.

Those, however, nearer a low Church model will need to define their authority otherwise, usually, according to the study, through the "burden" of "puritanical standards."[24] Often this leads them to shy away from intimate and personal friendships within the congregation, as such relationships would be seen to undermine their authority. The Hammond study was done in 1972 and a lot has changed since then in the realm of cultural and Church norms. I have however found no similar contemporary studies. Within my study in qualitative research of nine Swiss Reformed pastors it was not clear whether such considerations played any role in the pastors' self-understanding of their ministry, but the questions involved are useful for our reflection. At what point do pastors feel they have fulfilled their pastoral task in their relationships within the congregation? And is a clear definition of such a task a help or hinderance to them? I shall look at these questions further on in this chapter, where the emphasis within the multi-faceted relationship of friendship is on freedom.

Returning to Berry's understanding of Buber's references to the "normative limitation" of mutuality involved in the priestly or pastoral task, he assumed, as mentioned above, that Buber understood the role as a sacerdotal one, thus making reciprocity in the relationship impossible. Noting that the concept of "normative limitation" is not just applicable to teacher, doctor, and priest relations but more broadly to all the helping professions, Berry then relativizes it somewhat, with the goal, as he writes, of increasing "the long-range usefulness of Buber's paradigm."[25] He points out that there is imprecision in defining a relationship purely along the line of a single quality or role one of the persons brings to the relationship. These are helpful for applying models to the structure of the relationship in order to understand them. However,

> there seems to be no way of gainsaying the fact that in the living out of relation the conscious use of models introduces a

24. Hammond et al., "Clergy Authority and Friendship with Parishioners," 189.
25. Berry, *Mutuality*, 58.

destructive, distancing and objectifying aspect. To employ a model is to relate to the other in terms of precedent categories, and involves the educator the therapist or the absolver in the danger of imposing himself or herself on the other as pupil, patient or penitent. To employ models brings into awareness the other in terms of such factors as behaviour, skill and intellect rather than genuine encounter and points up the problem of what has been called the "power shadow," that is the problem of dealing with motivation "to help" another which can be an unconscious assertion of oneself over the other.[26]

Each of the persons involved in a helping relationship needs to be seen on the same human plane and this mutual confirmation of one another's humanity can be attended to without "eliminating all dimensions of one-sidedness."[27] Where each person sees the other as a "whole" person, where their psycho-physical unity is accepted, then a complicated but pragmatically real form of mutuality can be present.

Berry describes such situations in the educative and therapeutic setting and then (as is of particular interest for this study) within the "sacerdotal" setting. He writes that since Vatican II,

> the Christian world has been moving toward recovering a more authentic notion of forgiveness in which the situation of the priest and penitent is not conceptualized in so individualistic a manner. Sin is acknowledged to be mutual, from both sides, and the absolution that is conveyed is not thought of simply as a substance dispensed from one toward the other, but a reconciliation and renewal which both minister to each other in the community of faith.[28]

Within the Swiss Reformed setting which, at least theoretically, has upheld the priesthood of all believers since the Reformation, the idea of Christians, even those with different roles within the body of Christ, ministering to each other should not be a surprising novelty. That it sometimes appears to be so will perhaps have to do with what Berry describes as the problem of structure. Structure provides the continuity necessary for human life, and because humans cannot be disembodied

---

26. Berry, *Mutuality*, 58.
27. Berry, *Mutuality*, 61.
28. Berry, *Mutuality*, 61.

spirits but have an "irreducible materiality,"[29] such structure is vital and cannot be disregarded as unimportant.

Yet structure—i.e. task, role, purpose etc.—has often been considered "the enemy of relation with its characteristic spontaneity and openness."[30] This might be seen to be the case with normative limitation, where the structure of the task given to the educator, therapist, or pastor hinders a fulness of mutuality. Yet Berry contends that this need not be the case. The choice, as he writes, is not between structure and relation, but between

> a concern with structure which makes for openness to relation and a concern with structure which closes off or reduces the possibility of relation. The other with whom one may stand in relation is a concrete, material thing or being, not an idea or essence. It is the wholeness of that thing or being with whom one is in relation . . . Structure itself is not the enemy of relation but only that attitude toward structure which regards it as guaranteeing and exhausting the meaning or possibilities for life.[31]

Reflecting on this within the theme of this study, such considerations point to the importance of the attitude that pastors, and indeed members of the congregation, will have in their relations and whether they regard the structure given to that relation as a helpful framework or as a rigid rule for encountering the other. An awareness that degrees of mutuality in structured relationships may be possible and desirable could be helpful in reflecting such an attitude.

The Differentiation Between "Relationship" and "Relation"

At this point, Berry helpfully differentiates between the way he uses the terms *relationship* and *relation*. *Relationship* is the place where "normative limitation" is, the one-sidedness of a helping encounter, a place defined by the "assertion of need and the arrangement to respond to that need: structure." *Relation*, however, is a more mysterious place which "points radically to the context of freedom" and which in its mutuality "is a response to the grace of being met."[32] Berry concludes that seen in

---

29. Berry, *Mutuality*, 64.
30. Berry, *Mutuality*, 63.
31. Berry, *Mutuality*, 64.
32. Berry, *Mutuality*, 66.

this light, there is no reason why a teacher, therapist, or pastor might not enter into a relationship structured by the task at hand, and may do so without a "prior determination of arbitrary limits and with an openness to the presence and increase of mutuality." As the normative limitation attaches to the relationship and not to the relation as such, the helping person can enter each encounter "with a kind of expectancy, a kind of reverence." For someone who has experienced relation, the structure provided by relationship and the necessary distance and integrity it preserves has a "new, non-threatening status," he suggests, and may be the vehicle or occasion for relation.[33]

In writing about mutuality Berry addresses three of the four essential elements of friendship described by the interviewees. Along with mutuality itself, his writing encompasses thoughts about openness and about freedom, where he refers to the radical context of freedom when "relation" happens. The element of affection though is not explicitly touched on, however implicit that may be in the actual mysterious occurrence of "relation" happening. The theme of affection and where it comes from might have been an interesting element for Berry to discuss assuming there is some active, emotional part felt by both sides involved, should "relation" start to occur within "relationship" and it is not only a response to the "grace of being met" by another person. However, of course, Berry is not studying friendship as such, and is trying to approach an understanding of how an "I-Thou" relation, as proposed by Buber, may be experienced.

His differentiation between relationship and relation is helpful in that there seems to me a parallel here to the differentiation between friendliness and friendship. The structures of relationship, or the structures of friendliness within an encounter can remain just that, in which case "relation" or "friendship" does not happen. They are, however, also structures which, through mutuality, openness, and freedom, and at least in the case of friendliness also affection, may lead to an experience of actual "relation" or "friendship." Yet the interwovenness or entangledness of the elements within and around each other point to a complexity which, as we have seen throughout this study, makes precise definitions of the processes of relation difficult.

---

33. Berry, *Mutuality*, 67.

Mutuality in Friendship in the Life and Work of Dietrich Bonhoeffer

Having approached theological reflection on the theme of mutuality from the viewpoint of Donald Berry's more philosophical and psychological thought about the concepts of relation worked out in reference to Martin Buber, we now turn to the theological work of Dietrich Bonhoeffer.

Within the vast body of literature surrounding the thought of Dietrich Bonhoeffer,[34] the aforementioned recent dissertation by Preston David Sunabacka Parsons, *A Friendship for Others: Bonhoeffer and Bethge on the theology and practice of friendship* is of much value for the context of this study, as is also the collection of essays edited by Christian Gremmels and Wolfgang Huber *Theologie und Freundschaft: Wechselwirkungen Eberhard Bethge und Dietrich Bonhoeffer* and the article by Eberhard Bethge, "Bonhoeffer's Theology of Friendship."

Approaching the Mutuality of Friendship and Its Fragility Through the Example of Dietrich Bonhoeffer and Horst Rössler

Something fascinating about discussion around Bonhoeffer is how his thought and his life are so intricately woven together. Friendship as a theme occurs occasionally throughout Bonhoeffer's work from *Sanctorum Communio* onwards, and a theological understanding of relations between people and between people and God is central in his work. But friendship is not a topic he addresses systematically. It is however hard to underestimate the importance of his friends in his work, especially in regard to Eberhard Bethge. Bonhoeffer himself uses the term "friend" sparingly[35] and in his correspondence is aware of fine degrees of relational differentiation.[36] Parsons shows instructively how Bonhoeffer's friendships differed and which were lasting and which were not. He highlights a perhaps lesser known friendship, that between Bonhoeffer

---

34. I take for granted that the reader is familiar with the main aspects of Bonhoeffer's life and work. For Eberhard Bethge's biography, see Bethge and Barnett, *Dietrich Bonhoeffer: A Biography*.

35. Compare the comprehensive list of mentionings of "friendship" or "friend" in Bonhoeffer's correspondence; Parsons, *Friendship for Others*, 175. Interestingly, Bethge in his article of Bonhoeffer's theology of friendship lists only a small number of friends: Hans Christoph von Hase, Walter Dreß, Franz Hildebrandt, and himself; Bethge, "Bonhoeffer's Theology of Friendship," 85–86.

36. Parsons, *Friendship for Others*, 61.

and Horst Rössler, and compares that to his friendship with Bethge. This comparison is helpful within our context of mutuality in friendship in showing at what point mutuality becomes difficult to maintain. I shall take up Bonhoeffer's relationship with Rössler first, make some theological points on the basis of it, and then turn to his friendship with Bethge.[37]

The friendship with Rössler dates back to Bonhoeffer's time as a student of theology in Berlin. From the correspondence between the two friends it is clear that they share a mutual affection and are indeed open and candid with each other.[38] They share their theological work with each other and feel free to argue and disagree with each other. However, their friendship breaks up at the end of 1934 and there is no more correspondence between them after Rössler reveals that he is working with Bishop Heckel, the head of the Church Foreign Office. Between 1928 and 1934 there are a number of letters shared between Bonhoeffer and Rössler and through these the process can be seen of how the friendship becomes increasingly strained through disagreements over eschatology and the Church's need for repentance. And then how, although Rössler seems to hope for their friendship to somehow be rescued, Bonhoeffer can no longer continue their mutual sharing given Rössler's involvement in supporting a Church system with the *Deutsche Christen* to which he believes there can only be resistance.[39]

It seems obvious here that the mutuality of friendship can only be upheld when all partners in the friendship trust each other to be loyal, a theme mentioned in the interviews by Beat, for instance, in his reference to Schiller's "The Pledge." Bonhoeffer no longer trusts Rössler to be loyal to him in a tense situation of opposing parties within the German Church which is rapidly deteriorating and which Bonhoeffer already recognizes as dangerous. Bonhoeffer no longer feels he has merely intellectual differences with Rössler, but that Rössler is betraying the gospel by siding

37. Although Bethge does not refer to Rössler as a friend of Bonhoeffers, Parsons sees good reasons, based on their correspondence together, to do this; Parsons, *Friendship for Others*, 175.

38. Bonhoeffer, *Dietrich Bonhoeffer Works* (DBW/E) 10:1/148, 216–17/261.

39. DBW/E 10:1/40, August 7, 1928; DBW/E 10:1/78, April 5, 1929; DBW/E 10:1/79, April 7, 1929; DBW/E 10:1/106, February 23, 1930; DBW/E 10:1/119, June 24, 1930; DBW/E 10:1/148, June 24, 1930; DBW/E 10:1/148, December 11, 1930; DBW/E 10:1/40; DBW/E 10:1/78, DBW/E 10:1/79, DBW/E 10:1/106, DBW/E 10:1/106, DBW/E 10:1/119; DBW/E 10:1/164, February 22, 1931; DBW/E 11:1/14, October 18, 1931; DBW/E 12:1/22, December 25, 1932; DBW/E 13:1/168, November 16, 1934; DBW/E 13:1/172, November 20, 1934; DBW/E 13:1/181, December 6, 1934. Compare also Parsons, *Friendship for Others*, 56–59.

with the *Reichskirche*. This alone is a huge strain on a relationship such as a friendship. Coupled with that, his fear would seem to be that instead of mutual support the friendship might be abused by Rössler to his own disadvantage and that of the Confessing Church more broadly.

The theme of the fear of abuse of the mutuality of friendship is one to which several interviews in this study referred. As her reason for not seeking friendships within her congregation, Nicole states, "I simply experienced that friendship was abused." And Beat, while talking about trust, mentions in passing from his pastoral experience how devastating divorces can be, when the mutual openness enjoyed by the couple ends and both sides know things about each other which "might destroy you." This fear of abuse, grounded as it often is in people's actual experience of betrayal and the hurt involved, either within their own relationships or within those of people to whom they have been close, makes this a very real and understandable stumbling-block when looking at the theme of pastoral friendship. On a theological level, there are two related points we find in Bonhoeffer's writing, which are helpful in thinking about mutuality in friendships and the abuse of it. They are the conviction of the mediation of Christ and the idea of what Bonhoeffer calls *Stellvertretung* in his thought around friendship.

The mediation of Christ and Stellvertretung in Bonhoeffer's thought around friendship

Regarding the first, Clare in the interviews uses a reference to Bonhoeffer herself in her critical thoughts about the motivation for choosing certain friends: "as Dietrich Bonhoeffer said, we are related to each other not just by our earthly nature." Bonhoeffer's ecclesiology is one which draws upon the biblical metaphor of the body of Christ. For him, the Church is

> *Christus als Gemeinde existierend*, the Church is Christ existing as *Gemeinde*, "[h]owever questionable its empirical form may be."[40]

Christ himself, says Bonhoeffer, is present in his body, whether that be individual believers, in friendships among Christians, in a local congregation, or indeed in the worldwide Church. Although the present community of the Church and indeed of all communities is marred by sin which alienates people from one another and causes hurt and pain,

---

40. DBW/E 1, 142/211.

"unbroken social community" was part of the *Urstand* or primal being and is also looked towards in eschatological hope in the Church.[41] Wherever Christ is present in a *Gemeinschaft*, a community, a proleptic foretaste of "sociality in its sanctified form"[42] happens and community is restored. Thus, although the mutuality of a specific relation may be broken, if the people involved are members of the body of Christ, Christ himself can be understood to be present and this allows for the hope and promise of restored forms of relation, which might otherwise be impossible.

This leads to the second point, which is related: that of *Stellvertretung* or representation, literally a "standing in for." Parsons writes,

> for Bonhoeffer, community (including Church-community) is subject to disintegration in the present through the encounter of others as strangers or alien. But there is a lasting, eschatological form of community, and through the reception of another person as Christ—in the kinds of practices Bonhoeffer will describe as theological *Stellvertretung*—a person is revealed in divine love, community is restored in the present, and a person's strangeness is overcome; this is described by Bonhoeffer here as an "eschatological foretaste of sanctification."[43]

How this *Stellvertretung* can be understood to have effect is through a mediating presence. Indeed, Bonhoeffer can relate this type of thinking directly to friendship, and, using Hegelian *Geist* language in *Sanctorum communio*, sees the "objective spirit" as mediator between two friends. He writes, "objective spirit . . . desires admission into a bond of friendship; the objective spirit also thrusts itself as a third entity right between the two who are bound together."[44] Later, in *Life Together* and more generally in the literature from the Finkenwalde period, Bonhoeffer identifies the mediator as Christ.[45] Thus the mediation of Christ is understood to be central both in relationships which are strained and difficult within the body of Christ and also in those which would already be identified as friendships.

The mediation of Christ in Bonhoeffer's thought can be seen as being reliant on *Stellvertretung* in two ways: First, through Christ's

---

41. DBW/E 1, 37–39/63.
42. Parsons, *Friendship for Others*, 38.
43. Parsons, *Friendship for Others*, 36.
44. DBW/E 1, 62/98.
45. DBW/E 5, 31/44.

accomplished *Stellvertretung* in his death and resurrection,⁴⁶ and second, through his ongoing *Stellvertretung* in the form of other humans in the present.⁴⁷ Imagining the mediation of Christ within relations within the body of Christ has the effect of taking away a certain amount of pressure from the individual to feel it is up to them to make every relation work on what Bonhoeffer calls a *leiblich-seelisch*, or physical-emotional level. Bonhoeffer differentiates the level of mediated spiritual community in Christ, brought about by Christ's *Stellvertretung*, from that of unmediated community, or what he calls self-centred or emotional community.⁴⁸ Such unmediated community can lead to "human enslavement, bondage, [and] rigidity" rather than "the freedom of Christians under the Word."⁴⁹ Within the context of this study of the pastor as friend, it is such experiences of "human enslavement, bondage, rigidity" which explain the fear of abuse of the mutuality of friendship, which the pastors talked about in the interviews, and which kept some of them from even contemplating having friendships within their congregations.

And yet Bonhoeffer does not reject such relations as having no place whatsoever within the Church. In fact, he regards "mixed" communities where the unmediated is mixed with the mediated by Christ as being healthier than those which attempt to build themselves as purely spiritual communities. This is because

> A marriage, a family, a friendship knows exactly the limitations of its community-building power. Such relationships know very well, if they are sound, where the self-centred element ends and the spiritual begins. They are aware of the difference between physical-emotional and spiritual community. . . .On the other hand, whenever a community of a purely spiritual nature comes together, the danger is uncannily near that everything pertaining to self-centeredness will be brought into and intermixed with this community. Purely spiritual life in community [*Lebensgemeinschaft*] is not only dangerous but also not normal.⁵⁰

Commenting on this, Parsons concludes, I think correctly, that for Bonhoeffer the conscious and intentional inclusion of forms of emotional,

---

46. See, for instance, DBW/E 4, 228/214 or DBW/E 4, 231/217.

47. See, for instance, DBW/E 4, 236/222 or DBW/E 5, 31/44. Compare also Parsons, *Friendship for Others*, 138.

48. "seelische Gemeinschaft," DBW/E 5, 32/45.

49. DBW/E 5, 32/44.

50. DBW/E 5, 33/46–47.

affectionate relation, such as friendship, are helpful and of utility to a community as an aid to discernment between what is spiritual and what is "normal."[51]

Before I turn to Bonhoeffer's relationship with Bethge, which illustrates this utility for the community, I return to his friendship with Rössler and the reasons why it ended and community was not restored, despite that for which Bonhoeffer's theology of the mediation of Christ and *Stellvertretung* might have led us to hope. Parsons names these reasons in terms taken from *Sanctorum communio* of what appeared to be missing from their friendship, namely

> acts of love and repentance . . . In the letters we have, we do not see that they offered themselves to one another sacrificially, in a partial or a complete way, neither is there evidence of the mutual forgiveness of sin, intercession, or repentance.[52]

Bonhoeffer's idea of ongoing *Stellvertretung* in the form of other humans in the present, representing Christ to each other, has, as its goal the mutual building up of each other in the body of Christ. For this to take place, sacrificial love in discipleship of Jesus needs to be something those involved are willing to practice, not through some sort of mechanical reciprocity of an all too simple and measurable "give and take," but yet with the longing and desire that community and mutuality will be strengthened and where it is lost can be restored through the presence of Christ. The process of such restoration is understood in spiritual terms as being made possible through authentic intercession for each other and through repentance before God and in asking for forgiveness from each other. Whether Bonhoeffer actually attempted such a reparation of his friendship with Rössler seems unlikely,[53] and it would have been made more challenging than it already was, for at the time they could not easily visit each other and only the avenue of letter writing was open to them for communication. Such a process of restoration is also only feasible where it is authentic and where those involved are willing to freely spend energy and time in giving themselves to it. It seems to have been the case that both Bonhoeffer and Rössler were not willing to do that.

---

51. Parsons, *Friendship for Others*, 140.
52. Parsons, *Friendship for Others*, 90.
53. Compare Parsons, *Friendship for Others*, 91.

The Mutuality of Friendship Through the Example of Dietrich Bonhoeffer and Eberhard Bethge and Spielraum

Much of the later theology found in Bonhoeffer's writing, formulated in the letters and poems of his correspondence with Bethge and with others, only became accessible to a wider public because of their mutual friendship. This friendship was first moulded in their "Life together" with others in the seminary of the *Bekennende Kirche* in Finkenwalde. It was in the last years of Bonhoeffer's life, in the discussion of theological ideas and concepts as well as of the everyday practical things surrounding both of their lives—Bonhoeffer's in prison and Bethge's outside in close contact with the wider Bonhoeffer family[54] and other friends—that Bonhoeffer's theology was further formed. And after Bonhoeffer's execution in 1945, it was Bethge who became what we might call a hermeneutical vehicle for Bonhoeffer's thought, as he edited and published the letters from prison, and gave lectures about Bonhoeffer all over the world. Bethge's understanding of his friendship with Bonhoeffer allowed him, in a certain sense, to establish his hermeneutical priority over the way others gave emphasis and interpreted Bonhoeffer. As his closest friend, Bethge was the one people trusted to "speak most truly about what Bonhoeffer intended to say within the ongoing reception and interpretation of Bonhoeffer's work in the post-war context."[55]

This was implicit in Bethge's work for many years and was also shown in his biography of Bonhoeffer, published in 1967. Yet he himself only wrote about their friendship later on in life.[56] The reasons he gives for this are important in the context of our study. First, as he himself says, he was not the only friend of Bonhoeffer. For instance, he mentions Franz Hildebrandt as another, and he was aware that they and others "are not free of jealousies."[57] Jealousy, as I wrote at the beginning of this study, and the fear of its consequences within a congregation, is one of the main reasons why pastors avoid having friends within that congregation, something also referred to by Nicole, for instance, in the context of

54. He married Renate Schleicher, who was the eldest daughter of Bonhoeffer's sister Ursula and her husband Rüdiger, on May 15, 1943.

55. Parsons, *Friendship for Others*, 21. See also Simpfendörfer, "Eberhard Bethge als Hermeneut," 51–88.

56. Bethge, "Mein Freund Dietrich Bonhoeffer," 13–28: Bethge, "Der Freund Dietrich Bonhoeffer und seine theologische Konzeption von Freundschaft," 29–50.

57. Bethge, "Mein Freund Dietrich Bonhoeffer," 14; "von Eifersüchten sind wir nicht ganz frei."

her experience of divisions caused in the church by the previous pastor having a group of "chosen" people. And Bethge feared that the consequences of jealousy amongst the surviving friends of Bonhoeffer might jeopardise the work of editing and publishing Bonhoeffer's theology, to which he felt a responsibility.

The second reason is that he regarded their friendship as something which was a *Stück des Unverfügbaren*, something which was a "part of something not available," which means he felt that he could not with integrity research that friendship academically, nor did he feel that he should have to want to do that.[58] This is reminiscent of Berry's understanding of mutual relation as a "more mysterious place" as opposed to the structure of relationship. And it also might remind us of parts of the interviews in this study where, for instance, Clare says she realises that the reasons for friendship may reach into depths of one's own person, which are not necessarily consciously available to oneself. Bethge puts this non-availability into the realm of "experienced human freedom."[59]

That leads us to another theological thought of Bonhoeffer in the context of friendship, besides the idea of *Stellvertretung* to which I shall return in the friendship between Bethge and Bonhoeffer: that of the *Spielraum*.[60] The *Spielraum*, literally "room to play," denotes a freedom within the otherwise defined mandates of social order. Bonhoeffer was developing his theology of the mandates in what would be later published as his "Ethics," as the

> main areas of life where formation takes place: marriage and family (*Ehe*), work (*Arbeit*), government and civic life (*Obrigkeit*), and Church (*Kirche*). Each of these, while thoroughly worldly, is constituted by God's command for it.[61]

In each of these areas, obedience to God's authority within them is expected and Bonhoeffer upholds that structure. The idea of the *Spielraum*, however, constitutes a space of freedom. In denoting it as "a realm closely associated with the Church and in which friendship finds a place

---

58. Bethge, "Mein Freund Dietrich Bonhoeffer," 16; "Aber ich wollte von dem Stück des Unverfügbaren sprechen. Und das heisst, dass ich über dieses Thema nicht nur nicht akademisch nachforschen und reden kann, sondern dass ich es auch nicht wollen darf."

59. Bethge, "Mein Freund Dietrich Bonhoeffer," 16; "erfahrene menschliche Freiheit."

60. DBW/E 8:2/102, 290–92/267–69.

61. De Graaff, "Friends with a Mandate," 392.

in the mandates,"⁶² Bonhoeffer writes that in the "concept of the Church [...] we can regain the understanding of the sphere of freedom (art, education, friendship, play)."⁶³ For Bonhoeffer then, the *Spielraum*, although "closely associated with the Church," encompasses all the realms of the mandates and brings a reparative wholeness to an otherwise overly and unhealthily rigid and regulated social order and world.⁶⁴ It was this rigidity in part which Bonhoeffer saw at work in the "Prussian world,"⁶⁵ and which he believed led the Churches of Germany as a whole to be incapable of responding to the threat of fascist authoritarianism.

This is helpful for our study. The mandates are the area of obedience and structure, an area defined by responsibility and obligation, and an area which understands itself to be within God's plan for human flourishing. Within the pastoral setting, these might be regarded as the professional expectations which are expected of pastors by their congregations, often formulated and stipulated by the churches in which they work, and which they expect of themselves. These professional obligations are good and necessary. Yet within those obligations the idea of the *Spielraum* opens up the concept that for wholeness and health, areas of "art, education, friendship, play" will not only be mutually beneficial for those involved but will also protect social relations as a whole from becoming overly rigid and thus stifling the very life they want to protect. For pastors, this might open up the possibility to see mutual and free friendships within their congregations not only negatively, as threatening and difficult for the social order in the church, but positively, as an outworking of a healthy *Spielraum*, which helps guard against an all too rigid and stifling atmosphere of dutifulness. I take this up further in the next chapter where I respond to the research findings.

Finally, the friendship between Bonhoeffer and Bethge is instructive for my research in regard to the concept of *Stellvertretung*. As described above, Bonhoeffer's idea of *Stellvertretung* was related to the mediation of Christ in two ways. First, in his death on the cross Christ takes the place of the sinner. He dies as a *Stellvertretung* and thus works redemption and secures liberty for those who follow him. This has consequences for the relationships of those in the body of Christ, as the other may always be seen as one for whom Christ has stood in. Second, in carrying on the

62. DBW/E 8:2/102, 290–92/267–69.
63. DBW/E 8:2/102, 291/268.
64. Compare Parsons, *Friendship for Others*, 96.
65. DBW/E 8:2/102, 291/268.

work of Christ's *Stellvertretung*, those following Christ in discipleship can mutually represent Christ to each other. This happens partly in those acts of love and forgiveness which we saw were missing in Bonhoeffer's and Rössler's friendship, but which were very real in his friendship with Bethge,[66] and, connected to this, in personal and mutual intercession. In this regard Bonhoeffer writes of Bethge, "I know from experience that your prayer for me is real power,"[67] and again, "[you] can pray for me like no one else. I want to ask you for this, and I also do the same for you every day."[68] The mutuality of their friendship is thus an intrinsic aspect of their mutual faith in Christ and of the power of his love and forgiveness.

In Finkenwalde, Bonhoeffer had already expected each of the members of the community to have a confessor to whom they could confess sin and then receive the forgiveness of Christ through that other person, and Bonhoeffer himself was expected to do the same. Bethge writes in his biography that Bonhoeffer privately confessed his sin to him.[69] This private confession one to another can be understood as a form of *Stellvertretung*. Bonhoeffer writes,

> [t]hose who confess their sins in the presence of another Christian know that they are no longer alone with themselves; they experience the presence of God in the reality of the other.[70]

It is the mutuality of the confession which characterizes the type of friendship described here between Bethge and Bonhoeffer. This corresponds with, for instance, the mutuality and openness which Ueli talks about in his interview, and of willing to be metaphorically naked before one's friend.

One further aspect of mutuality and *Stellvertretung* in the friendship between Bonhoeffer and Bethge needs to be mentioned. It is something which could also have relevance in understanding friendship in the pastoral setting. It is often referred to as that which is dialogical in a relationship, that is, mutual counsel or intellectual or personal discussion. Bonhoeffer and Bethge enriched each other's thought and wisdom through their sharing of ideas and reflections. They developed thoughts

---

66. In this regard, Parsons cites a difficult episode in which Bonhoeffer afterward sought reconciliation with Bethge; Parsons, *Friendship for Others*, 145–46.

67. DBW/E 16:1/68, 125/136.

68. DBW/E 8:2/73, 187/179.

69. Bethge and Barnett, *Dietrich Bonhoeffer: A Biography*, 506.

70. DBW/E 5, 97/113.

and concepts in a dialogical manner and each could help clarify the other's position by asking relevant questions. For instance, Bonhoeffer writes in a letter to Bethge, "in countless questions you have decisively helped me by your greater clarity and simplicity of thought and judgment."[71] This was not only in intellectual matters regarding theology, but also in practical matters of everyday wisdom and decision-making. However, it was in theological counsel that it would have its greatest impact.

As Bethge had been so involved in the later years in their mutual task of wrestling with theological and philosophical concepts, and as Bonhoeffer had sent to him his writings from prison, it fell to Bethge to become Bonhoeffer's *Stellvertreter*, his representative, after his friend was executed in April 1945. He became, so to speak, the closest thing to Bonhoeffer's own voice. When Bethge wrote or said something related to an interpretation of Bonhoeffer's thought, it immediately had a weight to it. Through being his friend, and not just an acquaintance or colleague, and through having already discussed and mutually developed many of the key elements in Bonhoeffer's theology with him, he was in a position to represent that theology more fully than anyone else. This did not mean that he was above criticism in regard to interpretation of Bonhoeffer, but it did mean that not every speculative idea that was thrown around could gain much traction if Bethge had shown why it did not fit into Bonhoeffer's thought.

Within the pastoral setting with which this study is concerned, the idea of pastors becoming a voice for friends who may have or be given little voice of their own is interesting. Some of Jean Vanier's work might be regarded as an example of such *Stellvertretung*. His voice, his articulation and formulation of reality and love in representing his friends Philippe and Raphaël in Trosly had weight to it and was able to become such a dynamic force in founding the l'Arche communities because it was formed in the friendship they had together, and was not solely the result of advocacy built on good intentions.

Summary

In this chapter section dealing with theological reflection on a mutuality within a pastoral relationship which is affectionate, free, and open, I have taken up the work of the Episcopal priest and professor of religion

---

71. DBW/E 16:1/68, 125/136.

Donald Berry and his interpretation of Martin Buber's "I and Thou" schema, which he interprets as mutuality. His work around the mutuality involved with the "helper," which he (referring to remarks by Buber) sees exemplified in the doctor, the teacher, and the priest or pastor, is instructive for this study. He argues that although the full mutuality of a free relation with no tasks attached to it is limited normatively within a task-motivated relationship such as that between pastor and parishioner, there are helpful and fruitful degrees of mutuality possible. These may in turn lead from an initial structured "relationship" into a more mysterious "relation." This movement I have compared to the possible movement from a relationship of friendliness to a relation of friendship.

Further, I have considered friendship and mutuality in the life and work of Dietrich Bonhoeffer. I first looked at his ultimately terminated friendship with Horst Rössler, where the dialogical and at times affectionate mutuality they shared became strained and then broke as a result of their different positions in the *Kirchenkampf* in the German Church in the 1930s. I then addressed Bonhoeffer's idea of *Stellvertretung* with its different meanings and the mediation of Christ in relations within the body of Christ and showed how these allow for mutual acts of love and forgiveness which are necessary if a friendship is to endure. I further referred to Bonhoeffer's idea of a *Spielraum* of freedom above and encompassing the various mandates of social order which God has ordained in the world. He himself refers to friendship as a component of this *Spielraum* and conjectures that it is necessary to balance out otherwise all too rigid understandings of relationships in the social order. Finally, I studied the friendship between Bethge and Bonhoeffer and show how the various aspects of *Stellvertretung* are shown in their relation and how fruitful such a friendship can be.

THEOLOGICAL REFLECTION ON A KIND OF AFFECTION WITHIN A PASTORAL RELATIONSHIP, WHICH IS FREE, OPEN, AND MUTUAL

The affection associated with friendship in the experience of the interviewees was one of "liking the presence and character of the other specific person." Beat, for instance, puts this clearly by stating that what characterized a friendship was "loving to be together." For all the interviewees, friendship had to do with the emotions, in that it was not just some generic form of care for others but a conscious caring for a specific person. This care was not specifically seen as an obligation or even a burden, but was experienced as enjoyment and delight in each other, an affection I have called free, open, and mutual.

Perhaps, as for Beat, the most obvious attribute of friendship for most people is that our friends are people whom we like. Sallie McFague, for instance, puts this succinctly, "a friend is someone you like and who likes you... a friendship is a relationship that at one level is simply mutual delight in the presence of each to the other."[72] Why we like our friends, however, is not always obvious. The reasons that lead to enjoyment of people are complex. Often friends are people who share our own interests and assumptions; they are, perhaps, "our type of person." Seward Hiltner, whom I quoted earlier in this chapter, perceptively writes that an awareness of one's own susceptibility to those with whom we naturally find it easy to be friends must be developed and active in the area of pastoral counselling.[73] In differentiating between friendship and friendliness, he points out that the mutuality of friendship involves getting something from the relationship. This "getting something" from the relationship for what he later calls the pastor's own emotional needs, or what we might perhaps less polemically put into a framework of mutual affection, Hiltner regards as problematic within the counselling situation.

The example he uses in his essay is of a young pastor who had come to him for advice. The pastor had counselled a young lady, the daughter of a well-to-do member of the church, who was meant to go to college, but turned up at church only two weeks after leaving for college. The pastor asks her in passing whether she is on holiday and she tells him that she is back for good. Later he "whispered to her that there must be a story here, and she whispered back that there certainly was and that she'd tell me about it sometime."[74] A few days later he "happens to be taking her home" after an evening meeting and then she tells him about her situation. He attempts to be a good pastor to her but is aware afterwards in reflecting on the encounter that he was not very successful in his efforts to help her. Hiltner points out that, although there was no apparent romantic

---

72. McFague, *Models of God*, 160.

73. Hiltner, "Friendship in Counseling," 28–34. Interestingly, perhaps, regarding the intuitive importance attached to the theme of friendship in the pastoral setting, this article was one of the first at the beginning of the journal in the very first appearance of the journal *Pastoral Psychology* in 1950.

74. Hiltner, "Friendship in Counseling," 29.

involvement, the pastor has a certain affection for the lady, of which he is not sufficiently aware, and which is not given due attention. He writes that the problem "seems to lie in the fact that this is partially a friendship situation not recognized by the pastor as such." The lady comes from a middle-class background, is similarly educated to the pastor; she is the kind of person with whom he "can share assumptions."[75] Such assumptions make for what Hiltner calls an "economy of effort, being able to take some things for granted, the assumption that things will be understood and agreed with, the existence of a large basis of agreement and mutual understanding from which to start." These things make it easier to like people, easier for there to be a relationship of affection relatively quickly. But these assumptions can also be a hinderance in understanding where people really are with their emotions and needs.

> The real point is, then, that an element of friendship in a counselling situation, if not recognized for what it is, may throw things off the track. The moral is not the renunciation of personal friendship, even in the pastor's own parish, but clearer insight into what is friendship as against friendliness, i.e., what relationships do something to meet the pastor's own emotional needs.[76]

Important here, in the context of this study, is that Hiltner does not conclude that there can be no friendships of pastors within their own parishes. But he insists that pastors be very aware of their own motivations and their own relational needs. Pastors who become aware of their own emotions and affections within an encounter should be able to differentiate how to act wisely and prudently.

There is certainly a lot of practical wisdom in what Hiltner writes. Yet I would suggest that the difference between friendliness and friendship is not as clear cut as Hiltner would like it to be. His definition of friendship is "a two-way relationship in which the emotional needs of two people get some satisfaction. It is fostered by shared likes and dislikes, tastes and distastes, assumptions for and against."[77] Friendliness, as quoted above, is the one-sided "approach of warmth, genuine interest, and real concern for people" which should characterize pastoral care in general. Yet if interest really is genuine and concern for people real, then it appears difficult to see how the emotions or affections of a pastor will

---

75. Hiltner, "Friendship in Counseling," 31.
76. Hiltner, "Friendship in Counseling," 32.
77. Hiltner, "Friendship in Counseling," 33.

not be involved. Hiltner appears to be aligning friendliness with a form of giving love and trying to seal it off from any type of receiving love, which might involve what he calls the emotional satisfaction of the pastor. This differentiation between different types of love is most often discussed in theological literature using the Greek terms *eros* (desire love), *agape* (self-sacrificial love) and *philia* (mutual love), topics I will investigate further on in this chapter.

Putting the giving and receiving of love in terms of emotional satisfaction may well be a legitimate way of describing such giving and receiving, yet it is more deeply about joy. When the Westminster Shorter Catechism, a text of importance in Reformed theology and formation, says that it is the chief end of humans "to glorify God and to enjoy him forever,"[78] it is putting the enjoyment of a communal relationship of love with God in an absolutely central position. Jürgen Moltmann, whom I have already mentioned in this study, suggests that it is this joy which motivated Jesus in his life of friendship:

> The inner motivation for Jesus' striking friendship with "sinners and tax collectors" lies in his joy, his joy in God, in the future, and in human existence. That is why Jesus celebrates the messianic feast of God's kingdom with them every time he eats and drinks with them. Jesus does not bring a dry sympathy, but an inviting joy in God's kingdom to those who are "reprobates" according to the law. Jesus celebrates the kingdom of God, which he claims as present in their midst, in a feast. That is why he refers to the kingdom, on more than one occasion, as the eternal "marriage feast": "Enter into the joy of your master." The respect that Jesus showed the contemptible through his affection, in that he ate and drank with them, is the right of grace, the full power of acquittal. Thus, Jesus combines affection with respect. He becomes the friend of sinners and tax collectors because of his joy in their common freedom—God's future.[79]

The invitation to joy in God's kingdom characterizes Jesus' relationships, a combination of affection with respect,[80] says Moltmann, not dry sympathy. This is important in the context of this study. Probably very few would regard a position of "dry sympathy" as ideal in the pastoral setting.

---

78. The Westminster Shorter Catechism; Question 1.

79. Moltmann, *Open Friendship*, 55–56.

80. This is Immanuel Kant's definition of friendship according to Moltmann. See Moltmann, *Open Friendship*, 51.

And yet the process of professionalization, which I mentioned critically in chapter one would seem to encourage just that—skilled counsellors and listeners, attuned to the complexities of the human psyche, respectful in their encounters with those they meet, but wary of affection and enjoyment of the other.

Affection for others for reasons of which we are not aware, can make us blind towards prudent and helpful ways of communication, and wariness in regard to our natural sympathies and antipathies seems, as Hiltner shows, to be sensible. And yet love without affection and joy is hard to imagine. And if the aim of pastoral care might indeed be summarized, as Alistair Campbell does, as being "to help people to know love both as something to be received and as something to give,"[81] then it will not be helpful merely to avoid entirely the question of affection and enjoyment, of liking people or not.

Thinking about friendship in a pastoral setting, it may be helpful to approach the subject of affection with reference to the concept of care which John Swinton uses, in quoting from the work of the philosopher and professor for biomedical ethics, Jeffrey Blustein. There, he differentiates between four uses of the word care: to care for (to have affection for), to have care of (to be responsible for) to care about (to be invested in) and to care that (to seek something good for the future). Swinton writes,

> it becomes clear that the type of caring which represents the character of God and which is ultimately manifested in the life, death and resurrection of Jesus, embodies all four of these meanings . . . Human relationships that seek to realise the *imago dei* must also somehow incorporate these four points within their caring relationships.[82]

In this dynamic process of caring, it might not be clear which of the four meanings is present or prevalent at different times, but at some point, a truly caring relationship should aim to exhibit all four meanings. Thus, in a pastoral setting, this may mean that the "having affection for" aspect, caring for people, might only be experienced after initial periods of caring about their welfare, having care of them within the parish or congregation, or caring that they flourish and develop spiritually. Such a model allows for sympathy, interest, affection, and joy to grow. And yet it also assumes that it is important that pastors care for—in the sense of

---

81. Campbell, *Paid to Care?*, 1.
82. Swinton, *From Bedlam to Shalom*, 46.

liking and having affection for—the people with whom they are in contact. Some pastors may naturally find it easier than others to like other people, yet the formation of a character capable of the affection and joy, seen in the open friendship of Jesus, might be part of what discipleship of Jesus brings with it and could be an area in which pastors might usefully seek growth.

Yet this possible movement in a caring relationship from friendliness to friendship is something which it is difficult to prescribe. The interviewees experienced and understood friendliness as something which pastors should display as part of their professional duty to be helpful as ministers of the church, regardless of their actual emotions towards the other person. Ministers of the church consider such friendliness as a professional duty to be part of their embodiment of Jesus' call to love one's neighbor and even one's enemy. The form of love initially involved in friendliness can be understood as that which does not expect anything in return, and in the theological literature it is mostly associated with self-sacrificial *agape* love.[83] The form of love however most closely associated with friendship is the mutual love of *philia*. Thus, it will be now be helpful for us to look a little more closely at affection and *philia*.

Affection and *Philia*

The form of love most associated with mutual friendship is *philia*, as distinct from the self-sacrificial type of love of *agape* or the desire of *eros*. The Jesuit theologian Edward C. Vacek contends that along with the self-giving quality and friendliness of *agape* and the desire and passion of *eros*, the mutual love of *philia* should be given greater weight in Christian thought as

> communion or *philia* is the foundation and goal of Christian life. This love is a power that creates unity and forms the human community ever more extensively and intensively. Indeed, all human love finds its culmination and ultimate goal in a community of solidarity with and in God.[84]

If, following this line of thought, the goal of love in general is the communion of *philia* love, one could, in a similar manner, argue that the

---

83. Compare, for instance, Rahner, "Love as the Key Virtue," 340; Taylor, *God is Love*, 308.

84. Vacek, *Love, Human and Divine*, 280–81.

natural goal or *telos* of Christian friendliness is a communion which opens up the possibility of friendship. Friendliness, in other words, approached from a concept of the importance of *philia* love, opens the way for a communal relationship, which is no longer defined by one-sided giving, but is capable of mutual affection, of both receiving and giving love.[85]

Within a love relationship experienced as *philia*, "the members love and are loved in terms of their special relationship. Their love flows from the relationship and is directed back to it."[86] So the love and affection experienced is mutual; that is, it is both a giving and receiving love. Indeed, the love becomes what we might call emergent in the sense that it becomes more than the sum of its parts—the giving and receiving of love. In Berry's terms, it becomes "relation," an experience of community, of love together. Vacek succinctly describes as follows an affectionate relationship that is mutual: "Someone loves me, I accept that love, I love that person, the person accepts my love, we form a community, we cooperate as members of that community."[87] This basic pattern, he contends, is analogously present in all *philia* relations. Although the question of whether the person first "loves me" or I first "love that person" is interesting in the context of pastoral ministry, in the context of mutuality it is not relevant, as the very core of mutuality is that the love at some point is felt and expressed equally from both sides. Vacek's attempt at a definition of mutuality is also interesting within the framework of this study as it combines the elements of friendship which we have found to be essential from the interviews. Within the wider picture of the affection of *philia* love, he describes mutuality as

> (1) a form of sharing life (2) through interaction of free persons (3) who communicate themselves to one another (4) in a way that is progressively involving.[88]

Thus, *philia* love is described as a mutual affection to which freedom and openness necessarily belong if it is indeed to be truly mutual. This

---

85. Compare, for instance, White, "Friendship," 18. "But friendliness, if it does not develop into friendship, remains a superficial kind of human solidarity. If, however, friendliness is open to God's grace and does develop into friendship, it will be transformed into a relationship of continuity, stability, and trust. It will also be distinguished by the fact that it is a mutual relationship."

86. Vacek, *Love Human and Divine*, 286; quoting Keenan, *Goodness and Rightness in Thomas Aquinas's Summa Theologiae*, 126.

87. Vacek, *Love Human and Divine*, 287.

88. Vacek, *Love Human and Divine*, 287.

form of sharing life is "progressively involving" as the relation develops, an observation that corresponds to the interviewees' accounts and descriptions of friendship. They spoke about the dynamics of relations in which they freely chose to spend time with the other persons and open up to them. And it also corresponds to Swinton's language use around the fourfold development of caring for people, which can involve a moving from a professional friendly type of care towards a more affectionate relationship.

I have described the affection involved in the friendships described in the interviews as a "liking" of the other specific person. Vacek's concept of *philia* love seems to correspond well with friendship as described by the interviewees. And yet the question of the relationship between friendship affection as love and friendship affection as liking is an interesting one. I shall reflect on "liking" first and then move on to "love."

Friendship Affection as Liking

In the interviews, Clare spoke self-critically of her reasons for "liking" the person whom she regarded as a friend:

> Sometimes I think some reasons why people can react to each other in a very personal friendly, open, trusting way are also grounded in factors which we would be ashamed of if we really knew them.

Although the experience of liking or disliking people is very real, the formulation of understandable reasons for that like or dislike proves to be strangely difficult for most people. Within the literature around the theme of this study, I have found little in-depth discussion concerning the affectionate liking of people. One exception is an essay by philosopher Elizabeth Telfer. In her thoughts around the nature of friendship, she writes of two conditions necessary for friendship: shared activity and what she calls the passions of friendship.[89] The first element of the passions is affection. She writes:

> Friends must have affection for, or be fond of, each other. I define affection as a desire for another's welfare and happiness as a particular individual. This desire is to be distinguished both from a sense of duty and from benevolence.[90]

---

89. Telfer, "Friendship," 250–67.
90. Telfer, "Friendship," 251.

The affection she defines corresponds with that which we have found to be essential in the experience of the interviewees. It is not merely general benevolence, which could be shown to anyone, but it is for a specific person. The concern connected with this affection is the motivation for wanting to do good things with and for the specific friend, and is not from a sense of duty or even pity.

The second element of the passions of friendship is what Telfer calls the desire on the part of the friends for each other's company, as distinct from a desire for company as such. This desire she divides into two attitudes: liking, and the sense of having something in common. "Liking is a difficult phenomenon to analyse," she writes, and is not necessarily equivalent to enjoying someone's company, as "we can for a time enjoy the company of people whom we do not basically like—indeed certain kinds of unpleasant people have their own fascination."[91]

She then attempts to approach the concept of liking through the idea of "finding a person to one's taste." This "quasi-aesthetic" attitude depends on attributes and mannerisms which the other person exhibits, something a number of the interviewees in this study mentioned in their descriptions of their friendships. And yet it is not obvious which attributes and which mannerisms will be given priority in weighing up whether one likes another person or not. Here, Telfer uses the helpful metaphor of one's reaction to a work of art such as a picture, in the sense that, in the end, one's reaction is to the thing as a whole, rather than to the separate colors and forms which make up the picture. She writes:

> Sometimes what we like is partly the way in which everything about the person seems to "hang together" and be part of a unified style; sometimes we enjoy a contrast, for example that between a mild unassuming exterior and an iron determination.[92]

Interestingly, Telfer distinguishes liking someone from the sense of having something in common with them. This, she writes, is possible since you can like people and yet not want them as friends because you feel you have no common interest or mutual way of communicating with each other.

In summary, says Telfer, friendship can happen when there is affection for each other, a liking of the person as that specific person, and when you have the feeling of having something mutually in common with

---

91. Telfer, "Friendship," 253.
92. Telfer, "Friendship," 253–54.

each other. Regarding the specificity of liking an individual, she points to Aristotle's truest form of friendship, in which in caring for someone because of their virtue the friends care for each other for their own sakes. Thus, the care is not bound to usefulness or even pleasure, but to relation amongst the persons themselves. There may be rational and identifiable reasons for a friendship associated with a person's attributes, but in the end the friendship depends on who the individual is:

> Thus, if I like James because he is witty, gentle, and good at making things, I like him not as one example of a witty, gentle, and craftsmanlike person for whom another such [person] might be substituted, but as an individual whose uniqueness defies complete classification.[93]

Helpful here is a reference to the discussion mentioned earlier around the theme of benevolence and the story of the Church fathers Basil and Gregory, who lived together in their younger years and considered each other close friends. Perhaps friendship affection as liking could tentatively be regarded as an Aristotelian concern, focused as it is on the specificity of the person with whom one is friends. Friendship affection as love, to which we turn in the next section, could perhaps similarly tentatively, be regarded as a more Platonic concern, where the focus is on the universality of the experience which shows itself within a specific situation. As we noted earlier when Basil became bishop of Caesarea he left his friend Gregory without even consulting him or taking him into his confidence. I quoted there from Philip L. Culbertson,[94] who I think perceptively described the crisis between the friends as an outworking of different, competing philosophical foundations around the trajectory and aim of friendship. Gregory thought in an Aristotelian manner, meaning he understood friendship as moving from a form of universal benevolence to many towards the particularity of a specific friend. Basil, however, represented more the Platonic approach which is concerned with moving from a particular affective attachment or liking of a friend towards a more universal love. But perhaps we do not need to see the two so much as competing but could say that love may be best expressed in the particularity of friendship and that we hope for a friendship which is universalising.

It might be tempting in the context of this study concerning theological reflection on Christian pastors' approaches to and practices of

---

93. Telfer, "Friendship," 255–56.
94. Culbertson, "Men and Christian Friendship," 149–80.

friendship within their congregations to locate the affection of liking particular persons as being within the realm of friendship, and to locate the more universal, benevolent affection of love within the realm of professional friendliness. But that would be to oversimplify the terms of liking and loving. Friends do not merely want to be affectionately liked, even though they enjoy that. When relations develop and grow, they are happy to regard their relation as a form of love. Similarly, those neighbors whom Christ exhorts us to love do not merely want to be loved benevolently as a type of universal humankind, but to be liked as the individual and particular people they are. With this in mind, I now turn to the affection of love within friendship.

Friendship Affection as Love

At the end of her essay on the value of friendship, Elizabeth Telfer quotes from C. S. Lewis and compares his writing about "What is the good of literature?" with her theme. Of course, asking about the value or the good of something is already a move away from the specificity of the thing itself towards a more universal understanding. Telfer herself notices this and issues a word of warning, pointing out that,

> too much dwelling on the values of friendship has its own dangers. It may lead people to concentrate on looking for friendships rather than friends, and to value the other person as a possible term in a relationship rather than as himself.[95]

Yet Lewis's words about literature lead appropriately to our discussion about friendship affection as love as he compares the effects of literature with those of love.

> We want to be more than ourselves . . . we want to see with other eyes, to imagine with other imaginations, to feel with other hearts, as well as with our own. It is not a question of knowing [in the sense of gratifying our rational curiosity about other people's psychology] at all. It is *connaître* not *savoir*, it is *erleben*: we become these other selves.[96]

Here, perhaps, we overhear echoes of Berry's idea of "relation." The love involved is mutual and full of openness to each other.

---

95. Telfer, "Friendship," 267.
96. Telfer, "Friendship," 267; quoting from Lewis, *Experiment in Criticism*, 137–39.

C. S. Lewis's *The Four Loves* describes affection, friendship, erotic love, and the love of God, which he calls charity. Friendship is thus for him a type of love, and yet one which is differentiated from the type of love he associates with affection. Affection he considers to be a modest love, something that happens without one really knowing it, which has to do with familiarity, a type of being fond of and liking someone.[97] Although attempting to differentiate affection from friendship, he does however clearly see that friendship, and indeed the other types of love among which he differentiates, are well-nigh impossible without affection.

> Affection, besides being a love itself, can enter into the other loves and colour them all through and become the very medium in which from day to day they operate. They would not perhaps wear very well without it.[98]

Here the element of time is of interest for our study. Regarding friendships, Lewis considers them to be formed as freely chosen relationships through reasons of common and mutual interest, and thus not initially connected with what he calls affection love. And yet for them to remain and develop affection will be vital if they are to "wear well." Thus, the question regarding causes of friendship comes to the forefront: Does one freely choose people as friends because one likes them and feels an affection to them? Or is it more the case that one freely chooses people as friends for other reasons and then, as the relation develops over time, the affection of love comes?

The interviews in this study give no clear answer to this. Denise, for instance, speaks about friendships starting to grow when she goes on holiday with people, but, as mentioned in the analysis, she does not give the reasons for her choosing with whom to go on holiday. Presumably she would not choose a person who irritated her, but it is not clear whether she already felt affection for a person before going on holiday with them, or only afterwards, having spent time with the person, and having gotten to know them by degrees, through increasing mutuality and openness. Nicole also took up this theme in her interviews, specifically in her reflections of experiences during the Lord's Supper. Eating and drinking together is helpful in forming relations, even in constituting friendship, and the, "experience of participating in a table community, especially with people who are a bit difficult . . . can at the end mean that

---

97. Lewis, *Four Loves*, 56–57.
98. Lewis, *Four Loves*, 57.

you might even enjoy each other." Here the affection of liking people may grow through time and through communal events, and yet it is not clear that Nicole would, even while perhaps enjoying the company of people celebrating Communion with her, actually regard them as friends. Affection might then grow from Christian love, but not necessarily lead to friendship relations.

Walter Jeanrond, in his *A Theology of Love*, takes up friendship affection as love in his reflections around the writings of the English Cistercian monk Aelred of Rievaulx (1110 to 1167). Although Aelred can be read in the tradition of Augustinian and Ciceronian reflections on love, the abstract love of God found in Augustine "makes way for the personal discovery of love in human friendship."[99] Aelred, in distinction from his predecessors and from Cistercian thought otherwise, regards affection and reason as necessary elements of perfect love. Here, love is not spiritualized in the sense of cut off from our physical or emotional nature. It is, however, put into an eschatological framework, as Aelred is very well aware of human limitation in the here and now. Thus reason,

> must sometimes compel choice when *affectus* is lacking or opposed. It is also why we are bid to love all people, even our enemies, although we cannot be expected to enter into friendship with all until the eschatological fulfilment of our restoration in heaven.[100]

Affection, indeed the affection of liking, should in this approach be part of what it means to love in a Christian sense, and although the fulfillment of such love will only be possible in the eschaton, it can be experienced and positively sought within our everyday friendships. And where affection is initially lacking, reason—and within that a conscious will to obey Christ's command to love others—should be a Christian's orientation.

For Aelred, friendship originates in the nature of God. Indeed, in book 1 of *Spiritual Friendship*, he alters the words from 1 John 4:16 that God is love to God is friendship (*Deus amicitia est*), thus allowing the sentence, "He who abides in friendship abides in God and God in him."[101]

---

99. Jeanrond, *Theology of Love*, 210.

100. Jeanrond, *Theology of Love*, 210; quoting from McGinn, *Growth of Mysticism*, 314.

101. Aelred, *Spiritual Friendship*, I,69. Compare, Jeanrond, *Theology of Love*, 211; quoting from Matarasso, *Cistercian World*, 171. Interestingly, the feminist theologian Barbara Kerney applies this to her understanding of Jesus and states, "Jesus, the

Here the role of affection in friendship love is seen positively and constructively, and yet he insists that it should be "led by reason, tempered by integrity and ruled by righteousness," and on top of that be tested by "loyalty, intent, discretion and patience."[102] Such affection, within the framework of the Christian command to love, is indeed a high calling, but it becomes a little more accessible when it is seen to be grounded within the mutual caring, shared joy, and "candid and free spirit" which characterize friendship.[103]

Within the ministry of the pastoral calling, affection therefore becomes not so much the fruit of heroic individuals attempting to like everyone and thus focussing their sometimes wild and nebulous emotions positively towards them, but a shared fruit in a mutual and open relationship stemming from the power of the friendship love of God. And the need to choose freely to whom one wishes to admit one's affections and with whom to be mutually open remains, as it is impossible, says Jeanrond, to develop friendship with everybody.[104] This sentiment is shared by Soskice, who writes, "You cannot be friends with everybody without evacuating friendship of all meaning,"[105] and is also echoed by the interviewed pastors.

Summary

In this chapter section dealing with theological reflection on a kind of affection within a pastoral relationship which is free, open, and mutual, I have addressed the thought of Seward Hiltner and his differentiation between friendliness and friendship, and have looked briefly at John Swinton's fourfold interpretation of the idea of *caring for people*, which includes affection for them. I have looked at the concept of *philia* love offered by the Jesuit theologian Edward Vacek, in which each one loves the other in terms of their special and particular relationship, and their "love

---

incarnation of God in the world, demonstrated how friendship is . . . the most godlike relationship that human beings can have with one another." Kerney, *Theology of Friendship*, 38.

102. Jeanrond, *Theology of Love*, 211; Matarasso, *Cistercian World*, 177; 183. Compare Aelred, *Spiritual Friendship*, II,57.

103. Jeanrond, *Theology of Love*, 212.

104. Jeanrond, *Theology of Love*, 212.

105. Soskice, *Kindness of God*, 160.

flows from the relationship and is directed back to it."[106] This mutual form of a free, open, and progressively involving *philia* love corresponds with the interviews regarding how the pastors described their friendships. Yet they described the actual affection within that love as a "liking" of the other specific person.

Regarding this affection as liking another person within friendship relations, I have referred to the thought of the philosopher Elizabeth Telfer to attempt to clarify something of what "liking" a friend might mean. She defines affection within friendship relations as "a desire for another's welfare and happiness as a particular individual. This desire is to be distinguished both from a sense of duty and from benevolence"[107] and indeed from pity. Further, she describes the type of liking found amongst friends as "finding a person to one's taste" and uses the metaphor of a work of art which one enjoys as a whole through the way everything in that particular work of art hangs together. These descriptions fit well with the descriptions from the interviews, yet the connection with affection as a form of love needs to be found.

To do this I referred to C. S. Lewis's writing of *The Four Loves* and the work of Aelred of Rievaulx as taken up by Walter Jeanrond in his *A Theology of Love*. Lewis differentiates affection love from friendship love, erotic love, and what he calls the love of God, or charity. Affection love, says Lewis, has to do with familiarity and also with available time. If friendship love, which, in Lewis' thought, is initially centred around common and mutual interests, is to develop and be kept healthy, then affection must grow and, as with all the loves, will become "the very medium in which from day to day they operate."[108] A growing affection, thus, can be understood as a connecting factor between the forms of love.

Aelred, the twelfth-century English Cistercian monk, was one of the few theologians of the Middle Ages to write about friendship with a positive regard for the affections. He understands perfect love, as both oriented towards God and as receiving its power from God, to be a mixture of reason and affection, and exhorts his readers in his *Spiritual Friendship* to search diligently for both in their relations to God and to one another. He sees the concrete form of the love to which Christians are called as embodied in real friendships, and he translates the text from 1 John 4:16 as "God is friendship," resulting in the phrase (as Jeanrond quotes), "He

---

106. Vacek, *Love Human and Divine*, 286.
107. Telfer, "Friendship," 251.
108. Lewis, *Four Loves*, 57.

who abides in friendship abides in God and God in him."[109] This allows for the idea that in relations inspired by the love of God in the discipleship of Christ, affections can have their place, and that where they are initially lacking, one may pray and hope for them.

THEOLOGICAL REFLECTION ON A KIND OF FREEDOM WITHIN A PASTORAL RELATIONSHIP, WHICH IS OPEN, MUTUAL, AND AFFECTIONATE

Freedom is vital for friendship relations. As we have repeatedly seen throughout this study, the free choice regarding with whom to be friends is essential for any authentic concept of friendship. The participants in the interviews all recognized a duty, arising from their pastoral profession and calling, in being friendly to people, but forced friendship they could not see as working. As Markus wisely said in his interview, "we do not have a duty to be friends with everyone. It is something we can choose, or they can choose." Regarding such choice, the philosopher Eliot Deutsch writes that freedom, or what he here refers to as personal autonomy, he regards as a condition for friendship even to be possible: "First and foremost among the conditions for friendship is some measure of personal autonomy."[110] Friendship is by its very nature a free relationship as opposed to an obligation. C. S. Lewis put it as follows: "I have no duty to be anyone's friend and no man in the world has a duty to be mine. No claims, no shadow of necessity."[111] And in a letter to his friend Eberhard Bethge, dated 23rd January 1944, Bonhoeffer writes about friendship in the context of thought about the three mandates he sees as basic for human relationships that:

> I believe that within the sphere of this freedom, friendship is by far the rarest and most priceless treasure, for where else is there any in this world of ours dominated as it is by the first three mandates (marriage, work, state)? It cannot be compared with the treasures of the mandates; in relation to them it is *sui generis*, but it belongs to them as the cornflower belongs to the grainfield.[112]

---

109. Jeanrond, *Theology of Love*, 211; quoting Matarasso, *Cistercian World*, 171.
110. Deutsch, "On Creative Friendship," 17.
111. Lewis, *Four Loves*, 103.
112. Bethge, "My Friend Dietrich Bonhoeffer's Theology of Friendship," 150.

Whether the cornflower is necessary to the grainfield in the sense of grain production is perhaps difficult to determine, but it makes the sight of the grainfield most beautiful and pleasant and it conveys something of the abundance and joy of creation, where there is freedom and space to be, apart from the strictures of necessity, functionality, and obligation. Yet if friendships are understood as relationships of choice and not of duty or obligation, and if friends are people with whom we choose to be, what might this mean within the pastoral setting of a local church? At first glance, this freedom to choose relations seems to be very much at odds with the professional ethic underlying the pastoral ministry, that pastors should be willing and capable of relating to anyone within their congregation or parish, or indeed anyone at all, whether they really want to or not. Such a willingness reflects the goodness and love of God, as described in Matthew 5:44f NIV:

> But I tell you, love your enemies and pray for those who persecute you, that you may be children of your Father in heaven. He causes his sun to rise on the evil and the good, and sends rain on the righteous and the unrighteous.

This (recall M. Craig Barnes' reservations regarding friendship in his parish, outlined in chapter 1) has been one of the main arguments brought against pastors having concrete friendships. These chosen friendships would be particular and mutual and would thus compromise the pastor's position as a minister to all, without respect of persons. As I pointed out, again in the first chapter, my own experience as a pastor in the Swiss Reformed Church around the subject of friendship was that friendships were private relationships you either had or did not have outside of your profession and calling as a pastor, and one of the main reasons for this was that as a pastor you were understood and indeed called to have relationships in your parish with your parishioners, which were given and not chosen. As a good pastor it was not a matter of personal freedom whether you had relationships with those in your congregation: it was a part of your professional duty. These relationships then, being professional, were not thought about in terms of choice or autonomy, but in terms of what was fitting and appropriate for a pastoral ministry to which you were called, but for which you were also paid.

Because of this common understanding that the pastor is a professional person who has an obligation through their ministry to relate in some way or other to the people within their congregation and parish, there is very little theological literature around the subject of freedom or choice in regard to pastoral relationships. Interestingly, however, the possibility of the development of friendship, one growing out of a professionally given and friendly relationship with a person, was a theme which a number of the interviewees could see as a possibility. Such development has to do with freedom for a pastor in the sense of making choices regarding time and energy, which go beyond those they understand as required and expected of them in their professional capacity.

The Freedom of "Special Choices" in a Pastoral Relationship

Very few publications deal with friendship within the pastoral calling and setting. But of interest among those few are the thoughts about friendship, counselling, and therapy of Samuel Southard, whose work I take up here. He compares friendship with the counsellor relationship, and writes:

> Friendship is a relationship of choice. So is counsel or therapy. Early in a therapeutic relationship there is a growing awareness of special choices, as more and more time and energy is invested in one person.[113]

This is reminiscent of Nicole's thoughts in the interviews, where she specifically mentioned her awareness of such investment of time and energy in particular relations compared with others.

Southard, defending his argument for the ethical and theological validity of "special choices," turns to Augustine and points towards the concept shared with other theologians such as Gregory of Nazianzus of the acceptance of particular friendship in anticipation of our finite pilgrimage toward universal love. The freedom to make free choices which may lead to friendship relations Southard describes as the movement of friendship. This, he says, begins with exclusive invitations. Such an invitation, "may be rooted in a perceived need, such as companionship, insight, healing, redemption. It is exclusive because one person admits something that should claim the intimate attention of another."[114]

Yet it can also have less to do with need and more to do with liking someone, a type of affection which he describes as, "a gently growing admission that one person is drawn toward the qualities of life in another."[115]

---

113. Southard, *Theology and Therapy*, 204.
114. Southard, *Theology and Therapy*, 204.
115. Southard, *Theology and Therapy*, 204.

This is reminiscent of Ueli's description in the interviews of his experience of growing friendship with the two people within his congregation he described as friends, as he talks of being drawn to them. It also points towards something which is formulated well by Dean Cocking and Jeanette Kennett in their text "Friendship and the Self,"[116] where they focus on the iterative dynamic of the self being drawn and moulded by friends, rather than being something static which either finds itself mirrored in the other or finds expression in the relationship simply through self-disclosure.

Having recognized a growing affection, the interplay of the themes of mutuality and openness also now start to play a role in Southard's description of the movement of friendship within the therapeutic setting. In the following excerpt, he considers the role of obligation which the exclusive invitation offered invites:

> The invitation may take the form of a person's confession of need in one area of life and acceptance by the other of that need and the desire to meet it for their mutual benefit in a response of willing obligation. Each is expected in some way to measure up to acknowledged benefits of the growing relationship. If expectations are not met, the friendship may cease.[117]

An openness together towards the growth of relations which are of mutual benefit is necessary if the relation is indeed going to be a friendship. Southard points out well how easily such a relation can be undermined if there are hidden expectations on either side, and he realistically recognizes the danger of what he calls "a neurotic extractive misdirection of friendship" if a person is only seeking a Christian counsellor in order to gain exclusive attention.[118]

The one-sidedness of a relationship may be held for time as "a cry for help implies dependence, and an answer may mean that one person is more adequate than another."[119] And yet if people become resistant to the movement of friendship towards a form of mutual vulnerability and are not open to the "righting itself" of the relationship as egalitarian, then the relationship should be defined as something else, but not as friendship. Regarding this mutual vulnerability, Southard sees its growth and development happening in what he calls increasingly intimate conversation,

---

116. Cocking and Kennett, "Friendship and the Self," 502–27.
117. Southard, *Theology and Therapy*, 205.
118. Southard, *Theology and Therapy*, 205.
119. Southard, *Theology and Therapy*, 206.

which he puts into the context of Jesus' openness with his disciples referred to in John 15.[120] But once again this can only happen authentically in an atmosphere of freedom, where both parties are able and willing to choose a responsible form of relation which can be regarded as a friendship.

Although it is not unusual in the counselling environment to sort out with the client at the beginning of the counsellor-client relationship what each one's expectations and prerequisites are, Southard's approach seems unusual in so far as he consciously and deliberately allows for the development of friendships. Indeed, he views these within the Christian context of the relationships as something to be welcomed, albeit very carefully and wisely monitored and made transparent.

Freedom to Fulfill the Pastoral Task

The questions I raised earlier in this chapter are pertinent here: At what point do pastors feel they have fulfilled their pastoral task? And is a clear definition thereof a help or a hindrance? Within the therapeutic, pastoral setting which Southard is discussing, it is not clear how often such a relation involving the growth and development of increasingly intimate conversation will be possible or desirable. As mentioned, the danger of neurotic misdirection and of transference and countertransference is something of which the pastor must be aware, both on the part of the other person and on the pastor's own part. Here it is wise to be careful of overburdening some relationships and to be willing to leave them at their present level—this both as protection for the pastor in regard to the overstraining of their emotional and energetic resources and in recognition that it is legitimate to regard the pastoral task as indeed sometimes being fulfilled without the necessity of further development of a relationship into what Berry called "relation."

A particularly helpful formulation of the aim of pastoral care within the context of friendship relations is that of Alistair Campbell. He describes that aim as being, "To help people to know love both as something to be received and as something to give."[121] A clear definition of what this may mean will differ from one context to another, and whether the task has been fulfilled or not is something pastors will have to judge for themselves. Helping people to know love as something to be received

---

120. Southard, *Theology and Therapy*, 205–6.
121. Campbell, *Paid to Care?*, 1.

and as something to give will involve strengthening them as individuals to use their inherent freedom as persons made in the image of God in making free and responsible choices regarding their relations. Ministers of pastoral care cannot force love upon people, but they can offer stable and friendly relationships in which the freedom to understand something about receiving and giving love may grow and develop. Regarding the possible nurturing of mutual friendship within such relationships, pastors will need wisdom in recognizing the strengths and weaknesses of those with whom they are in relationship, as well as their own strengths and weaknesses.

The discernment regarding what degree of apparent choices made by people are really freely chosen is a hazardous subject, and it is presumptuous for pastors to make judgements regarding the motives of those with whom they are in relationship. And yet perhaps such judgements may at certain times and in certain circumstances be necessary. Southard writes a cautionary word for those involved in pastoral care: "A depleted self is not yet free to really choose responsible friendship."[122] Part of a therapeutic process in pastoral care will be, as I mentioned above, the building up of a person's selfhood and their confidence and ability in making sensible and responsible choices.

Oftentimes, though, people who look for pastoral care and counselling want and need help and may be suffering from spiritual and mental health issues, which pastors should develop competence in recognizing. A perception that there may be any number of benign or malignant motives and reasons for a person to appear to be trustworthy or not is surely sensible. Nevertheless, any attempt to try and establish at what point a person can be inwardly free enough to choose to be a responsible friend seems to me to be doomed to failure. As we have seen in the interviews, friendships, and specifically responsible friendships, are described as free, affectionate, mutual relations characterized by an openness in personal matters to each other. Without these essential elements, the interviewees would not regard the relation as a friendship. However, the measurement of degrees of freedom or mutuality or affection or openness is something peculiar to each unique friendship.

Some people's illnesses or character may make certain elements within their relations easier or more difficult. In his interview, Ueli referred to this in describing his experiences with a person in his

---

122. Southard, *Theology and Therapy*, 213.

congregation who had been involved in a serious accident and had sustained head injuries. These injuries had had a detrimental effect on the person's perception and social competence, and had led them to a point where other members of the congregation found it increasingly challenging to relate to the person. And yet even in challenging circumstances and with people whose communicative capabilities are for one reason or another limited, friendships can be developed and enjoyed, and thus it would seem foolhardy, in general, to put a limit on people's capacity for friendship by measuring to what degree they might be free to choose such friendships.

Wise pastors will be aware of the element of mystery surrounding people's freedom and character and yet still have the acumen to avoid a possibly destructive naivety when dealing with them. This, I believe, is what Southard is getting at when he remarks on the "depleted self." Such naivety can be destructive when the pastor is drawn into some form of psychological game or manipulation without an awareness of what is happening, for such manipulation will tend to curtail the freedom, mutuality and openness of the relationship. Where pastors are alert to such possible games and attempts at manipulation, whether consciously undertaken or not, they will have more freedom in their choice of response and may find suitable ways to minister authentically and wisely within a given relationship.

In this connection, Southard uses the phrase "redemptive friendship" to refer to a type of friendship which is willing to invest in others, "to encourage others to find love through honest companionship instead of secrecy and self-hate."[123] Such a redemptive friendship is characterized by a freedom which is open, mutual, and affectionate, and Southard sets it against co-dependent relationships where, as he writes, "security is maintained through clinging to other people."[124] He sees such a form of friendship within a context of wisdom and brings it into connection with therapy or *therapon*, which he defines (quoting Thomas Oden and LeRoy Aden) as "highly personal, sympathetic, confidential acts of service."[125] Thus, redemptive friendship in the context of wisdom

---

123. Southard, *Theology and Therapy*, 254.

124. Southard, *Theology and Therapy*, 212.

125. Southard, *Theology and Therapy*, x; quoting Oden, *Kerygma and Counseling*, 148; Aden and Ellins, *Church and Pastoral Care*, 39.

includes many elements of modern therapy, such as shared respect, empathy, mutual understanding, but it goes further than what is commonly understood as therapy by including, in taking up the account of Jesus with his disciples in John 15, an "emphasis upon sacrifice, spiritual values, and commitment in friendship."[126]

The freedom for pastors to invest, if they wish to, in forms of redemptive friendship within their congregations is a theme to which I will return in the next chapter concerning responding to the research.

Freedom and the Expectation of Reciprocity

One further aspect of mutual freedom is of interest to this study. To what degree do pastors expect something in return when they freely choose to deepen a relationship? Often there may be an intuitive perception that the other person may also be interested in such a deepening of the relationship, but it may not be clear what the expectations of reciprocity are. Alan Kirk has written helpfully on ancient rules of reciprocity in the context of a study on Luke 6:27–35.[127] He quotes from Marshall Sahlins,[128] who posits three main genres of reciprocity in relationships—general reciprocity, balanced reciprocity, and negative reciprocity—and also cites Natalie Zemon Davis's summary of these as "gift, sale and coercion."[129] These are all forms of reciprocity which may be found in pastoral relationships. General reciprocity is described as free "open-ended, generous sharing, typically construed in the language of unconditional giving." It is regarded as "gift" and there is no obvious or overt form of accounting.[130] In that sense it "expresses at the material level the personal trust that is the heart of friendship." There is, however, within this personal trust an implicit obligation to "make a return," something which Kirk, quoting

---

126. Southard, *Theology and Therapy*, x.
127. Kirk, "Love Your Enemies," 667–86.
128. Sahlins, *Stone Age Economics*, 198.
129. Kirk, "Love Your Enemies," 675; Zemon Davis, *Gift in Sixteenth-Century France*, 129.
130. There is a body of literature around the term "gift." In theology, the most recent opus is by John Barclay, *Paul and the Gift*. Barclay points out in his prologue that his focus is on divine gift-giving, and that neither "the formation of community through reciprocity" nor "the mutuality of gift and need in the body of Christ" are investigated in his study. Barclay, *Paul and the Gift*, 4.

Julian Pitt-Rivers, calls "the paradox of friendship."[131] Such a return may manifest itself on one level as gratitude, with the potential however of "more tangible reciprocation."[132] Balanced reciprocity, which Davis sums up as "sale," "features overt concern for equivalence of exchange, with obligations spelled out and fulfilled within set time frames."[133] Negative reciprocity, summed up by Davis as "coercion," is synonymous with exploitation, when there is an attempt to get something for less than its perceived worth, or even retaliation, in which, in terms of social psychology, some form of negative action is returned and harm intended.

Within the pastoral relationship, considerations around the area between general reciprocity and balanced reciprocity seem to be of most interest to us within this study. Negative reciprocity, either as exploitation or as some form of retaliation, would be the type of "return" which pastors, in their desire to follow Christ, would attempt to avoid at all costs. They would, however, need to be aware of their own potential to exploit relationships as well as that of others wishing to exploit them. A relationship of balanced reciprocity would perhaps best describe the professional, pastoral counselling situation. The structure of the relationship is one of clear tasks and boundaries, with set time limits and the "sale" of pastoral and spiritual expertise, which should be helpful for the client.

The free choice to invest more time and energy into a relationship, and then, over time, more affection, indicates a move towards a form of general reciprocity, where the "return" is no longer obviously balanced. In the forms of friendship investigated in this study, as long as the trust remains that if help in some form be needed it will be given for the sake of the friendship, then the open-ended, generous sharing characteristic of general reciprocity is present. The interviewees in this study talked of this, but also of how they found it difficult to sustain friendships if they felt that the other side was exploiting this free generosity, or if a negative reciprocity was taking over from the desired general reciprocity.

A further form of reciprocity is important within the context of this study—that of gratitude. Kirk mentions gratitude as a form of reciprocal giving within the structure of a general reciprocity. In this context, he introduces the Greek term *charis*:

---

131. Kirk, "Love Your Enemies," 675; Pitt-Rivers, "Kith and Kin," 97.
132. Kirk, "Love Your Enemies," 675.
133. Kirk, "Love Your Enemies," 677.

> The dynamic of open-ended exchange of benefits among friends—that is, generalized reciprocity—coheres around the term *charis* which designates both the concrete favours that friends do reciprocally for one another, and the gratitude shown in return, a gratitude that we have seen is the affective dimension of the diffuse obligation to reciprocate. The term highlights the qualitative aspects of the relationship, bringing into view the graciousness, trust and voluntariness crucial to this kind of mutual exchange. Thus *charis* is the vital principle of friendship itself.[134]

This amicable love has the potential within a friendship to bring about a sense of gratitude which Kirk refers to as the "affective dimension of the diffuse obligation to reciprocate." Such gratitude is something to which I imagine most people will be able to relate positively, and which pastors experience in their relationships. In classical literature, it is regarded as vital to healthy friendship relations. Seneca, for instance, writes that "we ought to be careful to confer benefits by preference upon those who will be likely to respond with gratitude," and he even writes, "I protest against the squandering of liberality upon the ungrateful."[135] However understandable at times such a sentiment by the stoic Seneca might be, perhaps even within the pastoral setting, the question of whether this is compatible with a Christian approach will need to be addressed.

Freedom and Gratitude Within a Christian Narrative

The Lutheran theologian and ethicist Gilbert Meilaender in his *The Theory and Practice of Virtue* writes an insightful chapter for the context of our study about gratitude as a virtue.[136] There, he points out well the tension involved in gratitude as an obligation and as a free response.[137] Gratitude to God is something which ought to characterize our lives, whether we feel grateful at a specific time or not. The gifts of God to us should elicit gratitude and thanksgiving, and it is our duty to be aware of this:

---

134. Kirk, "Love Your Enemies," 678; compare also Barclay, *Paul and the Gift*, 576–79.

135. Kirk, "Love Your Enemies," 679; Seneca, *De Beneficiis*, 1.10.4–5; 1.15.3.

136. Meilaender, *Theory and Practice of Virtue*, 152–53.

137. For further discussion of this tension see also Barclay, *Paul and the Gift*, 11–65; Gulliford et al., "Recent Work on the Concept of Gratitude," 285–317; Konstan, *In the Orbit of Love*, 95–128.

> That, indeed, is one of the reasons for liturgy. It gives us the fitting word which we, subject in our lives to the law of undulation, might not find within our passing moods and feelings.[138]

And yet "it is too simple just to say that receiving a gift obligates the recipient to show gratitude in return."[139] The language of virtue, he contends, helps one to see that gratitude in the end is not just an obligation or duty, but an attitude, a way of being, which permeates the whole of one's life. This leaves numerous ways of acting freely in choosing how, when, and in what form gratitude may be shown. When giving gifts to others, it also leaves one the freedom to not demand gratitude in return.

> Gifts should not be burdens. Recipients must in some way remain free. . . . If something is really a gift, there cannot be strings attached. . . . If I give you a gift and then condemn you for ingratitude, my criticism suggests that the gift was not really free, that I was seeking to bind you to some return. It suggests, that is, that I did not intend to set you free by my gift. . . . if I think myself obligated to show gratitude for your gift, I do not really experience it as a gift. I am not set free by it. And any gratitude I show will be only an isolated deed of gratitude, not an expression of my character and the way of life to which I am committed.[140]

Having asserted that a giver cannot demand gratitude for a gift, if it is indeed a gift, Meilaender wisely points out that that is not the same as saying that we should not be hurt if the gifts we give are not acknowledged gratefully. As he writes, "we are Christians not Stoics . . . our ideal is not invulnerability,"[141] and it is right to be aware of our status as needy beings, who are in need of such signs of affection as gratitude. Real giving, which is freely given and sets people free, and real receiving, which is spontaneously and freely grateful, will not be shaped by obligation but by love. This is the type of love shown by God in the gift of himself, "This gift has set us free—even to renounce the Giver and crucify him."[142] This love does not accuse us of failing in our obligation of gratitude, even as it simultaneously woos us and longs for the mutuality of friendship love.

---

138. Meilaender, *Theory and Practice of Virtue*, 158.
139. Meilaender, *Theory and Practice of Virtue*, 158.
140. Meilaender, *Theory and Practice of Virtue*, 170.
141. Meilaender, *Theory and Practice of Virtue*, 171.
142. Meilaender, *Theory and Practice of Virtue*, 174.

Meilaender closes his chapter on the virtue of gratitude with a meditation on Matt 18:21–35, in which he talks about the ungrateful servant at the end of the parable. The servant, having been forgiven much by the master himself, cannot find it in his own heart to act out of gratitude and forgive those who are in debt to him. Those who see this are disturbed, and rightly so, and report it to the master. In the parable, the master hands over the ungrateful servant to the torturers until the debt is paid. This, says Jesus, is what the heavenly Father is like. Meilaender writes:

> Can this be the last word about God? Can it be true that when his gifts do not elicit gratitude, he hands the wicked servant over to the torturers there to remain until the last penny of the debt is paid? Indeed, it is true. This is in truth the very last word about God. For whom does the Father hand over to the torturers? . . . Is it not Jesus who, though he was rich yet for our sakes became a debtor? He is the one the Father hands over. He it is whom the Father will not release until the debt is paid. This is the mystery of grace, of a gift which demands and requires nothing in return, not even gratitude. This gift of God is really a gift, perhaps the only real gift ever given. It is not cheap, but it is free. . . . This God . . . is the One who now says to us: freely you have received, freely give.[143]

Perhaps Christian pastors, shaped and moved by this type of freedom, will find ways of living out free and mutual friendships within their congregations, which are characterized by open-ended, generous sharing, something which Southard calls the "full sharing of the highs and lows of life."[144]

Summary

In this chapter section dealing with theological reflection on a freedom within a pastoral relationship that is open, mutual, and affectionate I have addressed observations by Samuel Southard regarding the freedom to make special choices to further certain relationships within the pastoral setting. Because friendship relations cannot be forced nor made a duty, they must be chosen. Southard describes such free choices as iterative invitations, which involve investing time and energy in one person. The reasons for these choices may have to do with "a gently growing admission

---

143. Meilaender, *Theory and Practice of Virtue*, 173.
144. Southard, *Theology and Therapy*, x.

that one person is drawn toward the qualities of life in another,"[145] or they may have other motivating factors such as the wish to help. There may be a one-sidedness to the relationship for a short while, yet this should not last long, and should develop towards a relationship characterized by mutual trust and openness. In this regard, Southard writes of "mutual vulnerability" and refers to the openness of Jesus with his disciples. If such mutuality does not develop, then the relationship may remain a counselling or therapeutic one but should not be misunderstood as a friendship.

In considering Southard's position, I pointed out that his use of the term friendship within the counselling pastoral context is unusual but instructive. It emphasizes the freedom both to develop friendship and to leave relationships within the realm of pastoral friendliness. In all situations pastors will need wisdom to be perceptive and aware of what they are doing and also of what is being done with them. They can simultaneously use their experience and training to avoid naively falling into manipulative behaviors by other people and yet also thank God for and enjoy the mysterious quality of friendship when they experience it, perhaps also with persons with whom they were initially unsure if such relations were possible.

In the context of freedom, I furthermore considered the tension surrounding the expectation of reciprocity when the development of a relationship towards friendship is offered. In discussing work by Alan Kirk, I took up the concepts of general, balanced, and negative reciprocity and what they might mean in the pastoral setting. While balanced reciprocity, with tasks and boundaries clearly defined and communicated, characterizes the professional counselling situation best, the choice to invest in friendship terms in a relationship would signify a move to general reciprocity with its quality of open-ended, generous sharing.

Finally, I looked at gratitude as a specific form of reciprocity and found the writing of the Lutheran theologian Gilbert Meilaender helpful within the context of this study. He regards gratitude as a form of virtue and searches for a way to uphold the appropriateness of expressing gratitude and even expecting it, and yet remaining free. In this endeavour, having seen how the ancient stoics connected love to gratitude, he points out that the gift of Christ is such that it is free, noting: "This is the mystery of grace, of a gift which demands and requires nothing in return, not

---

145. Southard, *Theology and Therapy*, 204.

even gratitude" and yet given by "One who now says to us: freely you have received, freely give."[146]

THEOLOGICAL REFLECTION ON A KIND OF OPENNESS WITHIN A PASTORAL RELATIONSHIP, WHICH IS MUTUAL, AFFECTIONATE, AND FREE

Frankness of speech, honest and intimate discourse with other people, has long been understood as an attribute of friendship relations. It was, for instance, an important *topos* in the Greco-Roman concept of friendship. Gail O'Day refers to the Roman philosophers Plutarch and Cicero in this regard and writes:

> Among Roman philosophers such as Plutarch and Cicero, friendship concerned not only what it meant to be a friend but how to distinguish between a true friend and its opposite, the flatterer (*kolax*) ... Philosophers advised ... on how to recognize social contacts who were not friends—those who had not the patron's interests at heart but their own. One of the distinguishing marks was the use of "frank speech" (*parrësia*). "Frankness of speech, by common report and belief, is the language of friendship especially."[147]

Such openness, such frank and truthful speech, is of prime importance in the New Testament. In John 15 the reason Jesus gives for calling his disciples friends rather than servants is that he has been open with them regarding everything the Father has revealed to him.

In the interviews for this study, all the participants were agreed that openness about very personal matters was essential in their understanding and experience of how friendship works. Ueli, for instance, talks in the context of his friendships of "sharing his heart" and of metaphorically "being naked." And Theo, in listing what he regards as the qualities of friendship, immediately mentions openness and honesty, and contrasts relationships moulded by such openness with those formed by the mindset of an accountant, where all is well so long as the right boxes are ticked and the formally correct words are said.

---

146. Meilaender, *Theory and Practice of Virtue*, 175.

147. O'Day, "Jesus as Friend in the Gospel of John," 147, quoting Plutarch, *How to Tell a Flatterer from a Friend*, 6. Compare also Fitzgerald, *Friendship, Flattery, and Frankness of Speech*.

In the previous chapter section, I quoted Samuel Southard regarding the wisdom involved in bringing elements of friendship in all freedom into the pastoral, therapeutic situation. He understood the sharing of the "highs and lows of life" as part of that realm of friendship. But what, if any, is the goal of such sharing? Or is it simply part of necessary human expression, something people automatically do when they feel a mutual, free affection with each other?

The Goal of Openness

Regarding the goal of openness, the classical Aristotelian view is that true friends will build each other up in virtue and that their open discourse with each other has that aim.[148] Indeed, the main aim of friendship is a form of self-love, which seeks growth in virtue through mutual openness with others one deems fit to promote such an undertaking.[149] As we have seen in the previous chapter section, Seneca felt it was a waste to spend time in benefitting those who would be ungrateful for such benefits and that likewise the open discourse encouraged in an Aristotelian virtue friendship should be focused on those with whom a mutual growth of virtue will most likely happen.[150]

Perhaps important for the context of this study in the pastoral setting is O'Day's suggestion that, in taking up John's Gospel, "plain speaking" should be the "language of the kingdom" and is an "act of friendship."[151] She brings this into the context of the pastor's responsibility to preach:

> Plain speaking, characterized by openness, boldness, and frankness, is an act of friendship because through such speech one enacts the love and openness that characterized Jesus' own ministry. . . . What does this mean for the theological and pastoral function of our preaching? It suggests that at least one possible function for preaching is to be a friend in one's preaching.[152]

She goes on to point out that preaching should be about truth and not flattery, and that telling a congregation what one thinks they want to hear using overly judicious phrases is not the plain speaking of friendship.

148. Compare, for instance, Roberts "Paulo Freire and the Idea of Openness," 80–81.
149. Aristotle, *Nicomachean Ethics*, VIII.
150. Seneca, *De Beneficiis*, 1.10.4–5; 1.15.3.
151. O'Day, "Preaching as an Act of Friendship," 19.
152. O'Day, "Preaching as an Act of Friendship," 19.

"Friendship," she writes, "requires bold, frank, open speech, a speech that is measured and assessed by its enactment of love, not its demonstration of power."[153] And, importantly, the plain speaking of friendship is something reciprocal. Thus, from the frank preaching of a pastor a community of friends should be growing in which each one can be honest and plain speaking with the other.[154] This, O'Day contends, has an eschatological component, which has to do with the coming kingdom of God:

> Plain speaking, the language of friendship, is the language of the kingdom, because in our plain speaking we announce with boldness the fullness of God's love and presence... We proclaim that in this moment, in this act of friendship, God's kingdom may indeed be near.[155]

Alistair Campbell writes similarly, albeit in the area of counselling in pastoral care, that although such counselling, in mediating acceptance of the other, has an affinity with Rogerian psychotherapy, it also has "a special quality derived from Christian hope" which has to do with a "future orientation which cannot remain content with the given, but seeks also . . . the end of the story." Thus,

> the physical presence and listening in pastoral care are rarely wholly passive, non-directive, or accepting in a non-confronting sense. They express a love which seeks truth, while yet conscious of the dangers of a judgementalism which can impede that search. Pastoral care offers an acceptance which is radical and revolutionary in its effects because it will not tolerate half-truths or evasions.[156]

Both frank speech and openness within the realm of preaching and within a counselling situation are probably something most pastors, at least in theory, would find good and desirable. These might lead towards the building up of communities characterized in their friendship by honest, direct and open communication, and the frank speech necessary to a concern for truth. But what degree of openness is fitting for a pastoral relationship otherwise?

Chloe Lynch writes about this type of openness within the framework of what she calls incarnational ecclesial leadership, which is

---

153. O'Day, "Preaching as an Act of Friendship," 19.
154. O'Day, "Preaching as an Act of Friendship," 18–19.
155. O'Day, "Preaching as an Act of Friendship," 19.
156. Campbell, *Paid to Care?*, 69.

concerned to bring the love of Christ into the realm of experienced reality through the pastor's own participation in that love:

> [By t]reating others as ends, not means to an end, this love presumes personal relationship between leader and follower, rather than a functional relationship giving primacy to role. Nevertheless, it does not presuppose unmitigated personal openness: the differentiation of both parties in this leadership relationship is honoured, as is relational finitude. What is core is a degree of personal vulnerability, a kenotic offering of self not without cost to the leader.[157]

Lynch, although emphasizing the personal element as vital in a pastoral relationship and referring to a "degree of personal vulnerability" and the "kenotic offering of self," does not believe that friendship in the pastoral relationship presupposes what she calls "unmitigated personal openness." However, an attitude of personal openness, even if not unmitigated, and even if "not without cost to the leader" will be necessary, it seems, if the term friendship is still to retain meaning within Lynch's concept. The amount of openness which is required and good for the relationship will be something the people involved will need to work out. Because she is specifically focused on the area of leadership within the spectrum of pastoral identity, Lynch thinks the differentiation of the roles of those involved in the pastor and parishioner relationship must be honoured, as well as "relational finitude," which I imagine refers to the impossibility of a pastor having the emotional energy to be invested in too many friendships which would require anything more than a cursory personal openness on their part.

Lynch tries here to negotiate the tension for pastors between on the one hand having a leadership role which is recognized and livable, but which in consequence does not allow for too much personal openness with most of those involved in a community, and on the other of keeping up the idea of relational and personal vulnerability with its emphasis on plain and honest speaking, which is vital to a form of friendship which is oriented towards the example of Christ. She writes openly about this tension in the last chapter of her book,[158] and points out wisely how helpful it will be to differentiate between a range of friendships of which ecclesial leaders are capable and to which they may be called. These are

---

157. Lynch, *Ecclesial Leadership as Friendship*, 187–88.
158. Lynch, *Ecclesial Leadership as Friendship*, 208–20.

nuanced, progressive in character and may fluctuate across the course of a relationship. Each will involve various amounts of personal disclosure and the willingness to show oneself to be vulnerable.[159]

The Ability to "Suffer" as Described by Jürgen Moltmann

What a willingness to become vulnerable might mean is approached in an interesting way for the context of this study by Jürgen Moltmann, at whose work we have already looked, around the theme of equality and friendliness. In his book *The Open Church*, he once again takes issue with the Aristotelian peer principle, which tends to promote an exclusivity in friendships among those who are the same. He takes up the famous phrase used by Aristotle, "Birds of a feather flock together"[160] and asks:

> But why? People who are like us, who think the same thoughts, who have the same things, and who want the same things confirm us. However, people who are different from us, that is, people whose thoughts, feelings, and desires are different from ours, make us feel insecure. We therefore love those who are like us and we shun those who are different from us.[161]

In contrast to this, Moltmann proposes how he thinks a community in the Church, amongst the followers of Christ, should work. He begins by taking up Paul's words from Romans 15:7, 13 (NEB): "In a word accept one another as Christ accepted us, to the glory of God . . . and may the God of hope fill you with all joy and peace by your faith in him, until, by the power of the Holy Spirit, you overflow with hope." Acceptance of one another in general, says Moltmann, is limited and has to do with our insecurity and deep-seated anxiety about ourselves. However, an understanding and orientation towards the way in which Christ has accepted us will lead us to having a new attitude:

> It opens us up for others as they really are so that we gain a longing for and an interest in them. As a result of this we become able actually to forget ourselves and to focus on the way Christ has accepted us.[162]

---

159. Lynch, *Ecclesial Leadership as Friendship*, 212–13; compare also Lafollette, *Personal Relationships*, 108–19.

160. Aristotle, *Nicomachean Ethics*, Book VIII, 1.

161. Moltmann, *Open Church*, 30.

162. Moltmann, *Open Church*, 30–31.

THEOLOGICAL REFLECTION ON THE ESSENTIAL ELEMENTS OF FRIENDSHIP 183

This openness, which helps us see others as they are and gain a longing for them, is characterized by an ability to suffer, for this is the way Christ has accepted us.[163]

An understanding of "suffering" is deeply important to Moltmann, and he uses the word "suffer" subtly and with connotations taken from the German verb *leiden*. M. Douglas Meeks in his introduction to Moltmann's book, points this out helpfully and shows the connection Moltmann saw in the word "passion" between the suffering of Christ (*Leiden*, as a noun, in German) and his "passion" as in the passionate devotion (*Leidenschaft* in German) of his life to the kingdom and reign of God. Indeed although "suffering" in modern English generally connotes something passive, the usage from Middle English, which was closer to German,

> implied an active as well as receptive power . . . ."Passion" and "suffering" mean not simply to be acted upon but also to be affected, changed, transformed, and matured by the lives of others. To be open, accessible, vulnerable is not the sign of passive impotence but the precondition of active historical life. Suffering also means the power to go outside of oneself and affect the other. And thus, it is the condition of love. One who is not empowered with suffering is not able to love, and vice versa.[164]

It is this capacity to suffer which, according to Moltmann, opens up life itself to us and frees us from the anxiety which would attempt to cramp and hinder us in our relations with others. If we are unable to suffer, then everything and everyone is difficult and nothing and no one can please us. But if we become absorbed in the passion of Christ, realizing and trusting in God's suffering love for us, which knows no bounds, through which Christ has accepted us, to the glory of God (see Romans 15), we are thus ourselves capable of suffering and, as Moltmann says, of forgetting ourselves.[165] This forgetting of ourselves is not understood and felt as a detrimental form of self-denial but as a step on the way towards a mutuality of acceptance within the community because Christ has accepted us. Such forgetting of ourselves is a question of focus. It means focussing on Christ's suffering love for us and trusting ourselves to this love and thus not focussing ourselves constantly on whether we feel good

---

163. Moltmann, *Open Church*, 31.

164. Moltmann, *Open Church*, 16; this active understanding of "suffering" is still present in the German language. The phrase "Ich kann Dich leiden"—literally "I can suffer you"—denotes that you actually like someone.

165. Moltmann, *Open Church*, 31.

or not at a particular point in time in a particular relationship. In regard to becoming absorbed in the passion of Christ and forgetting ourselves, Moltmann tries to spell out what a form of openness could mean, first of all in what he designates as a "messianic lifestyle,"[166] and then in "open friendship."[167] Both of these are helpful in this study around openness in the context of friendship within the pastoral setting.

Openness in the "Messianic Lifestyle" and in "Open Friendship"

The messianic lifestyle is characterized as a life worthy of the gospel.[168] Such a lifestyle is not legalistic, understood as principally determined by prohibitions and restraints, leading to a repressed, narrow-minded and anxious life in which we "have the gnawing feeling that we must and ought to be someone other than who we really are."[169] Rather, the messianic lifestyle is one of liberation in which, entrusting and opening ourselves to the leading of the Holy Spirit, we are able to give ourselves up and accept ourselves with all our limitations, thus being freed to live with God in what Moltmann calls the "covenant of freedom."[170] He compares this lifestyle with that of artists who are called to shape their lives in such a way as to express something of the beauty of divine grace and the freedom of divine love. This shaping is not seen as under the law but under the gospel, and thus we do not become masters ourselves but "through our openness and our suffering God becomes our master."[171] Thus Christians living messianically can speak freely and, where they can, set others free as well.

Under the title "open friendship," Moltmann initially makes reference to a children's book by Joan Walsh Anglund, called *A Friend is Someone Who Likes You*,[172] which speaks peacefully about an atmosphere of "open friendship" which holds the world together. This atmosphere in the world is one which does not have to be produced and cannot be possessed but is waiting to be discovered, and it likes you. It is a world to

---

166. Moltmann, *Open Church*, 37–49.

167. Moltmann, *Open Church*, 50–63.

168. Moltmann quotes here from Phil 1:27—"Let the manner of your life be worthy of the gospel of Christ."

169. Moltmann, *Open Church*, 38.

170. Moltmann, *Open Church*, 38.

171. Moltmann, *Open Church*, 39.

172. Moltmann, *Open Church*, 50.

which children in general have more access, but which over time tends to fade from our experience because "we no longer open our hearts."[173] Yet wherever friendship is experienced, it allows friends to "open up to one another free space for free life. Friends are not free without each other, but only with each other."[174] This opening up is also for the sake of joy in life, as we feel how good it is to share our happy experiences and enjoy others joy, without self-interest and envy. From such sharing of joy, shared suffering follows as trust is built up.[175] We find here in Moltmann's thought all four of the essential elements of friendship, as experienced by the pastors interviewed in this study, namely, mutuality, affection, freedom, and openness interwoven with each other.

Moving on from general thoughts around "open friendship," Moltmann now turns his attention to Jesus. Taking up the titles of dignity and office given to Jesus by the Church over the centuries, those of prophet, priest, and king, he finds them wanting in describing the new fellowship with God and with each other that is manifest and embodied through Jesus, a fellowship which is characterized by mutuality and openness. Thus, he suggests adding the "title" of friend, although he points out that "friend" as such, being a truly relational word and not a one-sided designation, cannot really be a title.[176] The reason for Jesus' friendship with people as described in the New Testament as with "tax collectors and sinners" (see Luke 7:34) "lies in his joy, his joy in God, in the future, and in human existence . . . Jesus does not bring a dry sympathy, but an inviting joy in God's kingdom."[177] And in John 15 it is once again joy, says Moltmann, which causes Jesus to be open and frank with his disciples, as he says in verse 11 shortly before he calls his disciples friends and no longer servants: "I have told you this so that my joy may be in you and that your joy may be complete." And so, in the fellowship of Jesus

173. Moltmann, *Open Church*, 51.
174. Moltmann, *Open Church*, 52.
175. Moltmann, *Open Church*, 50.

176. Moltmann, *Open Church*, 55; this is also of interest, of course, in terms of the validity of the use of the term "friend" for the pastor within a church, if the term comes to be used almost as a title given to that pastor. For further discussion regarding the use of the three classic titles for Jesus with reference to a fourth as "friend," see Adiprasetya, "Revisiting Jürgen Moltmann's Theology of Open Friendship," 177–87. Here, Adiprasetya suggests the use of the three terms "friend, servant and stranger" as an alternative, but also as what he calls a continuation and deepening of the classic titles (priest-friend / prophet-stranger / king-servant).

177. Moltmann, *Open Church*, 55.

the disciples become friends of God and they experience him as such a friend. And from this,

> open friendship becomes the bond in their fellowship with one another, and it is their vocation in a society still dominated by masters and servants, fathers and children, teachers and pupils, superiors and subordinates.[178]

Returning to the classic titles of dignity given to Jesus, those of prophet, priest, and king, Moltmann laments that these "highly exalted and official terms" have often concealed the simplicity of the friendship Jesus offers and have led the Church and her officials to maintain an exalted air which has been a hinderance to the openness of fellowship and friendship. He writes:

> It would be well if the Church, Church officials, and those taken care of by them finally recalled that together they are no more and no less than a "fellowship of the friends of Jesus."[179]

Defining the Church as no more and no less than the fellowship of the friends of Jesus will have consequences in the way people within that fellowship, including those in positions of authority and leadership, relate to each other. It is to those consequences that Moltmann now turns.

Openness Within the "Fellowship of the Friends of Jesus"

In his conclusions regarding what such openness within the fellowship of the friends of Jesus might mean in the actual life and workings of the Church and in the way Church officials view their calling and tasks, Moltmann contends in order to live "open friendship," one must deprivatize the romantic, mainly western, notion of friendship where the public sphere and the private sphere have been sealed off from each other, and where the only friendship regarded as such is that of intimate or "bosom" friends. Forms of friendship may thus be developed that have space and legitimacy within the public realm.[180] He does not explain how this might be practicable, but the way something like this may even start to happen is once again connected to joy rather than to duty. The idea that people

---

178. Moltmann, *Open Church*, 57.

179. Moltmann, *Open Church*, 60.

180. For a contemporary discussion of this, see Kotze and Noeth, "Friendship as a Theological Model." Also Slade, *Open Friendship in a Closed Society*.

will start to live in open friendship because it "has to" happen is a wayward thought for Moltmann. As he writes:

> It does not "have to" happen at all. It happens wherever men and women are seized by joy in God, in people, and in the world.... It is not by sympathising with others but by rejoicing with them that they will be won.[181]

Joy in God, in people and in the world, says Moltmann, is the driving factor in friendships which are open. The messianic lifestyle Moltmann commends depends on trust in the Holy Spirit and an overflowing of hope (see Romans 15), and the necessary openness is held by one's ability to "suffer" people, which, as we have seen, is understood as an active as well as a passive power.

In considering Moltmann's thought further, it is this trust and hope which mirrors God's prevenient grace in dealing with humans and which is manifest in Jesus' dealings with his disciples in John 15. John Fitzgerald, Professor of New Testament and Early Christianity in the Department of Theology at the University of Notre Dame, shows this well in his description of the Johannine conception of friendship. Normally, both in antiquity and today, and indeed as witnessed to by the experience of the interviewees within this study, a friend is regarded as someone who has shown themselves to be trustworthy and reliable. One therefore opens up to them with personal and even otherwise secret matters. Openness follows on from the confidence in the one deemed to be a friend, a confidence that the things about which one has been open will not be communicated to others and will not be used against one; revelation in this sense presupposes friendship. Jesus, however, turns this around and reverses the standard logic. Here, revelation creates friendship. In theological language, it is prevenient grace at work rather than any demonstrated reliability by the disciples which creates friendship. Indeed, the disciples will soon demonstrate how unreliable they are when Peter denies Jesus and the others abandon him.[182]

The ground of friendship in the Johannine literature of the New Testament is love, and more precisely the love of God the Father communicated and embodied in the love of Jesus which, as an act of grace, is freely given to the disciples. Following on from this grace and love, the disciples are exhorted to remain in that love if they want to remain

---

181. Moltmann, *Open Church*, 62–63.
182. Fitzgerald, "Christian Friendship," 285–86.

friends of Jesus, and are reassured that the comforter or "paraclete," the Holy Spirit, will be with them. Being such disciples entailed loving one another as Jesus had loved them (see John 15:12). As Fitzgerald writes, "Without discipleship, without abiding in love, friendship with Jesus and with one another was simply impossible."[183] The love Jesus characterized, the love the disciples were told to emulate and live in as friends of Jesus, is built upon the prevenient grace of God, which opens up before it is clear that the other will reciprocate and what form that reciprocation might take. While freely taking the first step in love, prevenient grace looks and hopes for mutual openness, because only in that mutuality will friendship blossom and flourish. Prevenient openness, inviting an openness which should become mutual if a form of friendship is going to happen, would thus seem to characterize the way Jesus exhorts his disciples to live.

What then might such prevenient openness mean for pastors in their relationships within the congregation? As we saw in the research findings, the interviewed pastors were aware that a certain degree of openness towards those with whom they had to do was necessary for them to function faithfully as pastors. This was shown in various ways. Stephanie, for instance, saw this openness in hospitality, creating welcoming communities where "what God wants with us" may then happen "through relationships." Beat understood his openness in terms of friendliness, where he communicates "openly, politely" and aware that he as a pastor should always, according to 1 Peter 3:15, be ready and able to give an answer to those who might ask him concerning the hope that is in him. Olivia wanted to be "100% approachable," but qualified this immediately, realizing that although some within the congregation might call their relationship with her a friendship, "I never really am in friendship, because I do not reveal everything about myself." Not revealing everything about herself is her protection against becoming a "much more vulnerable person," something she feels would compromise her ability to be approachable in the way she would like to be.

Thus, although the pastors interviewed expressed their conviction that openness is a core quality in their work and in their own way of being in the world, most of them shy away in their congregations from the great degree of personal openness which characterizes friendship, as they describe it, for fear of a vulnerability which might ultimately be detrimental to them fulfilling what they understand to be their pastoral task.

---

183. Fitzgerald, "Christian Friendship," 286.

Those who did have relations with others in their congregations which they considered to be friendships kept these relations restricted to only a small number, one or occasionally two people. With these people they felt sufficiently confident to open up about personal matters, although from the interviews it is not entirely clear what that meant in reality. Even when Ueli talks about becoming "naked" within friendships, it is unclear whether that is ultimately more an ideal for which he strives and what that nakedness entails in terms of very private personal revelations.

But making the sharing of very private matters the test of pastoral friendship is perhaps not really the crux of the matter. Prevenient openness shown by ordained pastors in the Church, as envisioned by Moltmann, is less about feeling the need to reveal all too personal things about oneself and more about what type of relational vulnerability may be appropriate within a Christian community committed to love, as embodied and taught by Jesus Christ. Here the goal of pastoral care proposed by Alistair Campbell, to which I have already referred, "to help people to know love both as something to be received and as something to give," can help give us direction. Pastors are accustomed to others being open and to becoming vulnerable with them. But learning to what degree mutual openness may be helpful towards that goal of pastoral care will involve free choices regarding how vulnerable they are willing to make themselves. For our purposes, Vanessa Herrick explores this theme instructively in her small booklet, *Limits of Vulnerability: Exploring a kenotic model for pastoral ministry*.

Openness, Freedom and the Limits of Vulnerability

Herrick defines vulnerability within the context of pastoral care. She cites Stephen Pattison,[184] saying that it is through the vulnerabilities and weaknesses of pastors that they can minister well to others. Vulnerability is then

> An openness to being wounded (physical or otherwise) which is the outcome of a voluntary relinquishment of the power to protect oneself from being wounded.[185]

Here, vulnerability is a choice, and Herrick puts this into the context of the life and person of Jesus, who, in trinitarian communion with the

---

184. Pattison, *Critique of Pastoral Care*, 151.
185. Herrick, *Limits of Vulnerability*, 3.

Father and the Spirit through prayer, and in reference to Philippians 2:5–11, chose to make himself vulnerable. Taking up the biblical narrative of Jesus, mainly from the Gospel of Luke, she highlights how dependent he was at the key moments of his life—birth, baptism, temptation in the desert, transfiguration, and passion—not only on his Father and the Holy Spirit, but also on his closest and most intimate circle of disciples. On the level of Jesus' human relationships, she refers here to what she calls "circles of intimacy," ranging from the comparative anonymity of the crowds attending Jesus' public ministry, to his disciples, to the seventy-two sent out, to the twelve apostles and then to the three who accompanied Jesus on the mount of transfiguration, Peter, James and John. It is within these "circles of intimacy" that Jesus exhibits "degrees of disclosure."[186] In the interviews conducted in this study, Markus referred to these concentric circles within Jesus' relationships as a help to him in ordering his own relationships in his congregation.

Jesus' dependence on others is shown most strikingly, says Herrick, in the passion narrative, where he actively becomes passive in his attitude towards those who are opposed to him. Here we are reminded of Moltmann's use of passion and suffering, with its both active and passive overtones. Here, Herrick quotes from William H. Vanstone's study on the verb *paradidōmi*, which means "to give, or hand over to another":

> What happens . . . when Jesus is handed over is not that he passes from success to failure, from gain to loss or from pleasure to pain; it is that he passes from doing to receiving what others do, from working to waiting, from the role of subject to that of object and, in the proper sense of the phrase, from action to passion.[187]

Herrick sees thus the working out of the love of Jesus, in which, secure in his relationship with God his Father, in the Holy Spirit, he is able to choose to open himself up to the possibility of being wounded. Taking up the Greek term *kenōo*, which means to empty or to make empty and is used in Philippians 2:7 to describe the active movement of Christ in becoming human and a servant, she goes on to offer what she calls a "kenotic model" for pastoral ministry. Wisely warning her readers from an all too naïve idea of transposing who Jesus was and what he said and did into who we should be and what we should say and do, she nevertheless speaks of a dynamic "imitation of Christ" responding to the Holy Spirit, where:

186. Herrick, *Limits of Vulnerability*, 11.
187. Herrick, *Limits of Vulnerability*, 12; Vanstone, *The Stature of Waiting*, 31.

> We should look to Christ (and for our particular purposes, to the self-emptying and vulnerable Christ), to provide us with a model for living and a model for good pastoral practice which *may* include making space for vulnerability within the pastoral relationship.[188]

Within her proposed "kenotic model," she notes five principles.[189] In the first, she emphasizes above all the need for a solid and secure relationship with God, mediated by the same Holy Spirit who worked in Christ. Then also the security of human relationships is emphasized, such as those within family or within the church, which "enhance our freedom to be vulnerable to others." Through such security we may then risk "varying degrees of disclosure amongst different circles of intimacy."

In the second principle, she notes the need to be aware of the Holy Spirit's leading towards appropriate responses to specific people. Thus, prompted by the Spirit, it may sometimes be necessary to be vulnerable with persons with whom we are in relation, and at other times the most caring approach may be one of critical distance.

The third principle refers to the necessary awareness that vulnerability may lead to pain and suffering and yet also growth. Those who pastor, she writes,

> can expect to be affected by those for whom they care. To enter into a pastoral relationship is to risk rejection, pain and suffering, for love demands an involvement with the other which, although it may be a key to growth, may lead also to both suffering with them and to suffering because of them.[190]

In the fourth principle, vulnerability may take the form of restraint or "passive activity." This is in some senses similar to principle two and refers to the acumen of being aware of what is appropriate with a specific person in the specific relationship between the pastor and the other. Thus, it may be helpful at times to speak of one's own experiences and needs and at other times more helpful to remain silent, even in the face of misunderstanding, rejection, or accusations.

And in the fifth principle, Herrick reiterates the necessity of a confidence in one's own freedom. Becoming vulnerable, sharing experiences,

---

188. Herrick, *Limits of Vulnerability*, 13; Herrick's italics.
189. Herrick, *Limits of Vulnerability*, 13–16.
190. Herrick, *Limits of Vulnerability*, 14.

even of weaknesses, failures, and needs remains a choice which pastors can freely make or freely choose not to.

Interestingly for this study, within Herrick's five principles in her "kenotic model" the four essential elements of friendship interwoven as described by the interviewed pastors, freedom, mutuality, affection, and openness, are very present and indeed vital to her understanding of good pastoral care. Throughout her writing there is an emphasis on the free choice of both pastor and the other regarding whether and how to develop and form the relationship. There is an acute awareness that the appropriate way of being and communicating with each other can only be worked out in a mutual fashion, one which is sensitive to the other. Her understanding of the love of Christ to which pastors are called is such that it will include specific affection with and for the specific other and not remain disinterested. And a willingness to be open both personally and emotionally is paramount in her understanding of how Christian pastoral care can be done well and in faithfulness to Christ.

Summary

In this chapter section dealing with theological reflection on a kind of openness within a pastoral relationship, which is mutual, affectionate, and free, I have taken up Jürgen Moltmann's criticism of the Aristotelian peer principle, which tends to promote an exclusivity in friendships of those who are the same. In contrast, his idea of the "open Church" is of one of the "fellowship of the friends of Jesus,"[191] who are capable of being absorbed into the passion of Christ and of suffering. This suffering is understood not only passively but also as something active, a concept Moltmann takes from the German verb *leiden*, which can be used both passively and actively. Such a capacity to suffer, held within our faith in the love of Christ for us which has no bounds, sets us free to forget ourselves and not be unduly afraid of vulnerability. Referring to the classic titles of dignity given to Jesus (prophet, priest, and king), Moltmann suggests adding a fourth title, that of friend. But he immediately qualifies this, as the word "friend" is essentially a relational concept and loses something of its meaning if used as a title. Moltmann further suggests that an understanding of friendship within the Church should not be confined to a private, intimate notion of "bosom friends" but should be

---

191. Moltmann, *Open Church*, 60.

opened up to the public realm. The realizing of such friendship cannot be regarded as a duty. It can only be achieved as a consequence of the joy people have in God, in others, and in the world, a joy which is hinged on trust in the Holy Spirit through faith in Christ.

Building on Moltmann's thought, I then referenced an essay by John Fitzgerald, which deals with the prevenient nature of Christ's openness with his disciples. In contrast to classic ways of regarding openness with others as a consequence of them having shown themselves to be trustworthy and reliable, Fitzgerald shows that Jesus, in the Johannine literature of the New Testament within the concept of love, turns things around. His revealing of himself to his disciples before and apart from them having shown themselves to be trustworthy is the basis for him calling them friends. Thus, friendship in this Jesus-like, Johannine approach is characterized by a prevenient openness which hopes and looks for mutual openness so that the relationship might flourish.

And finally, I discussed Vanessa Herrick's thoughts around the limits of vulnerability and what a kenotic model of pastoral ministry might look like. Herrick refers to the Gospel of Luke's accounts of how Jesus, at key moments of his life, showed his dependency on God his Father, the Holy Spirit and on his most intimate circle of friends. She highlights how he maintained circles of intimacy, with Peter, James, and John being those closest to him. Through the security of his relationship with God and also with his closest friends, Jesus' freedom to be vulnerable with others was enhanced. This freedom, prompted by the Holy Spirit, allowed him to respond appropriately to people, whether in openness, affection and mutuality, or otherwise.

SUMMARY OF THEOLOGICAL REFLECTION CONCERNING THE ESSENTIAL ATTRIBUTES OF FRIENDSHIP AS THEY EMERGED FROM THE RESEARCH FINDINGS

In this chapter I reflected upon the four essential elements of friendship which emerged from the data analysis and their interplay with each other described by the interviewees. This reflection involved detailed discussion of:

- a mutuality which is affectionate, free, and open, with reference to the thought of Donald Berry, taking up the work of Martin Buber, and to the theme of mutuality in the friendships and work of Dietrich Bonhoeffer, as reflected upon by Preston David Sunabacka Parsons;

- an affection which is free, open, and mutual, with reference to the work of Seward Hiltner, John Swinton, Edward Vacek, Elizabeth Telfer, C. S. Lewis, and Walter Jeanrond, who constructively takes up Aelred of Rievaulx;
- a freedom which is open, mutual, and affectionate, with reference to Dietrich Bonhoeffer, Samuel Southard, Alan Kirk, and Gilbert Meilaender; and
- an openness which is mutual, affectionate, and free, with reference to Gail O'Day, Alistair Campbell, Chloe Lynch, Jürgen Moltmann, John Fitzgerald, and Vanessa Herrick.

Using the knowledge and understanding gained from my theological reflection in this and the previous chapter, I now take on the fourth stage of the pastoral cycle in the next chapter, that of responding to the research. Once again aware that despite giving rich descriptions of experiences and sensitivities of individuals around a theme qualitative research does not claim to yield results which are scientifically generalizable, I shall attempt to find in my research elements of transformative resonance, using the term offered by Swinton and Mowat, which I consider useful and vital in approaching the questions I posed around friendship in the pastoral setting in the first chapter of this study.

5

Envisioning Revised Forms of Practice in Pastoral Friendship Within a Local Congregation

THE FOURTH STAGE OF THE PASTORAL CYCLE: RESPONDING TO THE RESEARCH

IN THE FIRST CHAPTER of this study, I described the fourth stage of the pastoral cycle, that of action or of responding to the research, as one of drawing together the various other stages of the research to produce suggestions as to how a deepening of understanding regarding the dynamics involved in a situation may be helpful in transforming it in ways which are authentic and faithful to the gospel of Christ. These suggestions are directed towards the questions I posed at the beginning of the study, and most specifically to the question I formulated there as: Could there be types of friendliness and friendship which can and should be actively sought and deepened in the ministry that ordained pastors have within their congregations? And if so, what might the dynamics of such friendliness and those of such friendships look like?

The qualitative research in this study using the hermeneutic phenomenological method has allowed us to deepen our understanding of the dynamics involved in the relationships designated as friendships by the interviewed pastors with other people in their congregations. Through my analysis in the research findings and theological reflection thereon in the previous chapters a number of themes have emerged, which I suggest will be helpful in envisioning ways in which models of pastoral friendliness and friendship which attempt to be faithful to the "plot"[1] of Christianity might be enacted and practiced by pastors within congregations without overwhelming them. Here I have considered it useful to consider under which of the forms of pastoral, congregational leadership referred to by Richard Osmer (see chapter 1) these suggestions might be most easily and effectively practiced: task competence, transactional, or transformational leadership. I have found these categories to be of help in my own reflection and work and can imagine that such a categorisation may be of help to other pastors as they consider and envision forms of pastoral friendliness and friendship within their specific setting and congregation. Improving task competence and transactional leadership qualities towards heightening the authenticity of the Church in its desire to live out relationships which are congruent with the discipleship of Christ may seem more accessible and appear less overwhelming than envisioning the "deep change" involved in a paradigm shift within a congregation or church towards which transformational leadership, as Osmer formulates it, is focused. Further, developing task competence and transactional leadership qualities may well lay the groundwork for and encourage forms of transformational leadership, which then do indeed work towards "deep change" and which prove to be fruitful and good for the Church.

Yet before I name and look at each of the emergent themes and consider through which forms of congregational leadership they might be most effectively approached, it is necessary to take up again briefly the subject of generalization and abstraction within qualitative research. We have already asked the question in chapter two about how valid it can be to look for generalizations from the results of qualitative research. How can the researcher use the findings of qualitative research within a certain situation to illuminate other contexts and situations? Swinton and Mowat, as quoted in chapter two, questioned the idea posited by Lincoln and Guba[2] that the qualitative researcher only provides thick descriptions of inquiries and has no responsibility to look for generalizations, and suggested that the terms identification and resonance would be helpful:

1. Swinton and Mowat, *Practical Theology and Qualitative Research*. 4.
2. Lincoln and Guba, *Naturalistic Enquiry*, 316.

> While the findings of qualitative research studies may not be immediately transferable to other contexts, there is a sense in which qualitative research should resonate with the experiences of others in similar circumstances. This resonance should invoke a sense of identification with those who share something of the experience.[3]

While, as they say, generalizability is not something which qualitative research in general is bound to look for, within the context of practical theology the goal of which is to be transformative in some way, in line with the challenge and message of the gospel of Christ, such "transformative resonance" means that data resulting from qualitative research frequently has implications beyond the immediacy of the research context.[4]

Furthermore, Swinton and Mowat point to the term "theoretical generalization" used, for instance, by Julius Sim,[5] which takes into account that the researcher, besides being interested in thick descriptions of experience by the people involved, also hopes that the study "will contribute to theory development with wider implications for other individuals and groups."[6] Philipp Mayring similarly suggests that moderate generalization is necessary and usually also the aim of qualitative research, and that it can be helpful as long as the results are regarded not as laws but as possible rules which may have any number of exceptions.[7]

Within this chapter, then, I will be making suggestions about how the understanding which has grown from the theological reflection of the data analysis around the question of what it could mean for pastors to have friendships within their congregations might be made fruitful for the praxis of the Church in its task of being faithful to the message and calling of Jesus Christ.

The nine themes which I suggest emerge from the theological reflection in the previous chapters and which I suggest might be fruitful for the task of responding to the research, are the following:

3. Swinton and Mowat, *Practical Theology and Qualitative Research*, 47.
4. Swinton and Mowat, *Practical Theology and Qualitative Research*, 47; in two of the qualitative studies presented in the book, such "transformative resonance" was experienced. Thus, for instance, in a study involving chaplains, during a feedback session with other chaplains, "several chaplains told us that they felt a resonance with the results of the study. That is to say, they identified with what we found and resonated with the perspectives that our study raised."
5. Sim, "Collecting and Analyzing Qualitative Data," 345–52.
6. Swinton and Mowat, *Practical Theology and Qualitative Research*, 48.
7. Mayring, "On Generalization in Qualitatively Oriented Research," 1–28.

1. Mutuality, affection, freedom, and openness, in their interplay, have been shown to be essential attributes of friendship. A growing understanding of the dynamics of these within pastor's relationships may be helpful in allowing them to build up competence in their congregational relations, without being detrimentally cautious or overconfident.

2. Pastors may learn to appreciate and welcome a mutuality of degrees, as referred to by Berry, in which a structured, pastoral relationship of friendliness with persons in the congregation may remain just that or, if mutually desired, lead to a more mysterious relation characterized by attributes of friendship.

3. Through Bonhoeffer's ideas of *Stellvertretung*, in which Christ is the mediator, and that of "mixed communities" where both mediated and unmediated relations are welcomed, pastors may learn to be more relaxed about the possibility of friendly relationships developing into friendships within their congregations, and they welcome that *Spielraum*. Indeed, through growing friendships, in certain circumstances they may themselves take on the role of *Stellvertretung* in an affectionate and faithful representation of their friends to others.

4. The encouragement of a concept of Christian love within the pastoral setting which does not rest solely on an understanding of self-sacrificial *agape* but which also and essentially includes the mutual affection of *philia* may be useful for pastors in their task of attempting to fulfill the aim of pastoral care as formulated by Alistair Campbell, "to increase love between people and between people and God" and to "help people to know love both as something to be received and as something to give."[8]

5. Pastors may take up the conviction, already formulated by Aelred in the Middle Ages, that in authentic relations inspired by the love of God in the discipleship of Christ affections may have their place, and that where they are initially lacking, they may be prayed for and hoped for. And yet pastors may also be sensibly and responsibly aware that they may freely choose whom they wish to admit to their affections.

6. Pastors are free to choose their friends and do not have a measurable duty or obligation to be friends or not be friends with people in their congregation. With this in mind, it may be helpful for them to

---

8. Campbell, *Paid to Care?*, 1.

train their conscious awareness of the use of this freedom, as such freedom works in different directions, both in choosing when and how to develop a relationship and in choosing not to.

7. The development of a heightened awareness around the presence of unspoken expectations of reciprocity and gratitude, both from pastors themselves as well as from those with whom they are in relations, may be useful. It might help pastors learn how to lead lives in tune with the Spirit of Christ, lives characterized by an authentic, open-ended form of generosity and sharing which is grounded in faith in the love of God and which seeks itself the growing, communal mutuality of *philia* love.

8. An active learning dynamic of being able to "suffer," in the sense about which Jürgen Moltmann writes, has the potential to strengthen pastors in their ministry. It might open pastors to a form of vulnerable, even "kenotic," living and being, which ultimately has a liberating effect as they develop, while entrusting themselves to the leading of the Holy Spirit, a responsible freedom to be themselves with and for others in their congregations.

9. The prevenient openness which characterized Jesus' relations with his disciples is grounded in the prevenient grace and love of God. Jesus' joy in his relation with God, through the Holy Spirit, was his motivation for both his celebration of life with his friends and his suffering for his friends. The idea of "open friendship" to which Moltmann invites both Church leaders and members of the congregation and which he regards as potentially transformative for the Church and the world can only be approached from this angle of overflowing joy through faith in Christ and not from an angle of pastoral obligation or duty. This may be encouraging for pastors, as it emphasizes the power of the Holy Spirit working through them and their faith rather than solely through their fulfillment of professional duties.

Before I turn to suggestions for working out these emergent themes within the pastoral setting in general, it is necessary to take into account the specific setting of this study in the Swiss Reformed Church and its structures for pastoral ministry. This is both necessary and useful within the framework of qualitative research, which has its focus on the specific and the particular.

THE PRAGMATIC SETTING IN THE SWISS REFORMED CHURCH

All of the pastors who participated in the interviews involved in this research study were ordained ministers (or soon to be ordained) working within the Swiss Reformed Church, and I myself am an ordained pastor ministering within that specific church. In chapter 2 I gave a short account of the context of the Swiss Reformed Church, as, regarding ecclesiology, a presbyterian-like setting. Here I want to describe a little more what that means in regard to the leadership role of pastors within a congregation and the dynamic of the relationships which are expected of them.

Each local congregation or *Kirchgemeinde* within the different cantonal Churches in Switzerland typically has a high degree of independence, although, as with most federally organized structures, the actual degree of independence varies from canton to canton. The decision-making frameworks are such that the pastor or pastors are also given a high degree of independence within their congregations with regards to their fulfillment of the everyday tasks and responsibilities of ministry. These tasks are formulated in a general manner in the *Kirchenverfassung* or Church constitution.

Within the Swiss Reformed Church in the canton of Basel-Stadt, for instance, where I myself work, the ministry expected of parish pastors is defined thus:

> § 87—The ministry of the pastors of the congregation consists in the proclamation of the Gospel according to the Holy Scriptures of the Old and New Testaments, the administration of the sacraments, pastoral care, teaching and the building up of the congregation. Through this ministry, they lead the congregation together with the other members of the Church council, the elders, in the sense of the Reformed understanding of ministry. Parish pastors are ex officio members of the Church council of their parish. . . . § 89—Parish pastors shall be elected by the parish assembly for an indefinite period.[9]

---

9. Verfassung der Evangelisch-reformierten Kirche des Kantons Basel-Stadt (November 2010), http://www.erk-bs-intern.ch/downloads/iv-a-verfassung-der-erk-bs.pdf—my own translation: "§ 87—Der Dienst der Gemeindepfarrer und Gemeindepfarrerinnen besteht in der Verkündigung des Evangeliums nach Massgabe der Heiligen Schrift des Alten und Neuen Testaments, der Verwaltung der Sakramente, der Seelsorge, dem Unterricht und dem Gemeindeaufbau. Durch diesen Dienst leiten sie die Gemeinde zusammen mit den anderen Mitgliedern des Kirchenvorstandes, den Ältesten im Sinne des reformierten Amtsverständnisses. Die Gemeindepfarrer und

Pastors are thus understood to be in a position of leadership within the congregation, together with the members of the local Church council, to which they belong ex officio, and which is a body constituted of members elected by the parish assembly. Pastors similarly are elected by the parish assembly and can also be removed by the parish assembly, should enough people with the right to vote in that assembly desire that.

Within a local congregation, in discussion with the members of the Church council, the tasks expected of the pastors are often worked out in more detail, and if there are a number of different pastors within a congregation, they commonly divide up the areas of ministry, which then allows each to lay more emphasis on a specific task, such as, for instance, work with older people, or with families and children.

The setting of the Swiss Reformed Church as an established church with its historical position in Swiss society means that a certain proportion of the population regards itself as Swiss Reformed, and by paying their annual church tax they remain members of the church even if they seldom attend any church services or take part in communal activities within the church. This means for most of the interviewed pastors that they are responsible for congregations which may have up to two thousand members, but those with whom they come into regular contact with at services or regular activities might be only five to ten percent of that large number.[10]

Regarding any expectations on relationships between a pastor or pastors and the congregation, both those in regular contact through services and activities and those not, there are no stipulations within the written rules of church governance other than that, as already noted above, of the minister's task of proclaiming the Gospel and administering the sacraments, which in the Reformed Church encompass Baptism and the Lord's Supper. Pastoral care (*Seelsorge*) is mentioned, as is teaching and the building up of the congregation (*Gemeindeaufbau*) but there are no further details as to the quality or type of relationships which may be helpful in fulfilling these tasks.

Gemeindepfarrerinnen gehören von Amtes wegen dem Kirchenvorstand ihrer Kirchgemeinde an. . . . § 89—Die Gemeindepfarrer und Gemeindepfarrerinnen werden von der Kirchgemeindeversammlung auf unbestimmte Zeit gewählt."

10. I take these numbers from a survey organized by the Swiss Reformed Church in Kanton Basel-Stadt of its members in 2017 regarding their preferences around the attendance of services and activities as well as their giving of time and finances to the Church. See: *Bericht ERK Mitgliederbefragung inkl. Executive Summary_01.12.2017.* https://www.erk-bs.ch/umfrage.

In recent years, due to the growing awareness regarding sexual abuse within the institutions of society and the scandals which have come to light in churches, for the most part in the Roman Catholic Church in Switzerland, pastors in the Swiss Reformed Church have been required to attend courses highlighting the subject and have also been required to sign a document which states their intent to be diligent in guarding against abuse both in their own behavior and in their observation of other's behavior within their congregations.[11] This is regarded as useful in helping avoid obviously unhealthy relational habits and for heightening the community's perceptive skills in regard to abusive relationships. It does not, however, address the question of how pastors might be positively formed and grow in healthy and Gospel-proclaiming relationships within their congregations.

Also, over recent years in the preparation for ordained pastoral ministry, both during studies and in the *Lernvikariat,* or time of curacy, more emphasis has been laid on character development and an awareness of one's own suitability for the ministry.[12] Students are required to undergo personality tests, which are then discussed and evaluated with mentors; the idea is to equip the individuals with a growing perception of their strengths and weaknesses in the varying fields of what ministry in the church involves. This then allows them to pay particular emphasis to skills which might be as yet underdeveloped. This seems useful in helping students realise whether they may or may not be suited for ministry in the Swiss Reformed Church. From talks I have had with students who have been through such tests, it appears to me that the emphasis seems to be more on guarding against the damage which certain people might inflict on themselves and the church if they were to be ordained into ministry, rather than how pastors might be positively formed in the dynamics of their relationships in a congregation.

Further education courses, offered and encouraged by the church for their ordained pastors, and indeed obligatory in the first five years after ordination, include courses on church development and leadership (*Gemeindeentwicklung und Leitung*) as well as those to do with education

---

11. In July 2021 my wife and I, for instance, as ordained pastors in the Swiss Reformed Church in Kanton Basel-Stadt were required to attend such a course and to sign a document 'Verhaltenskodex mit Verpflichtungserklärung zur Prävention von Grenzverletzungen und sexuellen Übergriffen' (Code of conduct with a declaration of commitment towards the prevention of boundary violations and sexual assault).

12. See: https://www.bildungkirche.ch/kirchliche-eignungsklaerung.

and spirituality (*Bildung und Spiritualität*).[13] Whereas the former focus on the learning of methods and practical techniques for church development and leadership, the latter are more focused on personal development and spiritual formation. Supervision and coaching possibilities are also offered to ordained pastors and others working in the church, and themes noted there include ones such as self-management (*Selbstmanagement*), coaching regarding the roles a pastor plays (*Rollencoaching*) and team-development (*Teamentwicklung*).[14]

It is perhaps here around these self-reflective and relational forms of education and formation encouraged by the Swiss Reformed Church that we come closest to the subject of this study. And yet, as noted in chapter 1, in the many years I have worked in the Swiss Reformed Church, I have not come across a course which deliberately takes up looking at the dynamics of friendship within the ordained ministry. Similarly, none of the interviewees in this study, neither those who have been in the ministry for a long time nor those who were recently ordained, mentioned having been part of a course organized by the Swiss Reformed Church where they had been led to think consciously about friendship in the church or about their calling and competence as pastors in this regard. Although I did not ask any questions specifically regarding such courses, a number of the interviewees expressed their surprise to me after the interviews that they had never thought about or reflected on the dynamics of friendship within their work. Given the intuitive importance of the topic and the degree of self-reflection which is demanded of professional pastors in many spheres of their ministry within such an established church, it does indeed remain surprising to me that the subject has been given so little attention. That this is the case was, however, one of the reasons which led me to work on this study and to attempt to gain understanding around the subject. And it is this gaining of understanding which leads me now to the formulation of possible fruitful themes for revised forms of practice in response to the research in this study around friendship in the pastoral setting.

---

13. See: https://www.bildungkirche.ch/kurse.
14. See: https://www.bildungkirche.ch/supervision-und-coaching.

FRUITFUL THEMES FOR REVISED FORMS OF PRACTICE AROUND FRIENDSHIP IN THE PASTORAL SETTING

In summing up the task of responding to research done in practical theology, Richard Osmer writes that it involves, "taking risks on behalf of the congregation to help it better embody its mission as a sign and witness of God's self-giving love."[15] The following themes which I suggest emerge from the analysis of the interviews and theological reflection in this qualitative research study can perhaps be seen as helpful in thoughtfully and hopefully fruitfully approaching "taking risks on behalf of the congregation" around the subject of friendliness and friendship in the pastoral setting within an ordained ministry. And if they, being applied, can help pastors to encourage their congregation "to better embody its mission as a sign and witness of God's self-giving love," while remaining faithful to the "plot" of Christianity, then they will indeed have been fruitful.

Seeking for Growth in Understanding Around the Dynamics of Friendship

As I have shown in this study through my data analysis of the interviews, the interplay of four attributes of relations the participating pastors designated as friendship have been seen to be essential. These are the ones on which I have reflected theologically in detail in the previous chapter, namely, mutuality, affection, freedom, and openness. As I pointed out in the previous chapter section concerning the specific, practical setting of this study within the Swiss Reformed Church, a number of the participating pastors expressed to me that they had not previously formally reflected upon friendship or its attributes and dynamics within their ministry. This has to do, perhaps, with the main emphasis which educatory programs in the Church have given to methods and techniques for "doing" pastoral work rather than understanding around "being" a pastor. Edward Zaragoza points this out while relating his basic assumptions for his thought in his book *No Longer Servants, but Friends*:

> (A further) basic assumption is that pastoral identity and practise are fundamentally relational and not simply functional. As such, any paradigm for ordained ministry must acknowledge

---

15. Osmer, *Practical Theology*, 29.

and involve a theology of who the pastor is (the pastor's "being") and not just a theology about what the pastor does (the pastors "doing"). However, it has been the functional "doing" side of pastors that has captured the attention of readers and therefore the interest of most writers.[16]

Yet, the idea of learning methods and techniques for how to "do" friendship for pastoral goals is something that I assume most pastors would find appalling. And well they might. For the very core of what they intuitively understand and celebrate as friendship has to do with mutuality and authentic, personal openness, which I have shown to be two of the essential attributes of friendship as described by the interviewees, and these cannot, with any integrity, be reduced to functions towards some higher goal which the pastor might have. Such a manipulative and functional understanding of friendship in the pastoral setting seems to me to be more a temptation towards the accumulation of influence and leverage in evangelisation and, perhaps, some base desire for power or for "being liked" than anything a pastor should want to aim towards. Andrew Root, professor for youth ministry and practical theology at Luther Seminary St. Paul, points this out in his instructive book *The Relational Pastor*:

> There is no means to an end in friendship because it is about persons, and personal relationships exist only for themselves. If I say, "I thought he was my friend but really all he wanted to do was sell me car insurance" we understand this as a violation. Friendship . . . has no functional end. The point is not an interest; the point is to be with and for, to share in the life of the other. "Friendship evangelism" which seeks to use friendship for the sake of meeting the interest of conversions, violates the personal; it ignores personhood.[17]

Nevertheless, while rejecting any concept of learning to "do" friendship for ulterior motives within the pastoral setting, a growing understanding of the dynamics of friendship within pastors' relationships in their congregations may be helpful for them in their learning of how to "be" pastors. Learning to differentiate the essential attributes of friendship and their interplay and the qualities associated with friendliness within pastors' congregational relations may allow them to understand better the intuitions and forces at work in those relationships, which may

---

16. Zaragoza, *No Longer Servants, but Friends*, 18.
17. Root, *Relational Pastor*, 65–66.

in turn allow them to act and react more suitably and competently within their ministry.

Put in terms of Osmer's pastoral leadership forms, which I have found helpful, this growing understanding around the dynamics of friendship might perhaps be best understood as a growth in task competence, in so far as the task is seen to be the development of relational understanding and not misunderstood as the actual making of friends. Whether or not and with whom a pastor wishes to build a friendship, to "be with and for, to share in the life of the other" as Root puts it, is not the issue at hand here. Rather, the competence which might be learned is one of differentiation and a growing perception of the dynamics of friendliness (benevolence, closeness, equality, faithfulness and hospitality) and of friendship (mutuality, affection, freedom and openness) or lack of them, involved in a relationship. The gain involved in such competence has to do with allowing pastors to be more comfortable within a variety of relationships in their congregations without being detrimentally cautious towards the way people wish to relate to them or overconfident and naïve in their assumptions about what is happening within an encounter.

Having suggested that a first part of the response to the research emerging from the findings of this study will have to do with a growing understanding of the dynamics around friendliness and the essential attributes of friendship, I now turn to a further eight suggestions which can also be seen as aspects of the task of responding to the research. Each of these has emerged from my theological reflection concentrated around the four essential attributes of friendship, with two concerning mutuality, two concerning affection, two concerning freedom, and two concerning openness, although as has been seen to be the case throughout this study, these attributes are almost inextricably interwoven with each other and my reflection on the elements of friendliness will also play a role.

Welcoming a Mutuality of Degrees

In the previous chapter I took up Donald Berry's differentiation of what he saw as Martin Buber's too polarised view of the fullness of mutuality in an "I-thou" encounter between two wholly independent individuals and its normative limitation within a task-oriented encounter, such as that of the pastor-parishioner. Berry pointed out, I think appropriately, that within most helping relationships, where one of the persons involved has a task within that relationship, although there will be a one-sidedness present, as long as each of the persons accepts and welcomes the other as a "whole" person in their psycho-physical unity, a nuanced and complicated but real form of mutuality can be present. According to Berry, the welcoming of this mutuality of degrees may make a positive difference in the quality of the relationship. Even though the relationship may be a structured one, i.e. one involving a task or role, a degree of mutuality is possible and may lead the way towards a deepening of a relationship.

Berry's differentiation between relationship and relation is useful and indeed pragmatic. As noted relationship is the place where the one-sidedness of a helping encounter is defined by the "assertion of need and the arrangement to respond to that need: structure." Relation, however, is a more mysterious place, which "points radically to the context of freedom" and which in its mutuality "is a response to the grace of being met."[18] It is here that Berry describes what he calls "a kind of reverence"[19] in an encounter when a structured relationship, such as pastors may have with a member of their congregation, is approached with an opening and welcoming attitude, which does not at the outset assume that no form or degree of mutuality will be possible. Within this attitude of "a kind of reverence" pastors may then learn to appreciate and welcome a mutuality of degrees, without feeling threatened or imposed upon. The relationship may well remain a structured one marked by the benevolence of pastoral friendliness and the distance and integrity such a structure preserves, even if there may be moments of closeness as offered situational companionship. Indeed, it is that distance and integrity which in turn may be the vehicle which allows a relationship, in all freedom, to gradually become more of a mysterious relation.

Perhaps Gordon Lynch's formulation of what he calls "moderated friendship" could be understood in a similar fashion to a mutuality of degrees, albeit with a more clearly set limit to it.[20] Using Aristotelian terminology, Lynch describes the pastoral relationship as one which, in his estimation, cannot be a friendship amongst equals, or we could say, using Berry's language, where fulness of mutuality cannot be given. Nevertheless, a form of "mutual regard" in a "moderated friendship" is possible and desirable, where the pastoral worker

18. Berry, *Mutuality*, 66.
19. Berry, *Mutuality*, 67.
20. Lynch, *Pastoral Care and Counselling*, 78–79.

gives emotional, practical and spiritual support to those for whom they care, in a way that they would not normally expect to receive in return from them. A person receiving pastoral care can demonstrate regard for the pastoral carer through valuing the carer's individuality and through a willingness not to make unreasonable or abusive demands upon the carer's energy. A pastoral relationship thus functions as a "moderated friendship" when it involves both a mutual regard between carer and care-seeker and the maintenance of appropriate boundaries within the relationship.[21]

A form or degree of mutuality within a pastor-parishioner relationship is thus also welcomed in Lynch's model, and it is, interestingly, this form of mutuality which allows him to use the phrase "moderated friendship" for his concept. His idea of "moderated friendship" however is more limited than that of Berry's mutuality of degrees as he does not entertain the idea of the pastoral relationship possibly moving from a structured relationship into a mysterious realm of relation. Indeed, he sees even a "moderated friendship" as under threat from those who might abuse the time and energy of the pastoral worker, and he recommends that pastors think carefully about how to work with "expectations, demands or attitudes from care-seekers (which) are unreasonable, excessive or unhealthy."[22] Combining the insights of Berry and Lynch, the welcoming of a mutuality of degrees might thus enable pastors to allow forms of mutuality to develop in their structured relationships, even to the point (to use Berry's language) at which relationship starts turning into relation, while simultaneously being aware of the very real potential for others to exploit their time and emotional energy.

Once again, this welcoming of a mutuality of degrees, which I suggest is good and useful, might, in terms of Osmer's pastoral leadership forms, be regarded as a development of task competence, for it encourages a wide field of authentic and potentially deep encounter. And yet it is also close to transactional leadership, which is based on the capacity of a pastor to work constructively with forms of mutual exchange. Learning to perceive and welcome degrees of mutuality could thus strengthen the pastor's ability for such transactional leadership. Finally, allowing and welcoming varying forms and degrees of mutuality in pastoral encounters and care may even be a form of transformational leadership involving "deep

---

21. Lynch, *Pastoral Care and Counselling*, 79.
22. Lynch, *Pastoral Care and Counselling*, 80.

Enjoying the *Stellvertretung* of Christ and the *Spielraum* for Friendship in "Mixed Communities"

The next suggested theme within the task of responding in the context of this study takes up my theological reflection around Dietrich Bonhoeffer's thought and life with reference to the dissertation by Preston David Sunabacka Parsons *A Friendship for Others: Bonhoeffer and Bethge on the theology and practice of friendship*. As I noted there, Parsons understands Bonhoeffer's thought on *Stellvertretung* as referring to the mediation of Christ in a twofold manner. First, on a soteriological level, through Christ's accomplished *Stellvertretung* in his death and resurrection, where he stands in for the world that God loves and wishes to redeem. And second, through his ongoing *Stellvertretung* in the form of a mediating spiritual presence within the body of Christ and the encounters amongst humans which take place there in the present. This Bonhoeffer understands in a manner that is well aware of the broken and disintegrating condition of much Christian community in the present, where believers still encounter each other as strangers and in many ways alien and yet where an "eschatological foretaste of sanctification" can occur and the other can be recognized and received as in Christ.[23] Christian community then has a dimension to it, in Bonhoeffer's approach, which has the potential, as one in which the mediation of the Spirit of Christ can occur, to rise above what is "normal" or what merely belongs to self-centred or emotional community. Having stated this potential, Bonhoeffer does not however reject or abrogate "normal" relations amongst people, among which he understands those including marriage, family, and friendships. Indeed, he thinks that healthy communities will be what he terms "mixed communities," where both relationships mediated by the Spirit of Christ and unmediated relationships, such as those of "normal" friendship, are accepted.

It is also here that the idea of a *Spielraum* or room to play, comes into play. Within the given structure of the social mandates which Bonhoeffer upholds, those of marriage and family (*Ehe*), work (*Arbeit*), government and civic life (*Obrigkeit*), and Church (*Kirche*), he understands the

---

23. Parsons, *Friendship for Others*, 36.

Church in particular as a place where a certain freedom may be enjoyed in areas such as art, education, play and, importantly for the context of this study, friendship. And as I wrote in the previous chapter, for pastors such a concept might be helpful in opening up the possibility of understanding mutual and free friendships within their congregations not only as threatening and difficult for the social order in the Church, but as an outworking of a healthy *Spielraum*, which helps guard against an all too rigid and stifling atmosphere of dutifulness.

I have entitled my suggested theme here as enjoying the *Stellvertretung* of Christ and the *Spielraum* for friendship in "mixed communities." I think the use of the verb *to enjoy* here is both suitable and thought provoking. In the language of the Westminster Shorter Catechism, to which I have already referred and which is a text of importance for Reformed theology, the chief end of humankind is "to glorify God, and to enjoy him for ever."[24] Within the context of Christ's work of redemption, his standing in for humankind through his death and resurrection and its consequences regarding communal relations within the Church and into eternity, I find the concept of enjoying God vital, and it is this enjoyment to which Moltmann also refers, as quoted earlier in this study. The idea of coming to enjoy the room given for relations of friendship within the body of Christ because the Spirit of Christ is present and mediating could be something which gives a new lease of life to pastors who may be caught between the sometimes stifling atmosphere of dutifulness and fear that they will exploited by members of their congregation imposing themselves on them. Perhaps through the lens of enjoying God pastors might learn to be more relaxed about the possibility of friendships within their congregations and welcome that room to play, the *Spielraum*, which is available to them through faith that the Spirit of Christ is already at work and is already mediating the friendship of God in Christ towards each member of the congregation. Indeed, through growing friendships in the communal enjoyment of God they may themselves, in certain circumstances, assist in the work of the Spirit of Christ and take the role of one who becomes a *Stellvertretung* in an affectionate and faithful representation of their friends to others.

In regard to forms of pastoral leadership, fostering a spirit of enjoying God together based on faith in the *Stellvertretung* of Christ and the presence of his Spirit in the congregation could be regarded as task

---

24. The Westminster Shorter Catechism; Question 1. https://www.westminsterconfession.org/resources/confessional-standards/the-westminster-shorter-catechism/.

competence, where pastors develop skills in recognizing when that enjoyment is being eclipsed by other elements and can help people to refocus their gaze on Christ. But it could also be understood as transformational leadership, where pastors can embody the enjoyment of God and open up for themselves and their congregations room to play, where friendships can freely blossom, but do not have to, in a mixed community of both spiritual and "normal" friendships. With such pastoral leadership, perhaps something along the lines of the "deep change" to which Osmer refers in the context of transformational leadership might start to happen in the realm of congregational relations.

Encouraging a Concept of Love Which Includes the Mutual Affection of *Philia*

The fourth theme I suggest in regard to possible revised forms of practice as a response to the research in this study is the encouragement of a concept of Christian love within the pastoral setting which does not rest on an understanding of self-sacrificial *agape* alone, but which essentially includes the mutual affection of *philia*. The interviewees, in describing their feelings around their friendships, often used language of "being" rather than "doing." This is summed up well, for instance, by Beat who in characterizing friendship talked of "loving to be together." I think most people might see friendship as a form of love, yet it is not that form of love they think about in regard to the love to which Christians are called. Within the categories of love, it is my experience in asking people to describe Christian love that they invariably respond with a description of a "doing" love, usually involving a certain amount of self-sacrifice. As I have said throughout this study, this is the form of love most often associated with *agape*. It is love which is willing to give up its very self for the loved one, and it is the form of love most often praised by Christian authors. And as Vacek correctly writes:

> When the Church thinks of saints, it thinks mostly of those who sacrifice themselves and not of those who nourish friendships . . . Theologians who reflect on love commonly emphasize those New Testament texts that highlight *agape*. They skip over the many texts that emphasize interpersonal relationships. They may say that covenant and community are central. But when they describe love, they focus on the kind of love one selflessly

offers to enemies, or strangers, or universal humanity. In a word, communal life is neglected.[25]

The love of *philia*, the mutual love which fosters and thrives in communal life, can perhaps best be described as a "being" love. It is that love which will love to do things for the loved one, but with the goal of their mutual and communal love being enhanced. It is the love perhaps signposted by Alistair Campbell in his formulation of the aim of pastoral care, "to increase love between people and between people and God" and to "help people to know love both as something to be received and as something to give."[26] Yet it is a difficult love to attain, for in its inherent mutuality, one is dependent on the other. With both *agape* and *eros* love, I can love even if the other does not love me, and yet *philia* only "works" if the love is mutual and focused towards that communal togetherness.

What I have entitled the encouragement of a concept of love which includes the mutual affection of *philia* is perhaps primarily directed at pastors who work in established churches such as the Swiss Reformed Church, where an individual's piety is, on the whole, their own concern and the ethical imperative to love one's neighbor is seen as a call to do good for others, but not generally understood as a call to communal togetherness.[27] Thus the encouragement of such a concept might involve renewed teaching by pastors that learning to take part regularly in a worship service and drink coffee or tea and talk to other members of the church afterwards or be part of a weekly bible study, prayer group, or house group with others, in other words practicing communal relationships by being with others, can well be understood as learning a form of Christian love, *philia*, and not just as an exercise directed towards the advancement of one's own relationship with God. Taking part in such activities is then not just a question of what spiritual or other advantage

---

25. Vacek, *Love, Human and Divine*, 280.
26. Campbell, *Paid to Care?*, 1.
27. Interestingly, the report at the end of the survey of its members done by the Swiss Reformed Church in Kanton Basel-Stadt in 2017 regarding their preferences around the attendance of services and activities as well as their giving of time and finances to the church, suggested that for the maintenance of healthy congregations more emphasis needed to be given to communal togetherness. The main reason given was because although the church still had a large number of members who paid their church tax but did not wish to take part in communal worship or activities, those were mainly older people and the younger generations who were still members of the church were more interested in being invested in feeling part of a community and being involved in that community. See ERK Basel-Stadt, *Bericht*, 31–33.

a person can get out of it, nor just a question of self-sacrificial giving of time and energy for others, but much more a question of what can happen when the communal love involved in "being" together within the congregation develops and grows. Such growth in communal love may not immediately mean that the congregation understands itself as one big group of friends, but it might be a space where an appreciation for each other can develop, where Christian hospitality which is welcoming and seeks the good of the other in an honest and open encounter with them can be exercised both by pastors and by others in the congregation.

Regarding the form of pastoral leadership involved in this theme of the recovery of the mutual affection of *philia* as a form of Christian love, it will possibly involve all three forms proposed by Osmer, namely task competence, and also transactional and transformational leadership. In the area of task competence, the ability to teach and preach well and to advance in exegetical and theological skill in expounding the biblical witness around Christian love might be important. Transactional leadership may be helpful where priorities need to be adjusted within the congregation to allow for a growing focus on the encouragement of communal togetherness as love. Finally, if within a congregation's exercise of Christian love the communal love of *philia* has long been neglected, transformational leadership may be needed; the pastor might be called to embody that love in a special way to encourage and facilitate the "deep change" necessary to allow the community to be faithful to its calling as part of the body of Christ.

Learning to Pray and Hope for Authentic Affection Inspired by the Love of God

The previous theme regarding the encouragement of the inclusion of a *philia* form of love as desirable and indeed necessary in a concept of Christian love within a congregation may, in theory, resonate with many pastors, as they see the need to strengthen communal togetherness. And yet one of the outworkings of *philia* love has to do with mutual affection, something which, as, for instance Clare talked about in her interview, is not something easy to understand or control, as the reasons we feel affection for some and not for others are foggy, to say the least. In the previous chapter I took up Walter Jeanrond's thought around Aelred of Rievaulx, who regarded affection, along with reason, as necessary elements of love.

Aware of human limitations regarding affection for others in the here and now, he nevertheless understood affection as an important goal of a Christian's exercise of love.

My suggestion is therefore that pastors take up the conviction, long ago formulated by Aelred, that in authentic relations inspired by the love of God in the discipleship of Christ affections may indeed have their place. Where such affection is initially lacking—and that may be in any number of relationships the pastor has within the congregation—it may be prayed and hoped for in faith in the power of God's love. This does not mean that pastors must attempt to become heroic individuals by trying to force themselves to like everyone, something which no one with integrity can even pretend to do. But it does mean that they should be open to the working of God's love which, Aelred reminds us, is a love directed towards friendship and a mutually affectionate relation. Learning to pray and hope for the shared fruit of authentic affection within relationships in their congregation may also help to heighten pastors' awareness of the many and varied causes of them liking or disliking others.

Such heightened awareness, I suggest, is an aspect of growth in task competence within pastoral leadership as pastors learn to reflect on their motivations regarding their likes and dislikes of members of their congregation. In a parallel manner to that mentioned above, this should not lead pastors to attempt to become heroic individuals of introspection. The aim is more, in faith in God's affection for them, to grow in character and knowledge of themselves, which may lead to a more relaxed, confident, and wiser way of approaching and interacting with others. To be sensibly and responsibly aware that they as pastors may freely choose whom they wish to admit to their affections while at the same time praying and hoping for God's friendship love to be at work in their relations is also an aspect of growth in pastors' task competence. This leads us to the next theme of freedom in which pastors may train themselves regarding friendships within their congregations.

Training an Awareness of Freedom in the Development of Relations

The theme of this sixth suggestion for revised practice in the Church emerging from this study is centred around training oneself in an awareness of freedom in the development of pastoral relations. While taking into account the themes I have already suggested above, it remains pivotal that while ordained pastors have various stipulated obligations and duties within their congregations, which they may or may not be paid to fulfil, they do not and cannot be obliged to be friends, or not be friends, with people in their congregation. As I wrote in my theological reflection around freedom, pastors remain free to choose their friends and the relations they wish to develop as friendships. This is crucial, for only thus can the essential attribute of freedom, which has emerged from the data analysis of this study, be maintained. I suggest that it is important for the integrity and wellbeing of pastors to take hold of this freedom, choosing to develop or not to develop relationships.

For pastors to train their conscious awareness of the use of their freedom may be a useful skill, as such freedom works in different directions, both in choosing when and how to develop a relationship or choosing not to. In this regard, Southard spoke of "special" choices which counsellors make in gradually investing more time and energy into relations with certain people. Such choices are taken continually and iteratively within the everyday course of pastoral relationships whether they are done intuitively or more consciously and deliberately. The suggestion here is that the conscious awareness of the freedom that pastors have be trained and heightened within such choices. Pastors can train themselves, as part of their task competence in leadership, to become more conscious of their choices and the reasons they make them, while realizing that their choices are only a part of those made while a relationship is developing, for the choices made by the other person or persons are also important and constitutive for the relationship, whether or not they lead to a relation involving attributes of friendship. Within the framework of the freedom they have, it might be helpful for pastors to learn neither to overestimate or underestimate the effect of their choices regarding time and energy on the others involved in the realm of encouraging friendship. Although in the end the way in which other people understand or misunderstand the words and actions of a pastor and react to them is up to them and is part of their freedom, it is also possible for pastors to train themselves in a realistic perception of how those words or actions may come across to the specific people to whom they are relating. This leads us to the next theme within the task of responding to the research, namely the awareness of expectations of reciprocity and gratitude either from pastors themselves or from those to whom they are relating.

Developing Generosity While Being Aware of Expectations of Reciprocity and Gratitude

In the previous chapter I addressed research concerning forms of reciprocity and posited that the terms suggested by Marshall Sahlins and quoted by Alan Kirk, of general, balanced and negative reciprocity,[28] or as Natalie Zemon Davis expressed them as "gift, sale and coercion,"[29] could be of use within pastoral relationships in the context of this study. "Coercion" in this setting would be close to abuse, either emotionally or sexually, and is something pastors should avoid at all costs. "Sale," or balanced reciprocity, perhaps best describes the professional, pastoral counselling situation in which the structure of the relationship is one of clear tasks and boundaries, with set time limits and the "sale" of pastoral and spiritual expertise which should be helpful for the client. Although I am sure many pastors would refrain from using the language of commerce to describe their professional ministry, this is a form of reciprocity in which (as emerged from the analysis of the interviews in this study) much valuable pastoral work is done and in which pastors feel comfortable. Yet the impetus towards something more than just the selling of one's professional expertise within the vocation of a Christian pastor was something all the interviewees both felt and communicated.

The language of grace, which is central and vital to the Gospel and to the discipleship of Christ, sits much better with the reciprocal form of the "gift" (or general reciprocity in Sahlin's terms) than it does with a purely balanced form. The "gift" is an open-ended, generously sharing form of reciprocity within which there is no obvious or overt form of accounting, and in terms of relationships it is most often brought into the context of friendship where through the mutual trust which is present friends do things for each other without immediate expectation of something in return. Yet within friendship and within the "gift" form of reciprocity there remains an implicit expectation that at some time something will be returned by the other, be that gratitude or affection or something more tangible. In friendship this makes sense as it is built on mutuality, which by its very definition involves give and take.

Regarding the task of responding to the research in the context of this study, I suggest that pastors will do well, as part of their task competence, to develop a heightened awareness around the presence of unspoken

---

28. Kirk, *Love Your Enemies*, 675; Sahlins, *Stone Age Economics*, 198.
29. Davis, *Gift in Sixteenth-Century France*, 129.

expectations of reciprocity and gratitude. This applies both to themselves and their expectations as well as to those with whom they are in relations. When pastors do, for instance, choose to spend more time and energy in certain relationships they may need to learn to make conscious to themselves what their motives are and what they expect from those relationships, and indeed to what degree they might be disappointed if the other person does not respond in the manner desired. Similarly, they might learn to try and perceive in which direction other people's expectations of them are moving as those others wish to spend more time with them and as far as possible make their thoughts regarding such expectations transparent. This may sound calculating and perhaps inhibiting for the building of relations. It does not have to be. There is a fine line between being responsibly aware of one's own desires and expectations and astute to those of others on the one hand and on the other being inauthentic and cynically suspicious in one's dealings with others.

There may be a tension, but there is not necessarily a contradiction in the suggestion that pastors may be learning to grow ever more astute and perceptive to the often undefined and unspoken expectations involved in human relations and wise in their dealings with them, and yet also be learning how to lead lives in tune with the Spirit of Christ. Such lives are characterized by an authentic, open-ended form of generosity in the sharing of their time and energy, which is grounded in faith in the love of God and itself seeks a growing, communal mutuality with others which exhibits the attributes of friendship.

It is, perhaps, most of all this tension to which the theologian and lecturer in pastoral studies Margaret Whipp is referring when she talks about the "lure of the friendship model":

> One of the great temptations . . . in the pastoral relationship. . . is to treat it as if it were a friendship. The lure of this model is understandable given the warmth of trust and intimacy in a good pastoral relationship . . . It is not unusual for pastoral relationships to involve some degree of shared human experience, and it is also quite common for pastoral contacts to take place in relaxed and informal settings. For these reasons, it can be easy for the minister to slip into the easy expectations of mutual friendship, forgetting the distinctive character and responsibility that comes with the pastoral role. . . . It is in the grey areas of

pastoral intimacy that the pastor needs to hold together both a warm heart and a clear head.[30]

Perhaps pastors practicing keeping "a warm heart" in their generous sharing of their faith in the community and in their relationship building and them learning continually better what having "a clear head" around the often messy expectations in human relations might mean will help that they do not fall foul to the "lure" of a friendship model. The development of skill in this area can help pastors develop a robust and healthy form of pastoral relations which is competently aware of the tensions without being afraid of forms of friendship.

Becoming Better at Being Able to "Suffer" People

The last two themes I suggest in response to the research findings have to do with the essential attribute of friendship which I have titled "openness." In the previous chapter I showed how Jürgen Moltmann emphasized an orientation to Christ's acceptance of us as the way to a new attitude of openness with each other, a new attitude which helps us to see others as they are, gain a longing for them, and which is characterized by an ability to suffer, for that is the way Christ has accepted us. Moltmann's use of the word to "suffer" is helpful here, as his use of the word has overtones of the German word *leiden* and shows that it is not just a passive verb but has an active element which points to the power to go outside of oneself and affect the other. In so doing, such a form of suffering with the other is a condition for love. He writes, "One who is not empowered with suffering is not able to love, and vice versa."[31]

An active learning dynamic of being able to "suffer," in Moltmann's sense, in pastoral ministry can be seen both as a growth in task competence and as transformational leadership. Regarding task competence, the growing ability to be empowered to "suffer" people may have the potential to strengthen pastors in their ministry as it becomes ever clearer that a certain type of "suffering" will necessarily belong to a Christian pastor's relations with others in so far as they are willing to love them. Pastors can perhaps learn from their "suffering" of those with whom they interact in their congregations, particularly when there are tensions and when they feel hurt, not to understand themselves so much as passive victims who

---

30. Whipp, *SCM Studyguide Pastoral Theology*, 146–47.
31. Moltmann, *Open Church*, 16.

must stoically clench their teeth and bear the pain but as people actively called to accept each other as Christ has accepted us. This in turn may help to open pastors to a form of vulnerable, even "kenotic" pastoral practice, as formulated by Vanessa Herrick in her booklet *Limits of Vulnerability: Exploring a kenotic model for pastoral ministry* (see previous chapter). Such practice might ultimately have a liberating effect for pastors engaging with it as they develop a responsible freedom to be themselves in an authentic manner with and for others in their congregations while actively entrusting themselves to the leading of the Holy Spirit.

Should pastors, having gained such task competence, be willing and able to embody such a freedom and openness with members of their congregation in the knowledge that this will involve the "suffering" in love of each other as members together in the body of Christ, then that might lead to a form of transformational leadership. It would involve the "deep change" Osmer writes about in congregations who might intuitively shy away from what they might perceive as too much openness and indeed from the idea of having to "suffer" others within the church. Pastors embodying such "deep change" would be "taking risks on behalf of the congregation" and it would be left to their freedom and wisdom, in consultation with their congregations, to discern whether and in what circumstances such risks might be good to take to help the congregation "better embody its mission as a sign and witness of God's self-giving love."[32] For it to endure, the paradigm shift would need to be freely embodied by the pastor and would encourage congregational change and a growth in the communal enjoyment of mutual *philia* love, while learning to be robust in "suffering" each other. This leads to the last of my suggestions.

Celebrating Together an Overflowing Joy of Belonging to Christ

The last theme that I want to suggest in response to the research findings has to do with a communal celebrating of faith in Christ which together with the ability to "suffer" people noted in the previous theme is the basis for Moltmann's vision of "open friendship" in the Church. As we saw in my theological reflection on the data analysis of the interviews engaging with Moltmann and John Fitzgerald, a prevenient openness characterized Jesus' relations with his disciples, and this was grounded in his confidence

---

32. Osmer, *Practical Theology*, 29.

in the prevenient grace and love of God. This confidence and joy in Jesus' relation with God, through the Holy Spirit, was his motivation for both celebrating life with his friends and suffering for his friends. This same joy that Jesus had is the driving factor in friendships which are open in the way that Moltmann envisions that. The messianic celebratory lifestyle which he commends depends utterly on trust in the Holy Spirit and an overflowing of hope as formulated by Paul in Romans 15:13.[33] Moreover, the requisite openness derives from the ability to "suffer" people, which is understood as an active as well as passive power.

The idea of "open friendship" to which Moltmann invites both church leaders and members of the congregation and which he regards as potentially transformative for the Church and the world can only be approached from this angle of overflowing joy through faith in Christ and not from that of pastoral obligation or duty. Recall his words, that

> It ("open friendship") does not "have to" happen at all. It happens wherever men and women are seized by joy in God, in people, and in the world.... It is not by sympathising with others but by rejoicing with them that they will be won.[34]

Such "open friendship" cannot itself become a task or duty for pastors to fulfil. And although that seems to make it less accessible, however desirable it might be seen to be, it may also be encouraging for pastors as it emphasizes the power of the Holy Spirit working through them and their faith rather than depending solely on their ability to fulfill their professional duties. However, I would suggest that it is "rejoicing with" others, or celebrating together an overflowing joy of belonging to Christ, that is an integral part of such leadership. Once again, the forms of leadership useful here could be seen to be task competence and transformational leadership.

Moltmann regards the nurturing of open friendships inspired by the overflow of hope and joy people experience in their faith in Christ as potentially transformative for the Church. In this regard pastors who embody such an overflow of hope and joy will be exercising transformational leadership by the very fact of them doing so. For pastors to be learning how to rejoice and celebrate their faith in Christ with others could in one sense be understood as task competence. But this does not seem quite appropriate. Perhaps it is more fitting to suggest that they be encouraged

---

33. Rom 15:13 (NEB): "and may the God of hope fill you with all joy and peace by your faith in him, until, by the power of the Holy Spirit, you overflow with hope."

34. Moltmann, *Open Church*, 62–63.

to take the time and space to nurture their spiritual health and realise the priority that they should give this aspect of their growth and health. Expecting themselves to exude joy and hope in Christ in their congregations, when they may only feel tired and empty, will probably not work.

This underscores, perhaps, how intertwined are the various themes I have suggested in the context of responding to the research, and how they may be approached as a gradual deepening and building of competence regarding an awareness of the various attributes of friendship and what encouraging them to blossom might mean. When pastors approach such efforts, they will be aware of their own limits and of what they believe themselves to be capable. Regarding the acquisition of task competence for pastoral leadership, Osmer notes how important humility is for this. This will show itself in two areas, first in pastors addressing the concrete needs of a congregation and not just following their own whims or desires, and second in relying on others when they become aware of their own limitations in a specific competency or field.[35]

It may belong to the humility of a pastor's task competence to learn to give others in the congregation space to give witness to the joy of belonging to Christ in times when they themselves find it difficult to exude joy and hope. Part of the communal celebration is after all experiencing joy overflowing within the community and this then works towards the building up and strengthening of others. Although pastors have a special responsibility within a congregation, they alone will not be able to create the conditions for the hope and joy of faith in Christ and belonging to God to overflow and enable the flourishing of relations which exhibit the attributes of friendship. As noted before, the very character of *philia* love is that it is based on mutual affection, freedom, and openness and that it thus cannot be guaranteed or created by one party alone, no matter how competent.

FURTHER THOUGHTS AROUND THE TASK OF RESPONDING TO THE RESEARCH IN THIS STUDY

At the beginning of this chapter, I recalled the questions I posed at the beginning of my study: Could there be types of friendliness and friendship which can and should be actively sought after and deepened in the ministry that ordained pastors have within their congregations? And if so, what might the dynamics of such friendliness and such friendships

---

35. Osmer, *Practical Theology*, 193–94.

look like? In response to these questions, it seemed important to me that pastors might see realistic ways of doing this without feeling constantly overwhelmed. In this chapter, I have formulated suggestions for possible revised forms of practice of pastoral friendliness and friendship within a local congregation. These have emerged from my theological reflection on the data analysis of the interviews using the hermeneutic phenomenological method in qualitative research. With each of these suggestions I have considered what type of pastoral leadership (Osmer) could be considered helpful in approaching them.

Although the vision of congregations in which the essential attributes of friendship might be embodied and at work would in many cases involve the "deep change" about which Osmer writes, and indeed a paradigm shift in the way the congregation might function, I have tried to avoid suggesting that transformational leadership is in all cases the best way forward. Although Osmer considers transformational leadership to be most necessary in mainline denominations,[36] it is a risky business and one which may involve prolonged conflict with any number of parties within a congregation as the pastor attempts to take as many people as possible with them on the voyage towards the envisioned transformed community. Pastors will need to ask themselves whether such a voyage is the best way forward within their specific congregations, whether they feel a calling to do this, and whether they have the necessary resources to undertake such a transformational journey without being overwhelmed by the task.

In most of the themes I have formulated here as possible revised forms of practice in pastoral friendship, I have attempted to place greater emphasis on suggestions of growth in pastoral task competence, or occasionally in transactional leadership, than on transforming leadership. Such development of awareness and skills concerning the dynamics of friendliness and the essential attributes of friendship seems to me at least initially to be more accessible and helpful for pastors than a call to a paradigm shift in their work. And perhaps some of the suggestions from the findings of this qualitative research may resonate with pastors in their attempts to be faithful to their calling to serve Christ and their congregations in a way which may in the end lead them to a form of transforming leadership which is both fruitful and sustainable.

---

36. Osmer, *Practical Theology*, 196.

6

Summary and Closing Thoughts

IN THIS FINAL CHAPTER I briefly recall the purpose of the research and the questions that motivated it along with a brief summary of the findings and an overview of the key contributions of this study. I shall also discuss briefly the limitations of this project and reflect on its implications with a view to future research and practice. I have suggested in the previous chapter that the findings of this research may have something relevant and important to say to the wider discussion on friendships that pastors might have in their congregations, and I shall conclude this chapter with some personal reflections.

PURPOSE OF THE RESEARCH AND A BRIEF SUMMARY OF THE FINDINGS

This research project was motivated by a desire to understand more clearly the phenomenon of friendship within a pastoral setting of a local congregation and how ordained pastors describe their experiences of such relationships which they designate as friendships. As discussed in the first chapter, my interest in the topics was the result of my own experience in my work as an ordained pastor in the Swiss Reformed Church and my realisation that the theme of friendship and its dynamics, although intuitively of great significance, was not something discussed or thought about as part of pastors' seminary or ongoing education.

Through contact, a number of years ago, with the work of John Swinton and Hans Reinders and their emphasis on the need for relationships of friendship within the Church, my awareness of the subject grew. Further, the New Testament witness of Jesus no longer calling his disciples servants but friends, and that no one has greater love than the one who lays down his life for his friends suggested to me that the *topos* of friendship might be important for disciples of Jesus, including those called to ordained, pastoral ministry.

This led me to formulate the questions in the first chapter:

- If the Church can be understood as a gathering place of Jesus' disciples, those he has chosen to call friends, would it not be strange if that did not also have meaning for the way in which we think about and practice Christian pastoring?

- If part of the vocation of pastors is to encourage and enable others within the body of Christ to live lives which reflect Jesus' call to discipleship, and thus lives open to friendliness and friendship with each other, what might this entail in their own relationships with those in their congregations?

- Could there be types of friendliness and friendship which can and should be actively sought and deepened in the ministry that ordained pastors have within their congregations? And if so, what might the dynamics of such friendliness and those of such friendships look like?

- If pastors have such friends, how do they experience having a friend or friends within their congregations, and what do these friendships mean to them?

Towards research into these matters, I used the framework of the pastoral cycle centred around the four stages of experiencing, of exploring, of reflecting and finally of responding. Having formulated the experience which led me to the research in stage one, in stage two I decided to work with a specific qualitative research method, that of hermeneutic phenomenology, which allowed me to explore the phenomenon of friendship as experienced and designated as such by ordained pastors in the Swiss Reformed Church in their congregations. I was thus enabled to gain understanding around friendship experiences of the individual pastors who agreed to take part in the interviews in my study. By inquiring phenomenologically into specific and particular lived experiences of relations which the pastors understood as friendships, and through the intentional fusion of horizons between myself and the participants, I described four attributes of friendship relations which, in their interplay, emerged from my research as being essential for the relationship to be regarded as a friendship. These were:

- Mutuality as an experience of reciprocal give and take in very personal areas of life;
- Affection as an experience of liking the presence and character of the other specific person;
- Freedom as an experience of choosing to want to be with and trust the other person; and
- Openness as an experience of honest communication of otherwise unspoken and unshared personal thoughts and feelings and a willingness to become vulnerable.

Further, I described five elements talked about by the interviewed pastors, which they regarded as part of the friendliness expected of them by themselves and often by others. These elements were often also involved in friendship, but they could equally well be part of a relationship which was friendly but which neither side would designate or understand as an actual friendship. These elements were:

- Benevolence as general goodwill and kindness to everyone with whom the pastors come into contact;
- Closeness as offered situational companionship to those who request it;
- Equality as the discipline consciously and self-reflectively to avoid letting prejudices cloud the professional and Christian treatment of people in the congregation;
- Faithfulness as loyalty to Christ leading to trustworthiness and reliability in other relationships; and
- Hospitality as the spirit of welcoming all who wish to be welcomed and inviting them into community.

Having described these attributes which emerged from my qualitative research, I turned, in the third stage of my research, to theological reflection of them, starting with a study around friendship from the

Hebrew Bible and the New Testament and then moving to reflection around the various elements of friendliness and then around those which had emerged as essential for friendship in their interwovenness. This reflection led me to the formulation in the fourth stage of the pastoral cycle concerned with responding to the research of nine suggestions regarding how pastors might be encouraged to approach friendship in their congregations. Here I was aware that the generalizability of results from research done using qualitative methods, which focus on the particular and the specific in a situation, must be approached with caution. The nine suggestions, which I made tentatively in response to the research, I formulated as:

- Seeking for growth in understanding around the dynamics of friendship;
- Welcoming a mutuality of degrees;
- Enjoying the *Stellvertretung* of Christ and the *Spielraum* for friendship in "mixed communities";
- Encouraging a concept of love which includes the mutual affection of *philia*;
- Learning to pray and hope for authentic affection inspired by the love of God;
- Training an awareness of freedom in the development of relations;
- Developing generosity while being aware of expectations of reciprocity and gratitude;
- Becoming better at being able to "suffer" people, and
- Celebrating together the overflowing joy of belonging to Christ.

UNIQUENESS OF THE CONTRIBUTION OF THIS RESEARCH

I noted in the first chapter that there has been very little qualitative research in practical theology into the experience and thought of ordained pastors around the theme of their friendships within a congregation, and indeed none with the same focus as my research in this study. Although theological literature in general around friendship has been growing over the last decades, there is also little literature that concentrates on friendship within the setting of ordained pastoral ministry.[1]

My focus on experiences of friendship by ordained pastors within their congregations, and my theological reflection on this, means that my research makes a unique contribution to the growing body of literature which focuses on an understanding of Christian friendship and its meaning for the health and growth of the Church. Further, in the particular context of the Swiss Reformed Church, a denomination less known for its warm fellowship[2] and more for its sober and rational approach to piety and ethics and the autonomy of its members, it was interesting to discover the potential which pastors saw in their congregations regarding a growth in forms of friendship which might be encouraging in their communal discipleship of Christ and have an impact on their witness to society.

LIMITATIONS OF THE RESEARCH

Having outlined the unique contribution of my research, here I shall reflect briefly on some of the limitations of the study. The first limitation is not strictly a limitation at all, but has to do with the method of research which I chose to use and which was so fruitful in gaining understanding around the theme of my study. Part of the fascination of qualitative research is its concentration on the specific and the particular, and thus part of the fascination of my own research comes out of the specific focus on friendship experiences by ordained pastors within their congregations in the Swiss Reformed Church. This concentration on a particular and small ecclesiological setting allowed me to delve deeply and reflexively with a view to gaining understanding. Having been able to do that, however, it opened my eyes to how enriching it might be to delve similarly deeply into the theme of friendship for ordained pastors in their congregations in other ecclesiological settings, both interdenominationally and ecumenically. For practical reasons concerning the size and breadth of the study, this was not possible.

---

1. Anne-Marie Ellithorpe points this out in her recent book, published in May 2022, and states, "The complexity of nurturing friendship within pastoral contexts is certainly worthy of further study." Ellithorpe, *Towards Friendship-Shaped Communities*, 215.

2. Bonnie Miller McLemore, for instance, refers to those in the Presbyterian Reformed tradition (which is similar to the Swiss Reformed), as the "frozen chosen." Miller McLemore, "Embodied Knowing, Embodied Theology," 749.

Another area which might possibly be seen as a limitation concerns a discussion around forms of communication. Before the crisis surrounding COVID-19 in 2020 and 2021 and the various public health measures the government in Switzerland took, including lockdowns and for a while a prohibition against people meeting and coming together for religious services, I had not considered what effect it might have on pastors in their relations if they were not free to meet other people personally or worship communally with them, apart from through digital forms of communication. The interviews were all conducted in person in 2018 and 2019 a number of months before the start of the COVID-19 measures, and in the early summer of 2020 I considered briefly whether I should conduct further interviews with the same participants to ask them about their experiences of friendship in their congregations during the crisis. However, I decided against this as I judged that such further interviews would make an already rich and complex study even more complex and that the question surrounding the means of communication used by pastors in their relationships in their congregations was not central enough to the questions that were the focus of my research to warrant further interviews. The present study therefore does not include such a discussion.

IMPLICATIONS FOR FUTURE RESEARCH AND PRACTICE

Emerging from my research, I suggest that further studies in qualitative research around the same theme of friendship experiences by ordained pastors within their congregations but in other cultural and ecclesiological settings could be of value for practical theology. Such studies might be helpful in gaining a greater understanding of the dynamics involved in pastoral relations in a variety of particular settings and could be of benefit to both pastors working in such settings and to congregations in their dealings with and their expectations of their pastors. As they grow more competent in their understanding of the dynamics of Christian friendship, it might also encourage pastors to discover a wider variety of relationships, including forms of friendship, which they, in freedom and in their discipleship of Christ, might pursue, enjoy, and encourage others to pursue within their congregations. This might help in making those congregations better able to fulfill their calling as places of faithful, communal witness to the love and joy of Christ as they learn to bear each other's burdens and live out authentic, open, and free lives together.

Further, as an implication of my research for future practice, it might be useful to encourage education regarding friendship and its dynamics in the courses for those in curacy and those in the first years of ordained ministry. Such education with a differentiated approach towards friendship in the pastoral setting, has sometimes been lacking. It could be of help, especially to young pastors, in encouraging them to live out their relationships within their congregations in a wise and prudent yet positive and joyful manner.

CLOSING THOUGHTS

I conclude my research journey through this study with a few personal thoughts. The title of this study "The pastor as friend?" is one which I have found has immediately fascinated people as soon as I mention it. Those who are not pastors themselves have shown a keen interest and have wanted to hear more about my research, but have been wary of saying too much themselves, possibly from a nebulous fear that I may ask them to start defining their relationship to me, as I am a pastor, or that I might start defining my relationship to them. Those who are pastors have similarly shown an immediate interest and have started to tell me of their own experiences around what they have often regarded as desired friendships in their congregations, the majority of which they themselves regard as challenging for the reasons I mentioned in the first chapter. Simultaneously, however, many of them have expressed the feeling that more of something like friendship would be helpful in encouraging the growth of the type of church communities they envision as being healthy.

During my research journey I have been able to develop a heightened and differentiated attitude of awareness around the subject of pastoral friendship in local congregations within the cultural setting with which I am familiar and within which I work. My research has shown that the whole area of friendships within the pastoral setting remains a complex issue which does not allow for simple answers to the question of whether pastors should be regarded as friends by their congregations. The conviction that there cannot be anything like a moral or professional obligation for Christian pastors to be friends with others in their congregations, even when there are perhaps any number of people who appear to desire such friendship, has grown throughout my research. The essential attributes of friendship which have emerged from my study—namely, mutuality, affection, freedom, and openness—do not allow for such an obligation. However, the conviction that there cannot be anything like a moral or professional obligation for Christian pastors *not* to be friends with others in their congregations has likewise grown, as this similarly would not be congruous with the research findings.

Thus, although my research findings and my theological reflection thereon do not allow for simple answers, they do lay the groundwork, as I have shown in the fifth chapter, for pastors potentially to grow in their relational and spiritual competence surrounding issues of friendliness and friendship, and this may in turn lead to forms of leadership which have a refreshing impact on congregations attempting to live faithfully to their calling in the discipleship of Christ. In my own vocation as a pastor within the Swiss Reformed Church, I have found that the understanding I have gained through my research has allowed me to approach the theme with more confidence and freedom, both to develop and not to develop relationships which might be regarded as friendships. Such confidence and freedom, fed by a growing awareness of the dynamics surrounding relationships moulded by friendliness and friendship, is importantly also nurtured by my understanding and faith that the Spirit of Christ is working in the Church and thus also in the congregation in which I am involved. That Spirit is the same Spirit through which Christ called his disciples no longer servants but friends, and who can, even through suffering, lead us to an overflowing joy of belonging to God. Such Spirit-worked joy, I believe, will lead to that which is good and healthy for the Church.

Bibliography

Aden, Leroy, and J. Harold Ellins. *The Church and Pastoral Care*. Grand Rapids: Baker, 1988.
Adiprasetya, Joas. "Pastor as Friend: Reinterpreting Christian Leadership." *Dialog* 57 (2018) 47–52.
———. "Revisiting Jürgen Moltmann's Theology of Open Friendship." *International Journal for the Study of the Christian Church* 21 (2021) 177–87.
Aelred of Rievaulx. *Spiritual Friendship*. Translated by Mary Eugenia Laker. Kalamazoo: Cistercian, 1977.
Ambrose of Milan. *De Officiis*. Translated by Ivor J. Davidson. Oxford: Oxford University Press, 2002.
Anderman, David E. "Conversation, Friendship, and Hospitality, Thoughts Toward A 'Weak' Ecclesiology." *Prism: A Theological Forum for the United Church of Christ* 24 (2010) 7–27.
Austin, Victor Lee. *Friendship: The Heart of Being Human*. Grand Rapids: Baker, 2020.
Ballard, Paul H., and John Pritchard. *Practical Theology in Action: Christian Thinking in the Service of Church and Society*. London: SPCK, 2006.
Barnes, Craig, M. "Pastor, Not Friend." *The Christian Century*, December 2012. https://www.christiancentury.org/article/2012-12/pastor-not-friend.
Barclay, John M. G. *Paul and the Gift*. Grand Rapids: Eerdmans, 2015.
Barry, William. *A Friendship Like No Other: Experiencing God's Amazing Embrace*. Chicago: Loyola, 2008.
Barth, Karl. *The Call to Discipleship*. Translated by G. W. Bromiley. Minneapolis: Fortress, 2003.
Bass, Dorothy, ed. *Christian Practical Wisdom*. Grand Rapids: Eerdmans, 2016.
Bayes, Paul. "Making Friends." In *Developing Faithful Ministers: A Practical and Theological Handbook*, edited by Tim Ling and Lesley Bentley, 15–28. London: SCM, 2012.
Bedford, Nancy E. "Speak, Friend and Enter: Friendship and Theological Method." In *God's life in Trinity*, edited by Miroslav Volf, 33–43. Minneapolis: Fortress, 2006.
Benner, Patricia. *Interpretive Phenomenology: Embodiment, Caring, and Ethics in Health and Illness*. Thousand Oaks, CA: Sage, 1994.
Bennett, Zoë et al. *Invitation to Research in Practical Theology*. Oxford: Routledge, 2018.

Berry, Donald L. *Mutuality: The Vision of Martin Buber*. Albany: State University of New York Press, 1985.

Bethge. Eberhard, and Victoria J., Barnett, ed. *Dietrich Bonhoeffer: A Biography*. Minneapolis: Fortress, 2000.

Billington, Wendy. *Growing a Caring Church: Practical Guidelines for Pastoral Care*. Abingdon: Bible Reading Fellows, 2010.

Bock, Kim Yong. "Minjung and Power: A Biblical and Theological Perspective on Doularchy (Servanthood)." *The Christian Century* (July 15, 1987) 628–30.

Bonhoeffer, Dietrich. *Dietrich Bonhoeffer Works*. 17 vols. Minneapolis: Fortress, 1996–.

———. *Discipleship* Translated by Barbara Green and Reinhard Krauss. Dietrich Bonhoeffer Works 4. Minneapolis: Fortress, 2015.

———. *Ethics*. Translated by Neville Horton Smith. New York: MacMillan, 1967.

———. *Ethics*. Translated by Reinhard Krauss et al. Dietrich Bonhoeffer Works 6. Minneapolis: Fortress, 2015.

———. *Letters and Papers from Prison*. Translated by Isabel Best et al. Dietrich Bonhoeffer Works 8. Minneapolis: Fortress, 2015.

Browning, Don S. *A Fundamental Practical Theology: Descriptive and Strategic Proposals*. Minneapolis: Fortress, 1991.

Buber, Martin. *Between Man and Man*. Translated by Ronald G. Smith. London: Kegan Paul, 1947.

———. *I and Thou*. Translated by Ronald Gregor Smith. Edinburgh: T. & T. Clark, 1937.

———. *The Knowledge of Man*. Edited by Maurice Friedmann. New York: Harper Collins, 1965.

Burgess, Robert G. *In the Field: An Introduction to Field Research*. London: Allen and Unwin, 1984.

Burt, Donald X. *Friendship and Society: An Introduction to Augustine's Practical Philosophy*. Grand Rapids: Eerdmans, 1999.

Cahalan, Kathleen, and James Nieman. "Mapping the Field of Practical Theology." In *For Life Abundant: Practical Theology, Theological Education and Christian Ministry*, edited by Dorothy C. Bass and Craig Dykstra, 62–85. Grand Rapids: Eerdmans, 2008.

Calhoun, Gerald J., SJ. *Pastoral Companionship: Ministry with seriously ill Persons and their Families*. New Jersey: Paulist, 1986.

Cameron, Helen, ed. *Talking about God in Practice: Theological Action Research and Practical Theology*. London: SCM, 2010.

Campbell, Alistair V., ed. *A Dictionary of Pastoral Care*. London: SPCK, 1987.

———. *Moderated Love: A Theology of Professional Care*. London: SPCK, 1984.

———. *Paid to Care? The Limits of Professionalism in Pastoral Care*. London: SPCK, 1985.

Carmichael, Liz. *Friendship: Interpreting Christian Love*. London: T. & T. Clark, 2004.

Chartier, Gary. *Understanding Friendship: On the Moral, Political, and Spiritual Meaning of Love*. Minneapolis: Fortress, 2022.

Cicero, M. Tullius. *De amicitia*. Translated by W. A. Falconer. London: Heinemann, 1923, repr. 1964.

Clebsch, William A., and Charles R. Jaekle. *Pastoral Care in Historical Perspective*. Lanham: Rowman and Littlefield, 1994.

Cluett, Elizabeth. R. and Rosalind Bluff, eds. *Principles and Practice of Research in Midwifery*. 2nd ed. London: Churchill Livingstone, 2006.
Cocking, Dean, and Jeanette Kennett. "Friendship and the Self." *Ethics* 108 (1998) 502–27.
Cooper, John M. "Aristotle on Friendship." In *Essays on Aristotle's Ethics*, edited by Amélie Oksenberg Rorty, 301–40. Berkeley: University of California Press, 1980.
Corley, Jeremy. "Friendship in the Hebrew Wisdom Literature." *Proceedings of the Irish Biblical Association* 38 (2015) 27–51.
Culbertson, Philip L. "Men and Christian Friendship." In *Men's bodies, men's gods: Male Identities in a (post-) Christian Culture*, edited by Björn Krondorfer, 149–80. New York: New York University Press, 1996
Culy, Martin M. *Echoes of Friendship in the Gospel of John*, New Testament Monographs 30. Sheffield: Phoenix, 2010.
D'Arcy, Martin Cyril SJ. *The Mind and Heart of Love: A Study in Eros and Agape*. Repr. Providence: Cluny Media, 2019.
Davies, Graham. "The Ethics of Friendship in Wisdom Literature." In *Ethical and Unethical in the Old Testament: God and Humans in Dialogue*, edited by Katherine J. Dell, LHBOTS 528135–50. New York: T. & T. Clark, 2010.
Davis, Natalie Zemon. *The Gift in Sixteenth Century France*. Madison: University of Wisconsin Press, 2000.
De Graaff, Guido. "Friends with a Mandate: Friendship and Family in Bonhoeffer's Ecclesiology." *Studies in Christian Ethics* 30 (2017) 389–406.
Denzin, Norman K., and Yvonne S. Lincoln. *Collecting and Interpreting Qualitative Materials*. Thousand Oaks, CA: SAGE, 1998.
Dietrich, Jan. "Von Der Freundschaft Im Alten Testament Und Alten Orient." *Die Welt Des Orients* 44 (2014) 37–56.
Dörnemann, Holger. *Freundschaft: Die Erlösungslehre des Thomas von Aquin*. Würzburg: Echter, 2012.
Dostal, Robert J., ed. *The Cambridge Companion to Gadamer*. Cambridge: Cambridge University Press, 2002.
Dulles, Avery, SJ. *Models of the Church*. Dublin: Gill and Macmillan, 1989.
Dunne, Ciarán. "The Place of the Literature Review in Grounded Theory Research." *International Journal of Social Research Methodology* 14 (2011) 111–24.
Dykstra, Robert. "Subversive Friendship." *Pastoral Psychology* 58 (2009) 585–86.
Eckholt, Margit, ed. *Freunde habe ich Euch genannt: Freundschaft als Leitbegriff systematischer Theologie*. Münster: LIT, 2007.
Edgar, Brian. *God Is Friendship: A Theology of Spirituality, Community, and Society*. Asbury: Seedbed, 2013.
Ellithorpe, Anne-Marie. *Towards Friendship-Shaped Communities: A Practical Theology of Friendship*. Chichester: Wiley-Blackwell, 2022.
ERK Basel-Stadt. *Bericht ERK Mitgliederbefragung inkl. Executive Summary_01.12.2017*. https://www.erk-bs.ch/umfrage.
Finlay, Linda. *Phenomenology for Therapists: Researching the Lived World*. Chichester: Wiley-Blackwell, 2011.
Fischer, Alexander A. "Freundschaft (AT)." *Das wissenschaftliche Bibellexikon im Internet*. 2007. https://www.bibelwissenschaft.de/stichwort/18617/).
Fitzgerald, John T. "Christian Friendship: John, Paul, and the Philippians." *Interpretation (Richmond)* 61 (2007) 284–96.

Fitzgerald, John T., ed. *Friendship, Flattery, and Frankness of Speech*. Leiden: Brill, 2014.

———. *Greco Roman Perspectives on Friendship*. Atlanta: Scholars, 1997.

Fletcher, Joseph. *Moral Responsibility: Situation Ethics at Work*. Philadelphia: Westminster, 1967.

Fowl, Stephen E. *Philippians*. The Two Horizons New Testament Commentary. Grand Rapids: Eerdmans, 2005.

Fredericks, Deborah. *The Leaders Experience of relational Leadership: A Hermeneutic Phenomenological Study of Leadership as Friendship*. PhD diss., University of Antioch, 2009.

Frère John, Taizé. *Eine Gemeinschaft von Freunden: Kirche neu entdecken*. München: Verlag Neue Stadt, 2012.

Fry, Jane, et al. "Muddying the Waters or Swimming Downstream? A Critical Analysis of Literature Reviewing in a Phenomenological Study Through an Exploration of the Lifeworld, Reflexivity and Role of the Researcher." *Indo-Pacific Journal of Phenomenology* 17 (2017) 12.

Fullam, Lisa. "Toward a Virtue Ethics of Marriage: Augustine and Aquinas on Friendship in Marriage." *Theological Studies* 73 (2012) 663–92.

Gadamer, Hans-Georg. *Truth and Method*. London: Bloomsbury, 2004.

Gaventa, Bill, ed. *Knowing, Being Known, and the Mystery of God: Essays in Honor of Professor Hans Reinders, Teacher, Friend, and Disciple*. Amsterdam: VU University Press, 2016.

Geerlings, Wilhelm. "Das Freundschaftsideal Augustins." *Theologische Quartalschrift* 161 (1981) 265–74.

Gerkin, Charles. *An Introduction to Pastoral Care*. Nashville: Abingdon, 1997.

———. *The Living Human Document: Re-Visioning Pastoral counseling in a hermeneutical mode*. Nashville: Abingdon, 1984.

Gill, Michael J. "Phenomenology as Qualitative Methodology." In *Qualitative Analysis: Eight approaches*, edited by N. Mik-Meyer and M. Järvinen, 73–94. London: Sage, 2020.

Giorgi, Amedeo. *The Descriptive Phenomenological Method in Psychology: A Modified Husserlian Approach*. Pittsburgh, PA: Duquesne University Press, 2009.

———. "The Theory, Practice, and Evaluation of the Phenomenological Method as a Qualitative Research Procedure." *Journal of Phenomenological Psychology* 28 (1997) 235–60.

Gonzalez, Michelle A. "When We Don't Choose Our Friends: Friendship as a Theological Category." *Theology Today* 69 (2012) 189–96.

Gooder, Paula. *Body: Biblical Spirituality for the Whole Person*. London: SPCK, 2016.

Gorsuch, Richard L. "The Pyramids of Sciences and of Humanities." *American Behavioural Scientist* 45 (2002) 1822–38.

Graham, Elaine, et al. *Theological Reflection: Methods*. London: SCM, 2019.

Greig, Jason Reimer. *Reconsidering Intellectual Disability: L'Arche, Medical Ethics, and Christian Friendship*. Moral Traditions series. Washington, DC: Georgetown University Press, 2015.

Gremmels, Christian, and Wolfgang Huber, ed. *Wechselwirkungen "Eberhard Bethge und Dietrich Bonhoeffer."* Gütersloh: Chr. Kaiser/Gütersloher, 1994.

Gula, Richard. *Ethics in Pastoral Ministry*. New York: Paulist, 2010.

Gulliford, Liz, et al. "Recent Work on the Concept of Gratitude in Philosophy and Psychology." *Journal of Value Inquiry* 47 (2013) 285–317.

Hale, Matthew. *Deification, Friendship, and Self-Knowledge*. Thesis, Abilene Christian University, 2015.
Hammond, Phillip E., et al. "Clergy Authority and Friendship with Parishioners." *Pacific Sociological Review* 15 (1972) 185–201.
Hands, Donald R., and Wayne L. Fehr. *Spiritual Wholeness for Clergy: A New Psychology of Intimacy with God, Self and Others*. Bethesda: The Alban Institute, 1993.
Hauerwas, Stanley. *A Better Hope: Resources for a Church Confronting Capitalism, Democracy, and Postmodernity*. Grand Rapids: Baker, 2000.
———. *A Community of Character: Towards a Constructive Christian Social Ethic*. Notre Dame: University of Notre Dame Press, 1981.
———. *In Good Company: The Church as Polis*. Notre Dame: University of Notre Dame Press, 1997.
———. *Sanctify Them in the Truth: Holiness Exemplified*. Nashville: Abingdon, 1999.
———. "Virtue, Description and Friendship." *Irish Theological Quarterly* 62 (1996) 170–84.
Hauerwas, Stanley, and Charles Pinches. *Christians Among the Virtues*. Note Dame: University of Notre Dame Press, 1997.
Hauerwas, Stanley, and Jean Vanier. *Living Gently in a Violent World: The Prophetic Witness of Weakness*. Downers Grove, IL: InterVarsity, 2008.
Heidegger, Martin. *Sein und Zeit*. Repr. Tübingen: Max Niemeyer, 2006.
Hempelmann, Heinzpeter. *Gemeinde 2.0: Frische Formen für die Kirche von heute*. Neukirchen-Vluyn: Neukirchener, 2011.
———. *Gott im Milieu: Wie Sinusstudien der Kirche helfen können Menschen zu erreichen*. Giessen: Brunnen, 2012.
Herbst, Michael. *Beziehungsweise: Grundlagen und Praxisfelder evangelischer Seelsorge*. Neukirchen-Vluyn: Neukirchener, 2013.
Herrick, Vanessa. *Limits of Vulnerability: Exploring a Kenotic Model for Pastoral Ministry*. Cambridge: Grove, 1997.
Heywood, David. *Reimagining Ministry*. London: SCM, 2011.
Hiltner, Seward. "Friendship in Counseling." *Pastoral Psychology* 1 (1950) 28–34.
Hintz, August W. "The Pastor as Friend." In *Bakers Dictionary of Practical Theology*, edited by Ralph Turnbull, 326–29. London: Baker, 1967.
Hofheinz, Marco, et al. *Freundschaft, Zur Aktualität eines traditionsreichen Begriffs*. Zürich: TVZ, 2014.
Holst, Jonas. "Philia and Agape: Ancient Greek Ethics of Friendship and a Christian Theology of Love." In *Love and Friendship Across Cultures*, edited by Soraj Hongladarom and Jeremiah Joven Joaquin, 55–65. Singapore: Springer, 2021.
Hongladarom, Soraj, and Jeremiah Joven Joaquin, eds. *Love and Friendship Across Cultures*. Singapore: Springer, 2021.
Houston, James. *The Transforming Friendship: A Guide to Prayer*. Oxford: Lion, 1989.
Hünermann, Peter. *Jesus Christus—Gottes Wort in der Zeit: Eine systematische Christologie*. Aschendorff: Münster, 1997.
Hunt, Mary E. *Fierce Tenderness: A Feminist Theology of Friendship*. New York: Crossroad, 1992.
Hunter, Rodney J., ed. *Dictionary of Pastoral Care and Counselling*. Nashville: Abingdon, 1995.
Husserl, Edmund. *Ideen zu einer reinen Phänomenologie und phänomenologischen Philosophie*. Berlin: De Gruyter, 1993; reprint from 1913.

Issler, Klaus. *Wasting Time with God: A Christian Spirituality of Friendship with God.* Downers Grove, IL: InterVarsity, 2001.

Jeanrond, Werner G. *A Theology of Love.* London: T. & T. Clark, 2010.

Jones, Alan. *Exploring Spiritual Direction.* Cambridge: Cowley, 1999.

Jones, L. Gregory, and Kevin R. Armstrong. *Resurrecting Excellence: Shaping Faithful Christian Ministry.* Grand Rapids: Eerdmans, 2006.

Kelly, Ewan. *Personhood and Presence: Self as a Resource for Spiritual and Pastoral Care.* London: T. & T. Clark, 2012.

Kerney, Barbara Lee. *A Theology of Friendship.* PhD diss., University of Durham, 2007.

Kimbriel, Samuel. *Friendship as Sacred Knowing: Overcoming Isolation.* Oxford: Oxford University Press, 2014.

King, Nigel, and Christine Horrocks. *Interviews in Qualitative Research.* London: SAGE, 2010.

Kirk, Alan. "Love your Enemies, The Golden Rule, and ancient Reciprocity (Luke 6:27–35)." *Journal of Biblical Literature* 122 (2003) 667–86.

Klaasen, John, JS. "Practical Theology: A Critically Engaged Practical Reason Approach of Practice, Theory, Practice and Theory." *HTS Theological Studies* 70 (2014) 3–7.

Klauck, Hans-Josef. *Gemeinde zwischen Haus und Stadt. Kirche bei Paulus.* Freiburg: Herder, 1992.

Koch, Günter, ed. *Dimensionen der Freundschaft. Oder: Wider den Egotrip (Würzburger Domschulreihe 8).* Würzburg: Echter, 1998.

Konstan, David. *In the Orbit of Love: Affection in ancient Greece and Rome.* New York: Oxford University Press, 2018.

Kotze, Manitza, and Carike Noeth. "Friendship as a Theological Model: Bonhoeffer, Moltmann and the Trinity." *die Skriflig* 53 (2019) a2333.

Kruschwitz, Robert B., ed. "Friendship: Christian Reflection." *A Series in Faith and Ethics* 27. The Center for Christian Ethics at Baylor University, 2008.

Kuhn, Thomas. *The Structure of Scientific Revolutions.* Rev. ed. Chicago: University of Chicago Press, 1970.

Kundert, Lukas. *Die reformierte Kirche: Grundlagen für eine reformierte Schweizer Ekklesiologie,* Zürich: TVZ, 2014.

Kunz, Ralph. *Der neue Gottesdienst. Ein Plädoyer für den liturgischen Wildwuchs.* Zürich: TVZ, 2006.

Lafollette, Hugh. *Personal Relationships: Love, Identity, and Morality.* Oxford: Blackwell, 1996.

Lamb, Richard. *The Pursuit of God in the Company of Friends.* Downers Grove, IL: InterVarsity, 2003.

Lapsley, Jacqueline E. "Friends with God?: Moses and the Possibility of Covenantal Friendship." *Interpretation* 58 (2004) 117–29.

Leech, Kenneth. *Soul Friend: The Practice of Christian Spirituality.* San Francisco: Harper and Row, 1977.

Lewis, Clive Staples. *The Four Loves.* New York: Harcourt, 1960.

Lincoln, Yvonne S., and Egon G. Guba. *Naturalistic Enquiry.* London: SAGE, 1985.

Lindseth, Anders, and Astrid Norberg, "A Phenomenological Hermeneutical Method for Researching Lived Experience." *Scandinavian Journal of Caring Sciences* 18 (2004) 145–53.

Lippitt, John. "Cracking the Mirror: on Kierkegaard's Concerns about Friendship." *The International Journal of the Philosophy of Religion* 61 (2007) 131–50.

Lohfink, Gerhard. *Wie hat Jesus Gemeinde gewollt?* Freiburg: Herder, 1982.
Lusungu Moyo, Fulata. "Traffic Violations: Hospitality, Foreignness, and Exploitation: A Contextual Biblical Study of Ruth." *Journal of Feminist Studies in Religion* 32 (2016) 83–94.
Lyall, David. *Counselling in the Pastoral and Spiritual Context*. Philadelphia: Open University Press, 1995.
Lynch, Chloe. *Ecclesial Leadership as Friendship*. Abingdon: Routledge, 2019.
Lynch, Gordon. *Pastoral Care and Counselling*. London: SAGE, 2002.
Malone, Thomas Patrick, and Patrick Thomas Malone. *The Art of Intimacy*. New York: Prentice Hall, 1987.
Marty, Martin. "What Friends Are For." *The Christian Century* 109 (1992) 985–89.
Mason, Jennifer. *Qualitative Researching: Second edition*. London: SAGE, 2004.
Matarasso, Pauline M. *The Cistercian World: Monastic Writings of the 12th Century*. London: Penguin Classics, 1993.
Maxwell, Joan Paddock. "Great Is Thy Faithfulness." *The Journal of Pastoral Care and Counseling* 57 (2003) 465–66.
Mayring, Philipp. "On Generalization in Qualitatively Oriented Research." *Forum Qualitative Sozialforschung / Forum: Qualitative Social Research* 8 (2007) 1–28.
McFague, Sallie. *Models of God: Theology for an Ecological, Nuclear Age*. Philadelphia: Fortress, 1987.
McGinn, Bernhard. *The Growth of Mysticism: Gregory the Great Through the 12th Century*, Vol. 2. New York: Crossroad, 1994.
McNeill, Donald P., et al. *Compassion: A Reflection on the Christian Life*. Garden City, NY: Image, 1983.
Meilaender, Gilbert C. *Friendship: A Study in Theological Ethics*. Notre Dame: University of Notre Dame Press, 1981.
———. *The Theory and Practice of Virtue*. Indiana: Notre Dame, 1984.
Miller-McLemore, Bonnie J. "Embodied Knowing, Embodied Theology: What Happened to the Body?" *Pastoral Psychology* 62 (2013) 749.
———. "The Living Human Web: Pastoral Theology at the Turn of the Century." In *Through the Eyes of Women*, edited by Jeanne Stevenson Moessner, 9–26. Minneapolis: Augsburg Fortress, 1996.
Miller-McLemore, Bonnie J., ed. *The Wiley Blackwell Companion to Practical Theology*. Chichester: Wiley-Blackwell, 2014.
Mitchell, Alan C. "The Social Function of Friendship in Acts 2:44–47 and 4:32–37." *Journal of Biblical Literature* 111 (1992) 255–72.
Moltmann, Jürgen. *Kirche in der Kraft des Geistes: Ein Beitrag zur messianischen Ekklesiologie*. Gütersloh: Gütersloher, 2010.
———. "Knowing and Community." In *On Community*, edited by Leroy Rouner, 162–76. Notre Dame: University of Notre Dame Press, 1991.
———. *The Church in the Power of the Holy Spirit: A Contribution to Messianic Christology*. Translated by Margaret Kohl. Minneapolis: Fortress, 1993.
———. *The Crucified God: The Cross of Christ as the Foundation and Criticism of Christian Theology*. London: SCM, 1974.
———. *The Living God and the Fullness of Life*. Translated by Margaret Kohl. Geneva: World Council of Churches, 2016.
———. *The Open Church: Invitation to a Messianic Life-Style*. London: SCM, 1978.
———. *The Trinity and the Kingdom: The Doctrine of God*. Translated by Margaret Kohl. Minneapolis: Fortress, 1993.

———. *Theology and Joy*. London: SCM, 1973.
Moltmann-Wendel, Elisabeth. *Rediscovering Friendship*. London: SCM, 2000.
Moran, Dermot. *Introduction to Phenomenology*. London: Routledge, 2000.
Morgan, George W. "Martin Buber and Some of His Critics (Review-Essay)." *Judaism* 18 (1969) 232–41.
Morrison, Glenn. "Pastoral Care and Counselling: Towards a Post-Metaphysical Theology of Friendship." Conference Paper: *The Association of Practical Theology in Oceania Conference*, Auckland, November 2006. researchonline.nd.edu.au/theo_conference/8/.
Murray, Stuart. *Church After Christendom*. Carlisle: STL, 2005.
Murray Beaumont, Stephen. *Pastor, Counsellor and Friend: Exploring Multiple Role Relationships in Pastoral Work*. School of History, Philosophy, Religion & Classics, The University of Queensland: PhD Thesis, 2012.
Newman, Elisabeth. *Untamed Hospitality: Welcoming God and Other Strangers*. Grand Rapids: Brazos, 2007.
Newson, Ryan Andrew. *Radical Friendship: The Politics of Communal Discernment*. Minneapolis: Fortress, 2017.
Noack, Winfried. *Gemeindeaufbau und Gemeindeentwicklung in der säkularen Gesellschaft*. Berlin: Frank & Timme, 2012.
Nouwen, Henri J. M. *Out of Solitude: Three Meditations on the Christian Life*. Notre Dame: Ave Maria, 1984.
———. *The Wounded Healer*. London: Darton, Longman & Todd, 1990.
Nygren, Anders. *Agape and Eros*. London: SPCK, 1932.
O'Day, Gail R. "Jesus as Friend in the Gospel of John." *Interpretation* 58 (2004) 144–57.
———. "Preaching as an Act of Friendship: Plain Speaking as a Sign of the Kingdom." *Journal for Preachers* n.d. (2005) 15–20.
Oden, Thomas. *Kerygma and Counseling*. Philadelphia: Westminster, 1976.
———. *Pastoral Theology: Essentials of Ministry*. San Francisco: Harper and Row, 1983.
Oliphant, D. G. *Intentional Friendship: A Philosophy of Pastoral Care*, PhD diss., University of Western Sydney, 2007.
Oliver, Gordon. "Speaking Christian: A Retrospective Journey in Practical Theology." *Practical Theology* 14 (2021) 454–466.
Olyan, Saul M. *Friendship in the Hebrew Bible*. New Haven, CT: Yale University Press, 2017.
Osmer, Richard. *Practical Theology: An Introduction*. Grand Rapids: Eerdmans, 2008.
Pakaluk, Michael, ed. *Other Selves: Philosophers on Friendship*. Indianapolis: Hackett, 1991.
Park, Samuel. "Pastoral Identity Constructed in Care-giving Relationships." *The Journal of Pastoral Care and Counseling* 66 (2012) 1–13.
Parsons, Preston David Sunabacka. *A Friendship for Others: Bonhoeffer and Bethge on the Theology and Practice of Friendship*. University of Cambridge, diss., 2018.
Paterson, Michael. "Discipled by Praxis: Soul and Role in Context." *Practical Theology* 12 (2019) 7–19.
Pattison, Stephen. *A Critique of Pastoral Care*. London: SCM, 1993.
Patton, John. *Pastoral Care in Context*. Louisville, KY: Westminster John Knox, 1993.
Peeters, Evelyn J. H. "Quality Pastoral Relationships in Healthcare Settings: Guidelines for Codes of Ethics." *The Journal of Pastoral Care and Counseling* 74 (2020) 42–52.
Pembroke, Neil. "Space in the Trinity and in Pastoral Care." *The Journal of Pastoral Care and Counseling* 65 (2011) 1–10.

Peterson, Eugene. *The Wisdom of Each Other: A Conversation between Spiritual Friends.* Grand Rapids: Zondervan, 1998.
Piper, Hans Christoph. *Gesprächsanalysen.* Göttingen: Vandenhoeck und Ruprecht, 1973.
———. *Klinische Seelsorge-Ausbildung (Heft 30).* Berlin: Berliner Hefte für Evangelische Krankenseelsorge, 1972.
Pohl, Christine D. *Making Room, Rediscovering Hospitality as a Christian Tradition.* Grand Rapids: Eerdmans, 1999.
Polanyi, Michael. *Personal Knowledge: Towards a Post-Critical Philosophy.* London: Routledge, 1958.
Prokes, Mary Timothy. *Mutuality: The Human Image of Trinitarian Love.* New York: Paulist, 1993.
Puthenkandathil, Eldho. *Philos: A Designation for the Jesus-Disciple Relationship.* Frankfurt: Peter Lang, 1993.
Quinn, Robert E. *Deep Change.* San Francisco: Jossey-Bass, 1996.
Reinders, Hans. *Receiving the Gift of Friendship: Profound Disability, Theological Anthropology and Ethics.* Grand Rapids: Eerdmans, 2008.
Rhodes, Stephen. "Jürgen Moltmann: The Comfort and Challenge of Open Friendship." *The Asbury Theological Journal* 49 (1994) 63–70.
Rome, Sydney, and Beatrice Rome, eds. *Philosophical Interrogations.* New York: Harper, 1970.
Root, Andrew. *The Relational Pastor: Sharing in Christ by sharing ourselves.* Downers Grove, IL: InterVarsity, 2013.
Rouner, Leroy S., ed. *On Community.* Notre Dame: University of Notre Dame Press, 1991.
———. *The Changing Face of Friendship.* Notre Dame: University of Notre Dame Press, 1994.
Rubin, Lilian B. *Just Friends.* New York: Harper Collins, 1985.
Ruffing, Janet, SM. "Spiritual Direction: An Instance of Christian Friendship or a Therapeutic Relationship?" *Studia Mystica* 12 (1989) 64–73.
Sahlins, Marshall. *Stone Age Economics.* Chicago: Aldine-Atherton, 1972.
Sanders, Patricia. "Phenomenology: A New Way of Viewing Organizational Research." *Academy of Management Review* 7 (1982) 353–60.
Schilpp, Paul, and Maurice Friedmann, ed. *The Philosophy of Martin Buber.* La Salle: Open Court, 1967.
Schwartz, Daniel. *Aquinas on Friendship.* Oxford: Oxford University Press, 2012.
Sherman, Nancy. *The Fabric of Character: Aristotle's Theory of Virtue.* Oxford: Oxford University Press, 1989.
Silverman, David. *Interpreting Qualitative Data.* London: SAGE, 2010.
Sim, Julius. "Collecting and Analyzing Qualitative Data: Issues Raised by the Focus Group." *Journal of Advanced Nursing* 28 (1998) 345–52.
Slade, Peter. *Open Friendship in a Closed Society: Mission Mississippi and a Theology of Friendship.* Oxford: Oxford University Press, 2009.
Smith, James K. A. *Imagining the Kingdom: How Worship Works.* Ada: Baker Academic, 2013.
———. *You Are What You Love.* Grand Rapids: Brazos Press, 2016.
Smith, Jonathan. "Beyond the Divide between Cognition and Discourse: Using interpretative phenomenological analysis in health psychology" *Psychology and Health* 11 (1996) 261–71.

Soskice, Janet Martin. *The Kindness of God: Metaphor, Gender and Religious Language.* Oxford: Oxford University Press, 2007.
Southard, Samuel. *Theology and Therapy: The Wisdom of God in a Context of Friendship.* Dallas: Word, 1989.
Spencer, Liz, and Ray Pahl. *Rethinking Friendships: Hidden Solidarities Today.* Princeton: Princeton University Press, 2006.
Spitzer, Lee B. *Making Friends, Making Disciples.* Valley Forge: Judson, 2010.
Steinhoffsmith, Roy Herndon. *The Mutuality of Care.* St. Louis: Chalice, 1999.
Sterling, Gregory E. "The Bond of Humanity: Friendship in Philo of Alexandria." In *Greco Roman Perspectives on Friendship*, edited by John Fitzgerald, 203–23. Atlanta: Scholars, 1997.
Sullivan, William, and Matthew Rosin. *A New Agenda for Higher Education.* Hoboken: Jossey-Bass, 2008.
Swinton, John. *Becoming Friends of Time: Disability, Timefullness and Gentle Discipleship.* London: SCM, 2017.
———. *Dementia: Living in the Memories of God.* Cambridge: Eerdmans, 2012.
———. *From Bedlam to Shalom: Towards a Practical Theology of Human Nature, Interpersonal Relationships and Mental Health Care.* New York: Peter Lang, 2000.
———. "Healing Presence: Reclaiming Friendship as a Pastoral Gift." *Contact* 126 (1998) 2–7.
———. *Raging with Compassion: Pastoral Responses to the Problem of Evil.* Grand Rapids: Eerdmans, 2007.
———. *Resurrecting the Person: Friendship and the Care of People with Severe Mental Health Problems.* Nashville: Abingdon, 2000.
Swinton, John, and Harriet Mowat. *Practical Theology and Qualitative Research.* London SCM, 2006.
Swinton, John, and Richard Payne. *Living Well and Dying Faithfully: Christian Practices for End-of-Life Care.* Cambridge: Eerdmans, 2009.
Telfer, Elizabeth. "Friendship." In *Other Selves: Philosophers on Friendship*, edited by Michael Pakaluk, 250–67. Indianapolis: Hackett, 1991.
Tiemstra, John P. "Professional Friends." *The Reformed Journal* n.d. (1983) 11–15.
Torrance, Iain. "Friendship as a Mode of Theological Engagement." *Modern Theology* 25 (2009) 123–31.
Turnbull, Ralph, ed. *Baker's Dictionary of Practical Theology.* London: Marshall, Morgan and Scott, 1969.
Vacek, Edward C., SJ. *Love, Human and Divine: The Heart of Christian Ethics.* Washington, DC: Georgetown University Press, 1994.
Vanier, Jean. *Becoming Human.* London: Darton, Longman and Todd, 1999
———. *Befriending the Stranger.* London: Darton, Longman and Todd, 2005.
———. *Community and Growth.* London: Darton, Longman and Todd, 1979.
———. *Jesus the Gift of Love.* London: Hodder and Stoughton, 1988.
———. *The Broken Body: Journey to Wholeness.* London: Darton, Longman and Todd, 1988.
Van Manen, Max. *Phenomenology of Practice: Meaning-Giving Methods in Phenomenological Research and Writing.* Abingdon: Routledge, 2014.
———. *Researching Lived Experience: Second edition.* Abingdon: Routledge, 2016.
Vanstone, William H. *The Stature of Waiting.* London: Darton, Longman and Todd, 1982.
Vernon, Mark. "The Ambiguity of Friendship." *Theology* 109 (2006) 403–11.
———. *The Philosophy of Friendship.* Basingstoke: Palgrave Macmillan, 2007.

Vesely, Patricia. "The Ethics of Reading: Friendship in the Old Testament." In *Friendship and Virtue Ethics in the Book of Job*, 74–104. Cambridge: Cambridge University Press, 2019.

Volf, Miroslav. *Exclusion and Embrace: A Theological Exploration of Identity, Otherness and Reconciliation*. Nashville: Abingdon, 1996.

Volf, Miroslav, and Dorothy C. Bass, eds. *Practicing Theology: Beliefs and Practices in Christian Life*. Grand Rapids: Eerdmans, 2002.

Wadell. Paul J. "An Itinerary to Glory: How Grace Is Embodied in the Communio of Charity." *Studies in Christian Ethics* 23 (2010) 431–48.

———. *Becoming Friends: Worship, Justice, and the Practice of Christian Friendship*. Grand Rapids: Brazos, 2002.

Wannenwetsch, Bernd. *Political Worship: Ethics for Christian Citizens*. Oxford: Oxford University Press, 2004.

Ward, Pete. *Introducing Practical Theology: Mission, Ministry and the Life of the Church*. Grand Rapids: Baker Academic, 2017.

———, ed. *Perspectives on Ecclesiology and Ethnography*. Grand Rapids: Eerdmans, 2012.

Weatherhead, Leslie D. *The Transforming Friendship*. Nashville: Abingdon, 1977.

Webb-Mitchell, Brett. *Christly Gestures: Learning to Be Members of the Body of Christ*. Grand Rapids: Eerdmans, 2004.

Wessling, Jordan. *Love Divine: A Systematic Account of God's Love for Humanity*. Oxford Studies in Analytic Theology. Oxford: Oxford University Press, 2020.

Whipp, Margaret. *SCM Studyguide Pastoral Theology*. London: SCM, 2013.

White, Carolinne. *Christian Friendship in the Fourth Century*. Cambridge: Cambridge University Press, 1992.

———. "Friendship Christian Reflection." *A Series in Faith and Ethics* 27 (2008) 11–19.

Williams, Alex. "Friends of a Certain Age: Why Is It Hard to Make Friends Over 30?" *The New York Times*, July 13, 2012. https://www.nytimes.com/2012/07/15/fashion/the-challenge-of-making-friends-as-an-adult.html.

Willig, Carla. *Qualitative Interpretation and Analysis in Psychology*. Maidenhead: McGraw-Hill, 2012.

Willimon, William H. *Pastor: The Theology and Practice of Ordained Ministry*. Nashville: Abingdon, 2002.

Wilson, Stuart Thomas. *Sketching a Scheme: A Friendship Model of Ministry as a Mediating Structure*. Lanham: University Press of America, 2005.

Wood, David. "The Recovery and Promise of Friendship." *The Princeton Seminary Bulletin* 27 (2007) 165–80.

Woodward, James, and Stephen Pattison, ed. *The Blackwell Reader in Pastoral and Practical Theology*. Oxford: Blackwell, 2000.

Wright, Nicolas T. "Mind, Spirit, Soul and Body: All for One and One for All, Reflections on Paul's Anthropology in his Complex Contexts." *Society of Christian Philosophers*: Regional Meeting, Fordham University (March 2011). https://ntwrightpage.com/2016/07/12/mind-spirit-soul-and-body/.

Young, William W. *The Politics of Praise: Naming God and Friendship in Aquinas and Derrida*. Milton Park: Taylor & Francis, 2007.

Zaragoza, Edward. *No Longer Servants, but Friends: A Theology of Ordained Ministry*. Nashville: Abingdon, 1999.

Zizioulas, John D. *Being as Communion: Studies in Personhood and the Church*. New York: St. Vladimir's Seminary Press, 2002.

www.ingramcontent.com/pod-product-compliance
Lightning Source LLC
Chambersburg PA
CBHW051052230426
43667CB00013B/2267

* 9 7 9 8 3 8 5 2 1 3 8 7 0 *